# not your mama's™ knit

## The cool and creative way

### by Heather Dixon

WILEY

Wiley Publishing, Inc.

For general information on our other products and services or to obtain technical support please contact our Customer Care Department within the U.S. at (800) 762-2974, outside the U.S. at (317) 572-3993 or fax (317) 572-4002.

Wiley also publishes its books in a variety of electronic formats. Some content that appears in print may not be available in electronic books. For more information about Wiley products, please visit our web site at www.wiley.com.

Library of Congress Cataloging-in-Publication data is available from the publisher upon request.

ISBN 13: 978-0-471-97382-9
ISBN 10: 0-471-97382-3

Printed in the United States of America

10  9  8  7  6  5  4  3

Book design by Elizabeth Brooks
Cover design by Troy Cummings
Interior photography by Matt Bowen
Illustrations by Joni Burns, Shelley Norris, and Jake Mansfield
Book production by Wiley Publishing, Inc. Composition Services

## Free bonus pattern available online!

Be on top of the smartest fashion trends with the Night Falls Scarf by designer Jane Thornley. To access your copy of the pattern, go to www.wiley.com/go/NYMknitting.

# About the Author

Photo by Jimbo Matison

Heather Dixon taught herself to knit at the age of six and never looked back. She studied knitwear design in Nottingham, England, and has had several of her pieces featured in the British press. After working as a freelance designer in Italy, she moved to New York City to become the designer of RELAiS Knitware, a line of contemporary ladies' sweaters. In her spare time, Heather designs a line of accessories, the patterns for which can be bought from her website, www.armyofknitters.com. She teaches a weekly knit clinic, is a regular at the Tuesday evening meetings of the New York Stitch 'n Bitch, and has patterns featured in *Stitch 'n Bitch Nation*, *The Happy Hooker*, *Inknitters* magazine, and the online magazine *Knitty.com*.

# Contents

## CHAPTER FIVE

## Twist and Shout: Knitting Cables and Bobbles

## CHAPTER SIX

## Painting by Stitches: How to Knit with Different Colors

## CHAPTER SEVEN

## It Ain't Over 'til the Fat Lady Pins: Finishing and Blocking

## CHAPTER EIGHT

## Everything but the Kitchen Sink: Embellishments

## CHAPTER NINE

## Oops, I Made a Big Booboo! Fixing Mistakes

## CHAPTER TEN

## 'Sall Greek to Me: How to Read a Knitting Pattern

# PART TWO
## ...And a Bag of Chips

### CHAPTER ELEVEN
## Heads Up!

### CHAPTER TWELVE
## Playing Footsie

### CHAPTER THIRTEEN
## Full Fluffy Jacket

### CHAPTER FOURTEEN
## Bag Ladies

### CHAPTER FIFTEEN
## Rug Rats

### CHAPTER SIXTEEN
## Home Buddies

# PART THREE
## Junk in the Trunk

### CHAPTER SEVENTEEN
## Make the Buy

## CHAPTER EIGHTEEN

# Knitters of the World Unite

## APPENDIX

Dedicated to the memory of my knitting mamas, Alice and Dora.

# Acknowledgments

I've reached the age where a large number of my friends are popping out babies left, right, and center. This book is my little baby, and the whole process has been like a pregnancy. First there was the flirtation with the lovely and talented Roxane Cerda at Wiley Publishing where the idea was conceived. Then came the morning sickness and sleepless nights worrying about whether I would be a good enough writer.

All my spare time was spent huddled under a blanket with laptop perched on my ever-growing belly—there was no time for healthy eating or exercise! My fabulous editor Lynn Northrup helped me to breathe and plan the chapters. I would have pulled out all of my hair without her gentle encouragement and guidance. The labor was long and at times quite painful but worth all the sweat and tears as now I get to be the proud parent of a beautiful little book. I'll watch it make its way out to where it will hopefully entertain, encourage, and enlighten knitters all around the world.

None of this would be at all possible without the wonderfully talented designers who contributed their gorgeous designs featured in this book—big, wet snogs to you all! Big thanks to Sharon Turner and Kristi Porter for their technical editing, and to Cindy Kitchel for reviewing all of the patterns and giving helpful suggestions.

Huge amounts of love and thanks to the members of my Tuesday night Stitch 'n Bitch NYC crew, everyone at The Point, and my Thursday evening students at Klatch for your friendship and encouragement, especially to Nadine Fishelson for knitting the enormous Bobbles and Balls and Jill Astmann for knitting the stitch pattern swatches. To Johanna Li, Jessamyn Lee, Michelle Mudry, and Jenn Wendell for editorial help and insightful content; to Debbie Stoller for advice and connections; and to Jill Roth for letting us stay in her country house!

Love forever to my wonderful friends Chris Crowley and Valda Girgensons for taking me in over Thanksgiving and not letting me lift a finger to help so I could keep knitting and writing—you're the best!

A big hug and kiss to Jimbo Matison for the last-minute photo session on your Brooklyn rooftop!

New York can be a scary and surprising place—I'd like to express my thanks to the kind man who leapt down onto the subway tracks to retrieve a cone of yarn I was knitting from which had jumped from my bag while I was waiting for my train one early morning. You are my hero!

To Glen Robinson, my beautiful and big-hearted boyfriend, thank you for working away in Montreal for the past few months where you wouldn't distract me—you can come home now!

Thank you to my parents, Tess and Jack, who failed to pull me from the couch, where I spent my youth knitting and watching old films, on sunny days with the curtains closed when I should've been outside running around in the fresh air! Are you proud of me yet?

Finally, thank you to knitters and crafters everywhere who continue to inspire us all with their fabulous creations—you make the world a more interesting place!

# Introduction

◆◆◆

# Breaking the Boundaries and Stereotypes

The craft section of any good bookshop is crammed full of knitting books to suit most tastes, with patterns from socks to hats and everything in between, knits for dogs, knits for your home, knits for just about everything, so what will make you buy this one?

Many of today's patterns are aimed at the young, street-wise knitter, emphasizing easy knits on big needles where the fancy yarns do all the work for you. This book aims to challenge the urban crafter who's looking for something a little different. It's targeted toward all abilities, from knitting beginners to the more advanced who want options to change some of the patterns to suit the individual. This book will show you how to exercise your creative options and learn to think and knit for yourself. The patterns in this book are rated by the time commitment you need to complete them:

- ◆ Flirtation Flirtation patterns are quick, easy, and great for experimentation.
- ◆ Summer Fling A Summer Fling requires a bit more of your time and concentration, but still has a fair amount of instant gratification.
- ◆ Love o' Your Life You'll put a lot of work into a Love o' Your Life pattern, but you'll also get a lot of enjoyment out of the finished product.

You've probably heard that knitting isn't just for grannies anymore. This is highlighted in a fabulous knitting encounter story from one of my knitting pals, Jessamyn Lee:

> *Recently I was riding the subway, happily knitting a luscious black cashmere scarf for my husband, when I noticed a pre-pubescent, unescorted skate punk kid staring at me, carefully studying my hands. He leaned up against the pole, occasionally brushing his bleached fauxhawk from his eyes, simultaneously balancing his*

1

skateboard under his free arm. I knit on the subways every day on my way to and from work, so stares from strangers are de rigueur.

At the next stop, the seat next to me became free, and Skate Punk Boy plopped down next to me.

"You know, I knit too," he mentioned as he secured his skateboard under his seat.

"Really? Who taught you how to knit? Your mom?" I inquired. Skate Punk Boy, digging furiously in his overstuffed backpack, explained that he was the only knitter in his family. Apparently, he was bored one day, thus prompting him to investigate demos and other instruction available online.

Impressed by his motivation, I asked Skate Punk Boy what sorts of projects he liked to create.

"Well," he began as he retrieved his knitting, an amorphous black blob, from his button-emblazoned backpack, "I'm really better with garter stitch. I would do more in stockinette, but my purl stitches are still a bit awkward."

"You sure know a lot of the knitting lingo. What are you working on?" I inquired.

Skate Punk Boy explained, "Nothing, really. I just like to knit. I don't have to actually make anything. I like the way it relaxes me and helps me concentrate. Maybe someday I'll make something I can wear, but for right now the relaxing is enough." His process-oriented attitude toward his craft was either utterly precocious, or the words of a future spiritual leader.

Bewitched and bewildered, I needed to discover exactly what inspired Skate Punk Boy. "So, where do you go to get yarn?"

"Oh! I love to buy yarn!" he replied enthusiastically. "Sometimes I get my mom or grandma to take me shopping. We usually go to craft stores in New Jersey. The stores in Manhattan are too expensive, but there's one downtown that I like. P & S * rocks!"

With a conspiratorial giggle, I acknowledged that, like many knitters, I spend too much money on yarn.

"Me too! At home, I have bags and bags full of stuff I've never even touched!" he beamed.

We reached my stop, and I had to get off the train, wishing my momentary friend luck in his future knitting endeavors. Birds of a feather really do flock together, despite odds like significant age differences. My only regret: I wished I got his phone number. I know some eligible, single knitters who would go for a smart, eloquent, centered knitter-man. Even if they have to wait a decade.

---

* P&S Fabrics—Fantastic needlework supply store in Manhattan.

With this knowledge, take a hold of your yarn and needles, wave them high in the air, and say with me, "I am knitter, hear me roar!"

# Humble Beginnings: The Diary of a Preteen Knitter

When I was younger, my mother made a lot of our clothes. I don't remember having anything new or shop-bought until I was in my early teens. (I have three older siblings, so I was dressed mostly in hand-me-downs.) She was, and still is, a very talented seamstress, much better than me, but I was embarrassed that I didn't have the same clothes as my friends. I remember the first pair of proper jeans that my dad brought back from a business trip to Spain. By the time they were the right size for me they were way out of fashion—flares were out, drainpipes were in—but I wore them anyway. Maybe that's where my fearless style came from. I no longer wanted to look like everyone else, but to make my own little statement by wearing different clothes.

## The Early Years

Coming from a big family and knitting from an early age (way before there was the Internet), the only knitting patterns in our house were a few of my grandmother's crumpled instructions from the 1940s and 1950s for very basic sweaters and cardigans. The cover always seemed to depict a pipe-smoking gentleman with a faraway look in his eye, or perfectly behaved children all buttoned up tightly.

As a punk rock-wannabe, this wasn't the look I was going for. I had to learn how to adapt. With the basic outline and measurements from these ancient patterns, I had the foundations from which I could build. I experimented with different needle sizes and thicknesses of yarn. I learned how to change necklines, sleeve lengths, and work with different colors. From a classic Aran pattern, I learned all about the fabulous possibilities of cabling.

## The 1980s

As soon as I was old enough to work a newspaper round, I had a little money to spend on more contemporary knitting patterns. It was during the 1980s that I fell in love with Patricia Roberts' take on color and texture. Her designs were like nothing I'd seen before—bold intarsias of fruits and faces, multicolor mohair bobbles on a fuchsia background, all styled and photographed like a fashion magazine. She helped open the door to different levels of creativity and inspired me to knit even more than I was already.

This was the 1980s: the decade of oversized sweaters in primary colors and sweater-dresses with wide necklines designed to fall sexily off one shoulder. Those boxy shapes were very easy to knit; it all just seemed to be straight tubes, a big one for the body and two narrower ones for the sleeves. I remember seeing an audience member on TV's *Top of the Pops* wearing a BodyMap skirt. I had to have one just like it, so I whipped out the needles and knitted up a ribbed two-tone pink tube, slipped it on, and folded over the top few inches to create the waistband. It couldn't have been an easier decade to be a sweater designer!

It seemed as though everyone in my school had a mohair sweater; the punks wore red and black stripes with well-placed holes "accidentally purposely" knitted-in, while the new romantics sported solid V-necks worn over their frilly shirts that tucked into their tightly waisted baggies. Just thinking about it brings back all the music of the era. I can't remember what we learned at school, but the clothes and the music are burned into my brain forever!

When it came time for me to leave school, I still didn't know what I wanted to be when I grew up. I loved to sing and act. (I still dream of a being a rock star!) Everyone told me that I should study fashion, but I disliked the fashion scene—those involved seemed so shallow and bitchy. I didn't want any part of it, except that I was always knitting and sewing—I couldn't stop creating clothes and being passionate about colors, textures, and silhouettes. I had no choice—it chose me!

I couldn't fight it any longer, so I gave in and went to fashion college, and it was fabulous! There were a few fashionistas, but they didn't bother me anymore. I found some "normal" like-minded souls, had some fun, and worked incredibly hard while doing what I loved!

I continue to learn new tricks as my knitting continues to evolve. Sometimes it tries my patience by not working out how I envisioned; other times it surprises me with its beauty. But my knitting is always there for me. Knitting is my best friend.

# • Part One •

## All That a Gal Needs

# Chapter One

◆◆◆

# Have It Your Way: Seeing Beyond the Pattern

Over the past three decades of knitting, and with hundreds of projects under my belt, I think I have only followed a pattern completely a handful of times—almost never with the yarn that the pattern called for. This wasn't necessarily because I feared conformity or lacked patience, but because I had limited materials to work with and wanted to create something uniquely "me."

Within this book, I hope to pass on a little of what I have learned over the years.

After showing you some of the tools you will need: needle types and sizes, a few of the many yarns you can buy, and then teaching the basic knitting techniques you'll need to start with, this book will guide you on how to adapt a pattern to make your knitted item turn out just the way you want. Make it individually yours, or follow the patterns exactly as they are written. (There are a number of things in here that I want to knit for myself!)

I'll offer simple ways to alter the look of the pattern. Just changing the colors, yarns, and trims of items can alter the look completely. The possibilities are endless!

The patterns in this book have been gathered from a variety of contributors; some of the designers are new to knitting themselves. My aim was to offer a collection of patterns to suit a wide audience and show how knitting is a diverse craft for a diverse crowd.

## God or Science? The Evolution of Knitting

Was God the first knitter? Is (S)He up there now, desperately trying to complete a new ozone layer because we wore a hole in the last one?

I'm joking about this, of course. But a lot has been said about knitting being "the new yoga."

I'm not a religious person—knitting is my religion and I practice it daily. I'd like to think of yoga as being my religion too, but if that were the case, I'd have a beautifully toned and flexible body instead of a ridiculously large yarn stash!

Strange as it may seem, there is a connection between knitting and yoga. Many knitters find peace and spirituality while clinking away with the needles. The simple rhythmic motion, the feel of the yarn running steadily though their fingers, the low chanting, "Knit one, purl two, slip, slip knit...ooooooooommm." Oh, I almost drifted off then, just writing this!

Knitters feel great satisfaction in completing a project, especially if it is a gift. We can proudly say, "Here, I made this for you; there's love in every stitch."

Some people say that knitting is like an addiction, as we get a buzz every time we buy yarn for a new project—the side effects being that as we spend so much time knitting, the housework suffers. But who cares about a little dust on the mantelpiece when you can make your own beautiful sweaters?

## The Not-So-Distant Past

Before the popularity of the knitting machine, all knitted items were made by hand. Working-class children learned how to knit from their mothers and grandmothers. They would knit for their families, usually learning a pattern by heart, then churning out the same item over and over again. If there was anything left after clothing their families, they would sell knitted items to help pay for food and other household necessities.

Although it was mainly the women in the family who took on the bulk of the knitting, men also knew how to knit. Their tasks were more masculine. Fishermen would knit their own sweaters out of heavy oiled wool, which made them somewhat waterproof. Those crafty sailors used knit and purl stitches to include their initials into the patterned yoke of their guernseys, thus enabling them to be identified if they fell overboard.

Knitting back then was very different from how it is today. As recently as the 1950s and 1960s, yarns and fabrics were relatively cheap. My grandmother made all the sweaters for her family, and just before she passed away, she completed all her projects. It was as if she knew her time was almost up. All of my grandfather's, father's, and uncle's sweaters were finished, elbows were patched up, and socks were darned. Not until the house was in complete order did she leave this life.

Nowadays we really don't *need* to knit. Machines can whip out sweaters much more quickly and cheaply than anyone can by hand. Knitting today is not the chore it used to be, but much more of a luxury pastime. Many people knit for relaxation. It helps us through hard times, it helps us concentrate, and it helps steady a restless mind.

In this computer-dominated age where machines do everything for us, we never need to leave our homes. We can buy everything we need over the Internet. Why do we even bother getting out of bed? Is it because we live in this age of time-saving devices that enable us to work longer hours to earn more money to buy more time-saving devices that we need to sit down, take some of that precious time, and create something beautiful and functional with our own two hands? It feels good to say, "I made it myself."

So forget about your worries and the pressures of everyday life. Pick up a soft bundle of fiber and your needles, snuggle into your comfy chair, and slow down for a change. Let your knitting guide you and indulge in your creativity.

## The Here and Now

Today, handicrafts are back in vogue. If only I had been born in this decade, I would be so much cooler in my original, lovingly created outfits. Even mass-produced items are being churned out with details giving them a homemade look.

New yarn shops are springing up all over the place. The coolest ones are part yarn shop, part café, so you can sip your mocha-choca-latte while perusing the latest in luxury yarns and browsing the pattern books, which are looking more and more like photography books than ever before.

Knitting is no longer a hobby you practice only in your living room. This is big business! I knit on the subway, while waiting in line at the bank or post office—I even knit while walking the streets of Manhattan and nobody seems to bat an eyelid.

Groups of knitters are gathering all over the world to share their hobby and their lives with other like-minded people. Internet groups have members thousands strong, swapping patterns and tips. Large numbers of these knitters are older ladies, for whom completing a sweater for little Jimmy, religiously following their patterns, is reward enough, but the army of new knitters whose numbers are growing daily want something *more*. More exquisite yarn, more exciting patterns. Knitters today have never had it better.

Now that you know a little about knitting history, I hope this book will entice you into becoming a more inventive, more fearless knitter as you experiment and enjoy taking knitting into the future.

# Chapter Two

◆◆◆

# Two Sticks and Some String

So you wanna knit, but what do you need to get started? Well, you *can* knit with your fingers and a packet of Twizzlers, but a pair of knitting needles and some nice smooth yarn will make things so much easier!

In this chapter I'll introduce you to some of the knitting needles and types of yarns that you can buy. I'll suggest which ones are good for beginners and others that are better suited to more advanced knitters. It's not only needles and yarn that you'll need, so I've included a list of items necessary for your knitter's tool kit.

## If It's Long and Pointy, You Can Knit with It

There are many different types of needles out there. You can buy straights, circulars, or double points, all of which come in a wide variety of materials and sizes. With so many choices, how can you possibly know which needles to buy? Here's a little info on the types of needles available. Keep in mind that with time and practice, you will develop a preference.

### Single-Pointed Straight Needles

These are what spring to mind when you hear the words "knitting needles." These are long straight needles with a point at one end and a knob at the other to stop the stitches from falling off. These are ideal for flat knitting and what I recommend beginners start with, because they can be easier to control if you have never knitted before. They are sold in pairs and come in a variety of lengths—most commonly 10 and 14 inches.

## Double-Pointed Needles

Commonly known as dpns, these are straight needles with — surprise, surprise — a point at both ends. If you need to knit tubular items with a small circumference, then this is what you will most likely use (although I find these glorified toothpicks too cumbersome and much prefer to use a long circular needle and the Magic Loop method — but more about that in Chapter 3, "Beginners, Start Your Engines: Basic Techniques"). Double-pointed needles are sold in sets of four or five and are usually shorter in length than straights. Their length varies depending on the manufacturer and materials.

## Circulars

My favorite — I would use them exclusively if I owned all the sizes, but that's just my preference. These babies are a pair of short straight needles joined by a flexible cord. They were originally used only for knitting larger tubular items, but they are also great for straight knitting, especially heavy items with lots of stitches, because the cord takes the bulk from the needles and lets it lay neatly in your lap. They are also perfect for knitting in tight spaces (while traveling, at the movies, at sporting events, or when you're stuck in an elevator), because the smaller needles need less movement, meaning that your elbows are less likely to flail about. Circulars come in a variety of lengths, most commonly 16, 24, 29, and 36 inches.

All needle types are available in the following materials:

- ♦ Aluminum If you want to be a super-speedy knitter, go for metal. Aluminum needles are often coated with chrome, nickel, or Teflon for a slick finish. That smooth surface helps those stitches fly off the needles. But beginners beware: The smooth finish that helps those stitches fly off the needles may mean you end up dropping your stitches!

- ♦ Plastic Usually cheaper, lighter, and quieter than metal, plastic is a good choice for beginners. Good-quality, plastic circulars are my needles of choice.

- ♦ Wood Ebony, rosewood, and birch make very attractive needles, but can be expensive. Bamboo is a little cheaper. These warm wooden needles are comfortable to hold and not as slippery as their metal and plastic counterparts, making them another good choice for beginners. They do need to be treated with care, though, because splintering will cause your yarn to snag, which can be a real pain in the neck!

## DIY Needles

If you're feeling super-crafty, you can make your own needles from pieces of dowel, available at any good hardware store.

Get the dowel cut to the required length, sharpen the point at one end (you could use a pencil sharpener or a craft knife for this), and stick a decorative knob on the other end. (Knob options include buttons, marbles, and beads — or have a go at making your own, but you will need something to stop your precious stitches from slipping off the end.) Sand down the dowel's surface until it's smooth and then rub it with paraffin wax. Voilà! Your own unique, handmade needles!

See the following table for the dowel diameters needed for your needle size. (Please note: Because these are handmade needles, the sizes may vary, so please make sure you knit a gauge swatch before plunging headfirst into your project.)

| Dowel Diameter (in inches) | US Needle Size | Metric Needle Size |
| --- | --- | --- |
| ⅛ | 2 | 2.75 |
| 3/16 | 7 | 4–4.5 |
| ¼ | 10 | 6 |
| 5/16 | 10½ | 6.5–7 |
| ⅜ | 13 | 9 |

## Where Width Is More Important Than Length

The larger the girth of your needle, the bigger your stitches will be; therefore, needles come in loads of different widths. When knitters talk about the size of their needles, it's the circumference that matters.

To knit a big bulky sweater out of super-chunky yarn, for example, you'll need a needle size that has a circumference of about 17 to 20mm; to knit a delicate lace shawl that will fit through your promise ring, you'll be knitting on something about 2mm or thinner. (You won't catch me with anything smaller than 3.25mm; I'm much happier about a 10mm. I'm so results-obsessed! The smaller the needle size and stitch, the slower the knitting will grow. I prefer projects with chunky stitches, using fatter needles, because the project gets finished more quickly. I don't have the patience for knitting a fine and featherlight lace shawl—but that's just me!) Now, I know what you're thinking: "A millimeter is such a tiny measurement, surely it wouldn't make a whole hill of beans difference whether I knitted on a 3mm or a 3.25mm. I mean, .25mm— that's nothing!" But it does make a difference—just you try it!

There are three different ways of sizing knitting needles: metric, Old English, and American. If you find or inherit some Old English needles and patterns (pre-decimalization), the patterns will quote Old English-size needles. Today, needles are made only in metric and American sizes, so a conversion table like the one shown in the appendix is a useful guide to check exactly what size you will need to complete a project. You can also keep track of which needles you own by marking them off on this handy table.

# The Long and the Short of It

Needle length...it's as simple as this: The more stitches you'll be knitting in a row, the longer your needle will need to be. Of course, you can squash a lot of stitches on a short needle, just like you can knit on a great big long needle with only a few stitches. A large project such as an afghan would require a lot of stitches compared to something narrow like a necktie, which would only have a few stitches per row.

Some people like to hold the end of one needle under their arm as they knit. I remember my grandmother knitting like this when I was little, but I never could get the hang of it. It all comes down to personal preference, and, in a lot of cases, what you already have in your kit!

# Stringing You Along

Yarn, yarn, glorious yarn! The fabulous stuff we love to knit with comes in a huge array of fibers and colors, not just wool as some people think. In England all yarn is commonly known as "wool" and yarn stores are still "wool shops," which, being a Brit, I find oddly comforting.

When you first step into a yarn store, you may be amazed by the enormity of the selection, but stay calm. Don't go for some fancy froufrou stuff with all the bells and whistles; it might look like it would be perfect for a scarf (and for someone with a couple of simple projects under her belt, I'm sure it would), but it's a nightmare for a beginner because you can't see the stitches clearly, making it almost impossible to pick up any that you will drop along the row (and we might lose you from our special clique if you get frustrated by your first attempts). Go for something smooth in a color that's light or bright so you can see your new stitches clearly.

## Choosing Yarn

From animal hair to plants to synthetics to novelties, yarn comes from a variety of sources. Here are some of the offerings available to tempt a knitter's palate. The price of yarn can vary widely. Synthetics are usually the cheapest, followed by vegetable-based yarns. Animal fibers come in as the most expensive, but, as with any rules, there are exceptions. Depending on the source, treatments, blends, dyeing, and spinning techniques used to produce the yarns, the prices are affected. It's important to take all of this into consideration when choosing your yarn. It's not always true that the more expensive yarns make a better product—buy the less expensive yarns to begin with, but don't buy something just because it's cheap. Shop wisely; you can find beautiful, high-quality yarns that won't break the bank! Given all the types of yarn out there, my advice is to buy the best yarn you can afford. You'll enjoy working with and get better results from a yarn that you like the look and feel of.

For beginners I recommend a smooth, soft yarn in a light or bright color. Sorry, all you Goth types, but it's too difficult to see the stitches in a piece of black knitting—it can make you cross-eyed when you don't know what you are looking for! I also suggest that beginners start with a heavy worsted or chunky yarn as the stitches will be bigger and more visible. The novice knitter is less likely to lose interest with a thick yarn that knits up quickly than a fingering weight yarn that takes hours to knit an inch. I wouldn't go with super-bulky, though, because those size 36 needles can be awkward to maneuver!

If you are unsure whether a yarn will be soft enough to wear next to your skin, hold it up to your neck. If it feels at all scratchy, choose another, softer yarn. You don't want to spend many hours working on an item of clothing if you are not going to wear it.

## Animal

Usually spun from an animal's coat, these protein-based fibers offer good insulation. Warm in winter and cool in summer, these soft bundles are the favorite of many knitters. Not only are animal fibers nice to knit with, they also make great clothing and are lightweight, absorbent, and stretchy.

- ♦ **Wool** The most popular of all the yarns, wool is spun from sheep's fleece. Many different breeds of sheep provide a variety of wool. The softest wool comes from merino sheep, but it isn't as strong as some of the less soft yarns, which contain more lanolin, making them more water resistant. (Did you know that the lanolin in your hand cream is really just the grease from sheep's fleece? So, if your hands are feeling dry but you've run out of hand cream, just find a sheep and give its coat a jolly good fondle! Mmmm, smooth hands.)

- ♦ **Mohair** This fluffy, warm, and lightweight yarn comes from a goat. It sheds and can be scratchy, so it's often blended with nylon or wool. Kid mohair is usually much softer.

- ♦ **Alpaca** One of my favorite fibers, this comes from an alpaca, a sort of shorter, stockier llama-type animal from South America. (I always imagine them to have two heads, thanks to the Push-Me Pull-You in *Doctor Doolittle*!) Their soft, light, and very warm hair comes in an array of wonderful undyed colors, from almost-white to the darkest brown with hues of caramel and chocolate in between. This fiber also takes dye very well. Alpaca is cheaper than cashmere and more expensive than wool, but does not retain its stretching memory very well, making it a better choice for shawls and scarves rather than sweaters.

- ♦ **Angora** This favorite of 1950s sweater girls comes from the very fluffy Angora rabbit. Although gorgeously soft, warm, and delicate, this yarn tends to shed very easily and is expensive, so it is often blended with other fibers.

- ♦ **Cashmere** From the hair of a cashmere goat, cashmere is one of the most luxuriously soft (and expensive) yarns you can buy. On its own it is simply delicious, although it does have a tendency to pill. Its softness goes a long way, so just a small amount blended with another fiber will make a beautiful, less-expensive alternative.

- ♦ **Silk** Unlike the other yarns in this group, silk doesn't come from an animal's hair but from the unraveled cocoon of the silk worm. This forms a long, lustrous fiber that drapes beautifully but does have a tendency to stretch with wear and needs special care for cleaning. Silk is often blended with other fibers for strength and to lower the cost.

♦ **Other** Other yarns from animal sources include the sumptuously soft and warm qiviut, which comes from the undercoat of the musk ox and the Australian possum, but because they are rare, these yarns can be very expensive. If you can gather enough of it, you can even knit with your pet dog or cat's fur, but it could take awhile to knit anything substantial from your hamster's coat!

## Vegetable

These durable, breathable cellulose fibers are spun from plant tissue. They don't offer as much insulation as animal fibers, but are cooler to wear and work with in the warmer months.

♦ **Cotton** There are many types of cotton; the best ones are Sea Island, Pima, and Egyptian. Cotton is very absorbent and quick drying, making it a good choice for baby items and washcloths. Mercerized (or pearl) cotton can be found in beautifully strong colors as it has been treated with sodium hydroxide to shrink it and increase its luster and ability to take dye. The chemical process also makes it stronger and resistant to mildew.

♦ **Linen** From the flax plant, linen is cool in warm weather but has a tendency to wrinkle, so it is often blended with cotton. Both cotton and linen have little to no elasticity, which is important to remember when choosing yarn for specific projects. This also makes it a little harder on the hands when knitting than animal fibers.

♦ **Other** Other yarns from plant sources growing in popularity include hemp—which can be similar to linen and bamboo—and soy. Both are soft and drape well.

## Synthetic

Man-made fibers are usually cheaper than their natural counterparts, and over the past few years there have been some exciting developments in this area. The knitting community has a large number of fiber snobs. These people will only knit with natural fibers and turn their noses up at the mention of a man-made yarn, but they may be missing out. Synthetics have come a long way and are not as nasty as they used to be!

♦ **Acrylic** Back in my youth, acrylic was just about all I could afford. It was available in the brightest colors imaginable and sold all over the place. The quality back then was not the best and it would squeak as I knitted. At intervals I would run my needles against my scalp to add a little natural grease, which helped the squeaking but didn't do my hair-do any good! Over the years, scientists have worked wonders and can now produce some fabulously soft yarns that have little of the old squeak factor. An acrylic/wool or acrylic/cotton blend, for example, makes a beautifully durable and affordable yarn.

- **Nylon** Nylon is a very strong fiber that is often added to natural yarns to add strength—making it an especially good choice for socks. Some of the fun-fur yarns popular today are 100 percent nylon.
- **Polyester** The majority of those froufy eyelash scarves you see around are made from this soft fiber.
- **Metallic** Any yarn with a bit of a glittery shine contains small amounts of metal. Metallic yarn is usually blended with another fiber; on its own it isn't very strong and can be quite scratchy.
- **Rayon** Although derived from wood, rayon is a man-made fiber. It has some of the qualities of a vegetable yarn, being absorbent, soft, and lustrous.

### Novelty

Many synthetic yarns are blended and spun to form novelty yarns, which can be fun to knit but look best when used in small items or on trims. They are good for scarves, bags, collars, and cuffs, but be careful: You could end up looking like Bigfoot if you overdo it! Choosing novelty yarns is not a good idea if you are a beginner. On the one hand, the unevenness of the knitting can hide a multitude of knitting mistakes, but on the other hand, it is very difficult to see the stitches clearly, so mistakes occur more often and are much harder to mend. If you're a beginner, it's much better to go with a smooth yarn that feels good in your hands.

- **Bouclé** Fibers are twisted together at different rates to form an uneven, bumpy yarn with big or small loops or gimps.
- **Chenille** Small pieces of cut yarn are held together with a binder to create a yarn that, when knitted, resembles velvet.
- **Eyelash** Very popular with the froufy-scarf brigade, these yarns are made by twisting fibers together and adding longer cut lengths of soft and light yarns at varying intervals to form the eyelash effect.

## Yarn Thickness

The table on the next page shows how different thicknesses of yarns are categorized. It also shows the most common needle sizes to use with each yarn and the number of stitches you would get in 4 inches. This is a guide only and not to be taken as the be-all and end-all.

## A Ball in the Hand Is Worth Two in the Bush

Manufacturers wind their yarns up in different ways to make them appealing to the public. The three most common offerings are the ball, the skein, and the hank.

As you might have guessed, a ball of yarn is round or oval. A skein is wound in a similar way to a ball, but has a longer, more sausage-like shape. The best way to knit from a ball or a skein is to find its beginning end from the center. Some manufacturers make this easy by having the end hanging out a little. Sometimes it is hidden under the yarn label. If you can't find the end on the outside, it may still be nestled in the ball or skein's core. The best way to find it is to gently stick your fingers in there and hunt around for it, hoping that you don't pull all its innards to the outside! If you can't find the beginning end, then just knit from the outside end, but this may cause your ball or skein to jump all over the room as you knit from it!

## Standard Yarn Weight System: Categories of Yarn, Gauge Ranges, and Recommended Needle and Hook Sizes (courtesy of www.yarnstandards.com)

| Yarn Weight Symbol and Category Names | 1: Super Fine | 2: Fine | 3: Light | 4: Medium | 5: Bulky | 6: Super Bulky |
|---|---|---|---|---|---|---|
| **Type of Yarns in Category** | Sock, Fingering, Baby | Sport, Baby | DK, Light Worsted | Worsted, Afghan, Aran | Chunky, Craft, Rug | Bulky, Roving |
| **Knit Gauge Range* in Stockinette Stitch to 4 inches** | 27–32 sts | 23–26 sts | 21–24 sts | 16–20 sts | 12–15 sts | 6–11 sts |
| **Recommended Needle in Metric Size Range** | 2.25–3.25 mm | 3.25–3.75 mm | 3.75–4.5 mm | 4.5–5.5 mm | 5.5–8 mm | 8mm and larger |
| **Recommended Needle in US Size Range** | 1 to 3 | 3 to 5 | 5 to 7 | 7 to 9 | 9 to 11 | 11 and larger |
| **Crochet Gauge* Ranges in Single Crochet to 4 inches** | 21–32 sts | 16–20 sts | 12–17 sts | 11–14 sts | 8–11 sts | 5–9 sts |
| **Recommended Hook in Metric Size Range** | 2.25–3.5 mm | 3.5–4.5 mm | 4.5–5.5 mm | 5.5–6.5 mm | 6.5–9 mm | 9mm and larger |
| **Recommended Hook in US Size Range** | B-1 to E4 | E-4 to 7 | 7 to I-9 | I-9 to K-10½ | K-10½ to M-13 | M-13 and larger |

* GUIDELINES ONLY: The above reflect the most commonly used gauges and needle or hook sizes for specific yarn categories.

Hanks are long loosely wound loops of yarn that are twisted and tied to secure. Ask whoever you bought your hanks from to wind them into balls for you. If they don't offer this service you can do it yourself by having a friend hold the loop of yarn over her hands as you wind. If no one is around to help, you can use your feet or knees as an anchor, then carefully wind up your ball from there.

To start a center pull ball, you'll want to hold an end of about 4 inches in the palm of your hand, then carefully wrap the yarn in a figure eight around your thumb and first finger until you have a good-sized piece. Take this off your fingers and keeping the end that was in your palm free, continue winding to form a nice round ball, but not too tightly, because that can stretch the yarn. Tuck the finishing end into the top layer of the ball and knit from the beginning end.

## Reading a Yarn Label

It may not look like much, but there's a lot of important information on a yarn label (see figure on next page).

In addition to the manufacturer's name, their contact information, and the yarn's name, the label should show the fiber content, which is useful to know in case you have an allergy or just a penchant for a particular feel of yarn.

Care or washing instructions let you know the best way to clean the item you will be knitting out of the yarn. You don't want a "dry clean only" yarn for baby items that will need to be washed regularly.

There should also be the weight and yardage of the single ball, skein, or hank, which is vital when figuring out how much you'll need, especially when subbing a yarn (see "Subbing Yarns" later in this chapter).

There may be symbols, which are useful to know if the yarn is from abroad and the information is in a foreign language.

If you are buying more than one skein of a particular type of yarn, it is very important that you check the dye lot number. This will normally be stamped on the label next to the color name, shade, or number. Yarn is dyed in large kettles and it isn't guaranteed that the manufacturer can match the exact color every time it is dyed; different dye lots of the same color can vary significantly. Always check the dye lot numbers and make sure they all match, so your project has a consistent color. What may look like two exactly-the-same colors when wound in a ball can stand out like a sore thumb when knitted up.

## Yarn Shopping

Large craft stores sell a variety of inexpensive, mainly synthetic yarns. If this is all you have access to, then you will probably be able to find a wool/acrylic or wool/cotton blend in a smooth yarn that will be good for starters. The staff at these stores may not be able to help you with

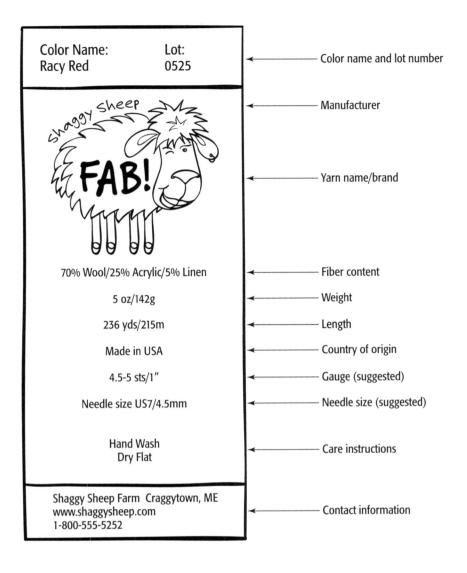

| | |
|---|---|
| **Color Name:** Racy Red | **Lot:** 0525 | ← Color name and lot number |

Shaggy Sheep

FAB!

← Manufacturer

← Yarn name/brand

70% Wool/25% Acrylic/5% Linen ← Fiber content

5 oz/142g ← Weight

236 yds/215m ← Length

Made in USA ← Country of origin

4.5-5 sts/1" ← Gauge (suggested)

Needle size US7/4.5mm ← Needle size (suggested)

Hand Wash
Dry Flat ← Care instructions

Shaggy Sheep Farm  Craggytown, ME
www.shaggysheep.com
1-800-555-5252 ← Contact information

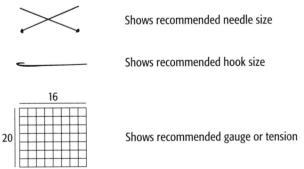

Shows recommended needle size

Shows recommended hook size

16

20

Shows recommended gauge or tension

What's on a yarn label?

knitting queries, so if you have one within reach I would highly recommend to trip to your LYS (local yarn store). Any good LYS will be stocked to the rafters with all types of tempting goodies as well as have specially trained staff to help answer any knitting-related questions. If you buy the yarn and pattern for a particular project at your LYS, the staff will usually be only too happy to guide you through it. Many a LYS offers classes and workshops where you can learn a new technique while meeting other people who share your hobby.

Once you have discovered which yarns you really enjoy working with, you can save a bit of money by buying over the Internet, but because you can't feel the quality or see the colors properly, I would only advise this if you are familiar with the particular yarn you are buying. My favorite place to buy yarn is at a yarn store—it's right there for me to take home immediately and get started on my project!

## Subbing Yarns

Designers suggest the yarn to use for a pattern, but it is not set in stone. Sometimes we have to use an alternative, whether because of price, availability, or because we already have yarn that could be used in its place. Using a different yarn than the one called for in the pattern can drastically change the look of a project—which is something I want to encourage, but only if that is your intention!

If you want to maintain the look of the original, then the first thing you'll need to know is whether you have enough yarn to complete the project. Watch the yardage required. Don't just go for the weight, because alternative yarns can differ greatly in this area. You'll want to use the same size of yarn as well—if the pattern calls for a worsted weight yarn and you use a fingering weight, for example, your finished item will look nothing like the pattern because the finer yarn will produce skinnier stitches, making the finished piece smaller than if you had used the required worsted weight yarn. Another thing to consider is the yarn type. Different fibers knit up very differently, so chose a yarn blend close to the one in the pattern, and *always* remember to knit a gauge swatch or the finished size may be nowhere near what you wanted.

# A Knitter's Tool Kit: Other Stuff You'll Need

Knitting needles and yarn are just the main tools of this trade. You'll also need at least a few of the following items if you really want to get serious about it. (If money's tight, or you don't mind roughing it a bit like me, I've added my cheapster alternatives, but a lot of knitters I know love all the gadgets you can buy.)

- **Scissors** Get a small pair for carrying with your project (folding ones are great).
- **Large-eye tapestry needle** For sewing up seams and tidying ends.
- **Crochet hooks** For picking up dropped stitches, weaving in ends, or crocheting seams. (You can manage with just a small one, but it's not a bad idea to have a few different sizes.)
- **Pins** Long, rustproof, color-headed ones are best. You'll need them to hold seams while sewing and anchoring pieces for blocking.
- **Tape measure** Get one that shows both inches and centimeters, because all the best designers use the metric system (heh heh!).
- **Stitch markers** You can find all sorts of fancy ones made from wire adorned with pretty beads, but I still use a loop of contrast-colored yarn, which works perfectly well for me.
- **Stitch holders** Again, I choose the cheap route here and hold my "live" stitches with a length of contrast-colored, smooth yarn, or I just shove them to the end of my needle until I need to work with them again.
- **Safety pins** Work great for holding a few stitches or as stitch markers. Choose ones without the coils, as they could get stuck in your yarn.
- **Point protectors** These both stop your stitches from falling off the needles when not in use and protect people and other things from being stabbed. They come in different sizes and some novelty shapes, but I find a cork works beautifully for this purpose.
- **Needle gauge** To check your unmarked needles for size. Also handy for checking the conversion of US and metric needle sizes.
- **Stitch gauge** For checking your gauge. Handy, but I still use a tape measure or small ruler.
- **Cable needles** These are very good at escaping, especially behind the sofa cushions! They can be sold in sets of three—a small, a medium, and a large—use the one that's the closest to your needle size. In a pinch you can use all sorts of other substitutes— a toothpick, pencil, hairpin, dpn, or circular—be imaginative!
- **Row counter** Nice to have, but I still jot down my rows tally-style in a notebook. That way I know exactly what I knit when it comes to working the second sleeve or sock, or repeating a particular part of the pattern.
- **Notebook** Write *everything* down—you never know when you'll need the information again. A notebook is also good for recording information about swatches and yarn.

- ◆ Pen or pencil  Do I have to explain this one?
- ◆ Bobbins  For winding small amounts of yarn when doing color work.
- ◆ Post-It notes  Great for marking your place in a pattern.
- ◆ Clear plastic storage bags  I've only just started to use these and I don't know how I managed without them. If you store your yarn in clear bags, you can see what's in there without opening the bag—who knew?! Now I keep everything in clear plastic storage bags. They are also perfect for transporting some of the smaller items on this list.
- ◆ Nail file  If you have dry skin or rough nails, it wouldn't be a bad idea to include one of these in your kit to smooth off those pesky hangnails that could snag on your yarn.
- ◆ Project bag  If you're a knitter on the move, you'll need something to cart all this stuff around in. You can buy project bags with all kinds of specially designed pockets, or you could just get something that looks good and is big enough to carry your current project(s).

# Chapter **Three**

◆◆◆

# Beginners, Start Your Engines: Basic Techniques

Now that you know all about knitting needles and yarn, it's time to pick them up and get started! But be patient—knitting for the first time is not as easy as most beginners expect. Just like learning any new skill, you'll need lots of time and practice to feel like you're getting somewhere. So keep at it, and in time you'll be one of the many millions of new knitters joining our wide circle every day.

## On the Casting Couch: Casting On

There are a few different ways to put your first stitches onto your needles. I will show you the two most common ways to cast on. Both of these methods start out with the very important slip knot. Here's how to make a slip knot:

1. Leaving a tail of approximately 4 inches, wrap the yarn around two fingers twice.
2. Using a knitting needle, pull the yarn at the back through the yarn at the front to form a loop.
3. Pull the end of the yarn to tighten the loop a little, leaving enough of a gap for inserting the second needle. There, you've just made a slip knot!

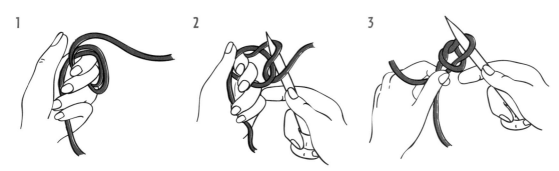

1  2  3

## The Cable Cast-On

This method of casting on gives a firm, neat finish. It's also good for starting a rib pattern. This is by far my favorite method—I very rarely use any other—but as with a lot of knitting, after awhile we develop preferences. You may find you prefer one of the other methods.

1. After making a slip knot on your left needle, insert the right needle through the loop from below and toward the back of the left needle.

2. With your right hand, wrap the ball end of the yarn around the back of the right needle in a counterclockwise direction, placing it between the needles.

3. Carefully slide the right needle down to pick up the yarn between the legs of the slip knot.

4. You now have a new stitch on your right needle. Place this new stitch onto your left needle above the slip knot. Pull the yarn a little to tighten.

5. To make the third and following stitches, instead of inserting your right needle between the legs of the last stitch on your left needle, insert the point of the right needle into the gap between the top two stitches on the left needle and repeat steps 2 through 4 until you have the required amount of stitches on the left needle.

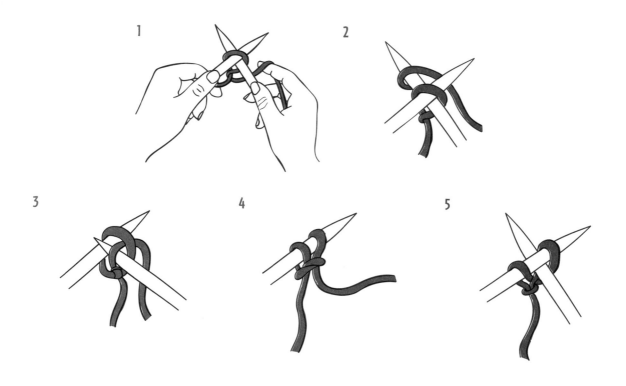

## The Thumb Cast-On

This method of casting on gives you more of an elastic start. It's used for the beginning of a pattern worked in garter stitch or stockinette stitch.

1. Make a slip knot, leaving a tail that is about 36 inches long, and place it on a needle. Holding the needle in your right hand, wrap the ball end of the yarn over your right forefinger.
2. Wind the tail around your left thumb from front to back and hold in place with your ring and pinky fingers.
3. Insert the needle under the yarn loop on your thumb.
4. Wrap the ball end of the yarn counterclockwise around the point of the needle, and then slide the point of the needle from back to front, pulling the loop through to form a stitch.
5. Remove your thumb from the loop and pull the tail a little to tighten.

Repeat steps 2 through 5 until you have the required amount of stitches.

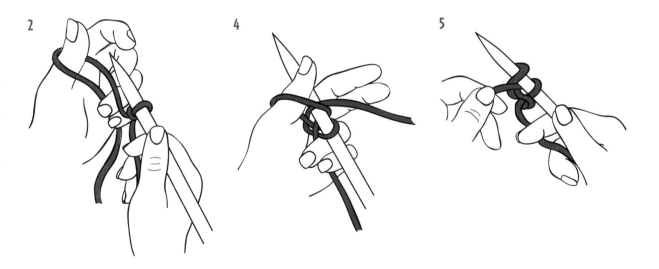

## Get a Grip! Holding the Yarn and Needles

You will probably feel very awkward holding your yarn and needles in the proper way, but it's better to start off holding them correctly as you will find it faster knitting this way once you get the hang of it. No one showed me how to do this until I was well into the swing of things and I felt like a complete beginner all over again, but I now knit much faster, thanks to a little patience.

The two most common ways to knit are the English method (also called the right-hand method, or "throwing"), and the Continental method (also called the left-hand method, or "picking"). Back when knitting was a necessity rather than the relaxing hobby it has become today and the finished item was more important than the process, it is believed that all knitting was worked in the Continental method, because that is the fastest way to knit once you have mastered the technique. The English method was developed when elegant society ladies thought it would look much more civilized to hold their needles points up.

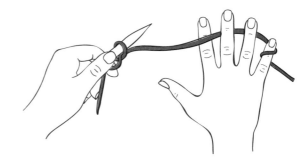

Holding the yarn

Depending on whether you chose to look elegant or are going for speed, your yarn will be held in a different way. Try out the different methods and choose the one you are most comfortable with.

To maintain even tension on your yarn while knitting, wrap the ball end of the yarn around your right pinky for the English method (see figure above) or around your left pinky for the Continental method.

## Bring It On! The Knit Stitch

Now it's actually time to go for it—give it all you've got and bring on the knitting!

## Ooops, I Made a Booboo #1: Common Mistakes When Casting On

Don't pull your stitches too tightly! I see beginners doing this all the time, so don't think it won't happen to you. You'll only be miserable trying to knit your first row, squeezing your needle through a gap that isn't big enough, and having a starting edge that pulls in too much.

Relax. You will have a more pleasant knitting experience if you loosen up a bit.

Once you've been knitting for awhile, you will just know when you're working at the right tension. The feel of the yarn on the needles will become second nature. But when you're just starting out, it's a good idea to cast on using a needle two or three sizes bigger than the ones you are going to use–but don't forget to switch to the correct size once you have all the stitches cast on, or you'll end up with something that looks like a fishing net!

## The English Method

We're going to start out with the elegant English method, so go ahead and cast on 15 stitches using whichever method you feel most comfortable with. Take a good look at these stitches and see how they are sitting on the needle. Imagine them as little creatures with legs, sitting astride the needle. It's important to know their front legs from their back legs as you don't want them to be all twisted and uncomfortable.

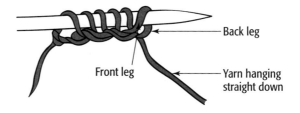

How the stitches should sit on the needle

1. Insert your right needle into the first stitch just like you did at the start of the cable cast-on: from below, between the legs, and toward the back.

2. Using your right forefinger, lift the yarn and take it between the needles from the back—as you did in the cable cast-on—pull the new stitch through, but instead of putting this new stitch on the left needle, keep it where it is and slide the old stitch off the left needle. You now have your first knit stitch on the right needle.

Repeat steps 1 and 2 until all 15 stitches have been worked and you have knitted your first row. Turn your work to the other side and do it all over again. Carry on working this way, knitting every row, and you have worked garter stitch, which is the name given to the pattern where you knit every stitch in every row.

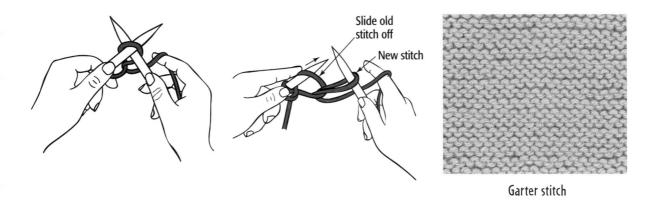

Garter stitch

## The Continental Method

If you can crochet, you may find this method easier, as you hold the yarn in a similar way. If you want to be a speedster, then this is the method for you.

1. Insert your right needle into the first stitch from below, between the legs and toward the back.
2. Using your left forefinger, lift the yarn and wrap it around the point of the right needle from front to back.
3. Pull the new stitch through and slide the old one off the needle.

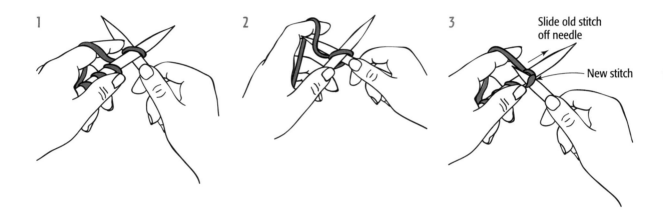

Repeat these steps until all 15 stitches have been worked. As with the English method, if you keep knitting every row this way you will have garter stitch.

Many items can be made in garter stitch, and if this is all you want to work with, you can whip out all sorts of scarves, washcloths, potholders, placemats, blankets, and throws. Of course, you'll need to know how to bind off your work, so let's get right on with it!

## How to Bind Off

Now that you've mastered the fine art of knitting garter stitch, you'll want to know how to finish it—just so you can start another piece. Binding off is the way to finish off your knitting by getting it off the needles and securing the stitches so they don't unravel, and at the same time making a neat edge. It's always a good idea to bind off in pattern (using the same stitch as you have just worked). Seeing as you have just mastered the knit stitch, that is the pattern we will use here.

## Standard Knit Bind-Off

The standard knit bind-off is an easy, quick way to bind off garter stitch and stockinette stitch on the right side.

As with casting on, it's good practice to use a needle two or three sizes bigger than the rest of your knitting for binding off. This keeps it from ending up too tight.

1. Knit the first two stitches in your chosen method, then use the point of your left needle to pick up the first stitch on the right needle and pass it all the way over the second stitch and off the right needle.

2. Knit another stitch onto the right needle and pass the first stitch over the second as before.

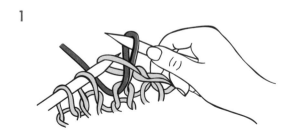

Repeat steps 1 and 2 until you have only one stitch remaining. Pull this stitch into a large loop and take it off the needle. Pass the ball of yarn through this loop and pull tight to secure. Cut the yarn, leaving a tail of at least 4 inches to weave into knitting.

## Knit 2 Together Bind-Off

This method was recently shown to me by one of my students, which goes to show that you can keep on learning new tricks, no matter how long you've been knitting!

1. Knit the first two stitches together.
2. Place the new stitch back onto the left needle.

Repeat steps 1 and 2 until you are left with one stitch. Pass the yarn though the loop and finish as you did for the first method.

## Binding Off in Purl or in Pattern

Once you have mastered the purl stitch, you'll want to use this method to bind off. It can be used for finishing the right side of the purl stitch or the wrong side of the knit stitch. Use the standard bind-off method, but work all stitches in purl or in pattern instead of knitting them—it's as simple as that!

# Purls of Wisdom: The Purl Stitch

Garter stitch rectangles are enough for some people, but if you really want to up the ante, then learning the purl stitch will open the doors to all manner of stitchery pockery!

Purling is like knitting, only in reverse. The needle is inserted into the front leg from above, then the loop is taken backward to form a new stitch. Look carefully at a knit stitch.

Below the needle is a V shape on the front and a bump at the back. When you purl, the bump falls to the front and the V to the back. You'll learn more about how to make patterns by alternating knit and purl stitches a little later on.

As with the knit stitch, purling can be worked in both English and Continental methods. We'll start again with the English method.

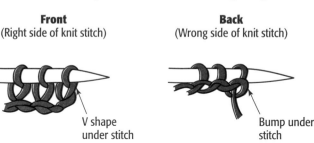

**Front**
(Right side of knit stitch)

**Back**
(Wrong side of knit stitch)

V shape under stitch

Bump under stitch

Anatomy of a stitch

---

## Ooops, I Made a Booboo #2: Common Mistakes When Knitting

You're happily knitting away when you notice something very strange: Not only is your knitting growing lengthwise, it's also getting wider! How can that be? You haven't been taught how to increase yet! It could be one of many reasons, the most common being the old "yarn hanging at the back making the first stitch look like two stitches" trick.

When you finish a row of knitting and turn it to start a new one, check that your first stitch is lying correctly on the needle. The yarn should be hanging straight down from your needle and not flipped over toward the back.

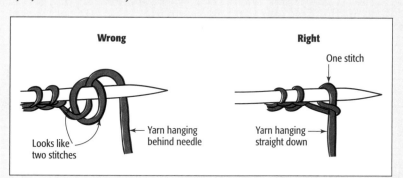

**Wrong**

Looks like two stitches

Yarn hanging behind needle

**Right**

One stitch

Yarn hanging straight down

This can also happen mid-row, so check your knitting regularly. Become familiar with the way the stitches are sitting on the needles. This will help you spot your mistakes—which don't for one moment think you won't make. I still make tons of mistakes, but knowing how to spot them is half the battle. I'll show you how to fix a few a little later on.

Be careful when you put your knitting down. It's always best to get to the end of a row before taking a break. Beginners often pick up their work mid-row, then go back the way they just came or knit with the yarn at the front instead of the back. These practices can have strange effects, which are not what you want at this stage.

## Beans on Toast: Purling the English Way

Cast on 15 stitches or continue working from your knitted piece.

1. Holding your yarn at the front, insert the point of the right needle between the legs of the first stitch from above and toward the front.
2. Using your right forefinger, lift the yarn, take it between the needles from above, wrap it counterclockwise around the point of the right needle, and bring it down.
3. Slide the right needle down and draw the new stitch toward the back through the old one.
4. Keeping the new stitch on the right needle, slide the old one off the left needle.

Repeat steps 1 through 4 until all 15 stitches have been purled. Turn your work and purl the next row, *or* alternate knit and purl rows and you'll have stockinette stitch!

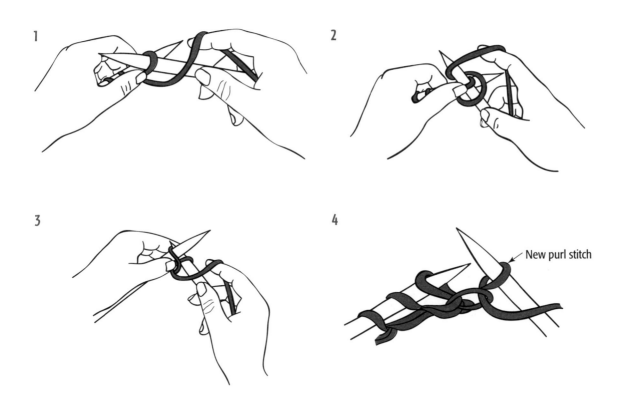

1

2

3

4

New purl stitch

## Coffee and a Croissant: Purling the Continental Way

Cast on 15 stitches as you did for the English method.

1. Holding your yarn at the front, insert the point of the right needle between the legs of the first stitch from above and toward the front.
2. Using your left forefinger, lift the yarn and place it between the needles, wrapping it counterclockwise around the right needle.
3. Slide the right-hand needle down, and draw the new stitch toward the back through the old stitch.
4. Keeping the new stitch on the right needle, slide the old stitch off the left needle.

Now that you can knit and purl, you can work up thousands of different combinations. With the aid of the list of abbreviations found in the appendix, try a few of the patterns in my Stitch Gallery at the end of this chapter—you'll be amazed at what you can achieve using just these two stitches.

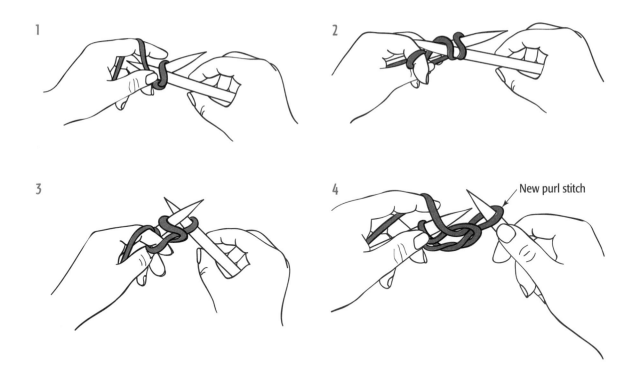

New purl stitch

# Getting the Round In: Working with Double-Pointed and Circular Needles

One of the main gripes of the knitters I know is the dreaded finishing—especially tidying up the loose ends and sewing up the seams. Sometimes it can take more time to put a sweater together than it takes to knit it, and often items that were lovingly knitted lay in the backs of closets or are stuffed under the bed because the knitter just can't face sewing up another seam. But there is a better way!

## Tube Way Army

Instead of knitting two straight pieces, one for the back and one for the front, then joining them to make a tube, why not knit them into a tube to begin with?

To do this you will need either a set of double-pointed needles (dpns), or a circular needle with a smaller circumference than that of the tube you will be knitting (unless you knit with the Magic Loop method—but more about that in a moment).

Start by casting on the required number of stitches. (If using dpns you'll have to divide the stitches evenly between the three needles.) If this is your first time knitting in the round, or you are knitting with a small needle, you may want to work straight for a couple of rows to keep the stitches from becoming twisted when you join the circle (see figure on next page). (If you do end up with a twist in your knitting, there isn't a special trick to untwist it, so be very careful when starting the first round.)

Once you feel confident that your stitches won't be twisted, it's time to join them. If you're using a circular needle, bend it around so the two points are in your hands as if you were knitting straight and the first and last stitches are close to the needle points. The right side of the knitting should be on the outside of the circle. It's a good idea to place a stitch marker at the beginning of the round, as it may not be so easy to spot after going around a few times.

The first stitch in every round will need to be worked tightly to stop a ladder-like gap from forming between the stitches, then carry on knitting in the round.

If you are working with dpns, you'll need to position the three needles into a triangle. Using your fourth needle, knit all the stitches from the first needle onto the fourth needle, then use the empty first needle to knit all the stitches from the second needle etc., round and round.

Another fabulous thing about knitting in the round is that you can knit in stockinette stitch without having to purl. As you will be knitting every round, the bumps will fall to the inside of the tube and the outside will be all lovely smooth stockinette stitch! You can work different stitch patterns in the round, too.

## The Magic Loop Method

I *love* the Magic Loop and I use it whenever I can. It's so painfully simple that I can't believe I didn't know about it years ago. Being able to knit any size of tube without having to swap to

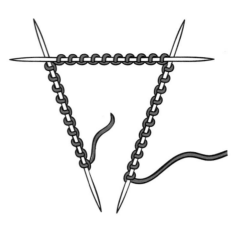

No twists in stitches: Cast-on for circulars (left) and dpns (right).

the dreaded dpns (which I never got the hang of, they would constantly stab into my palms), has changed my life forever!

You'll need a fairly long circular needle; don't try it with anything shorter than 24 inches. You might find that you need a 40-inch one, but anything around 36 inches will work well. Always use a good-quality needle with a smooth join from needle to cable—anything that will stop the stitches from sliding smoothly will drive you completely bananas. I speak from experience!

Cast on your stitches as usual, then divide them equally by pulling out a loop of cable from between the center stitches. This will be your first loop.

Slide the first half of the stitches close to the point of the needle end in your left hand. Now, still keeping a loop of cable between the gap in the center of your stitches, slide the stitches on the other side further to the center of the cable until you can bend around the point of the needle in your right hand so that you are able to knit without putting any strain on the stitches. This will form your second loop.

Keeping the cable with your last stitch stuck like glue to the first stitch with your left hand (this ensures there won't be a ladder-like gap at the joins), knit the first stitch tightly and keep it close to the point of your right-hand needle. Continue to knit the remainder of the stitches on this side of the first loop. Then turn your work to the right so that the second half of the stitches are facing you. Slide these stitches close to the point of the needle and the rest of the stitches onto the cable and continue to knit in the round.

And that, my fine knitting friends, is all there is to it—it's magic!

If you'd like more information about the Magic Loop, Bev Galeskas and Sarah Hauschka have written a great booklet. You'll find it online at www.knitpicks.com/books/itemid_30340/books_display.aspx.

# Knit One, Purl One: Gallery of Stitch Patterns #1

Practice all that you have learned so far by knitting the following patterns that use knit and purl stitches.

## Garter Stitch

Knit all rows.

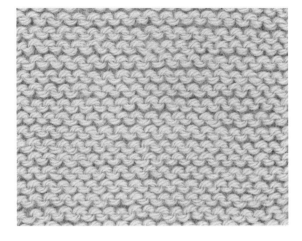

## Stockinette Stitch

**Row 1 (RS):** Knit.
**Row 2:** Purl.
Rep rows 1 and 2.

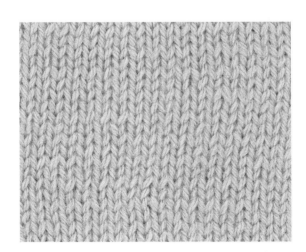

## Seed (Moss) Stitch

Even number of sts:
**Row 1 (RS):** *K1, p1; rep from * to end.
**Row 2:** *P1, k1; rep from * to end.
Odd number of sts:
**All rows:** K1, *p1, k1; rep from * to end.

## Fisherman's Rib

Even number of sts:
**Row 1 (RS):** *K1, p1; rep from * to end.
**Row 2:** *K into the st below the one on the needle, p1; rep from * to end.
Rep row 2 until length required.

## Diagonal Ribbing

Multiple of 12 sts:

**Row 1 (RS):** K1, *p4, k4: rep from * to last 5 sts, p4, k1.

**Row 2:** K4, *p4, k4: rep from * to last 2 sts, p2.

**Row 3:** K3, *p4, k4: rep from * to last 3 sts, p3.

**Row 4:** K2, *p4, k4: rep from * to last 4 sts, p4.

**Row 5:** P1, *k4, p4: rep from * to last 5 sts, k4, p1.

**Row 6:** P4, *k4, p4: rep from * to last 2 sts, k2.

**Row 7:** P3, *k4, p4: rep from * to last 3 sts, k3.

**Row 8:** P2, *k4, p4: rep from * to last 4 sts, k4.

Rep rows 1–8 until length required.

## Lattice Stitch

Multiple of 6 sts +1:

**Row 1 (RS):** K3, *p1, k5: rep from * to last 4 sts, p1, k3.

**Row 2:** P2, *k1, p1, k1, p3: rep from * to last 5 sts, k1, p1, k1, p2.

**Row 3:** K1, *p1, k3, p1, k1: rep from * to end of row.

**Row 4:** K1, *p5, k1: rep from * to end of row.

**Row 5:** As row 3.

**Row 6:** As row 2.

Rep rows 1–6 until length required.

# Chapter Four

◆◆◆

# Shape Shifters: Increasing, Decreasing, and Other Fancy Things to Do with Your Knits and Purls

There are only so many scarves and potholders any sane person can make. Sooner or later you're going to have to learn how to increase and decrease if you want to knit anything more than just a big swatch! These techniques can be a little fiddly at first, but follow the directions carefully and you'll be shaping up a storm of matching right and left slants!

## Increase the Love: Basic Increasing Maneuvers

We'll start with a few basic increasing methods. These will all add an extra stitch each time they are worked. Practice increasing and notice how the different methods affect the appearance of your knitting. Most patterns will tell you which method to use when increasing, but others may leave it up to the knitter to choose. When you know how an increase will look, you will best be able to decide which technique will suit your project.

- **Yarn forward (yf or yfwd) or yarn over (yo), between two knit stitches** While working the knit stitch, your yarn is hanging neatly at the back of your work. A very simple way of making a new stitch is by bringing the yarn forward and then knitting the next stitch. This will form a loop over the right needle, which is then worked as a new stitch in the next row. (With beginners this often happens unintentionally!) (See figure 1.)

- **Yarn round needle (yrn) or yarn over (yo) between two purl stitches** When working the purl stitch, the yarn will be hanging at the front. Take the yarn over the right needle to the back, then bring it forward back under the right needle and purl the next stitch. This will form a loop on the right needle, which is worked as a new stitch on the following row. (See figure 2.)

- **Knitting into the front and back of a stitch (kfb)** Knit into the front leg of the next stitch as normal, then, without taking it off the needle, knit into the back leg of the same stitch, then slide them off the left needle together. (See figure 3.)

- **Purling into the front and back of a stitch (pfb)** Similar to kfb, except you will be purling into the front and back of the stitch before sliding them off the left needle together. (See figure 4.)

- **Make 1 (m1)** Between the stitch on the left needle and the stitch on the right needle there is a horizontal "bar" of yarn. Insert the point of your right needle from front to back under this bar, twist it around, (either toward the left or the right, depending which way you want the new stitch to slant), and place in on your left needle, then knit or purl it through the back leg as if it was the next stitch. If you don't twist it before putting it on the needle you'll have a nice big hole where the bar used to be! (See figure 5.)

- **Lifted increase** Insert the point of your right needle into the top of the stitch below the next stitch on the left needle and knit it, then knit the stitch above. This should give you an almost invisible increase.

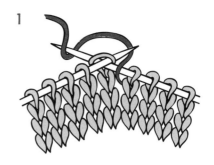

1

Yarn brought forward to front
from back between needles

2

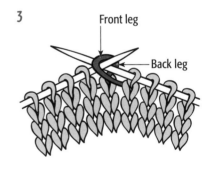

Yarn taken over the needle
to the back then under
needle to the front

3

Front leg

Back leg

4

Front leg

Back leg

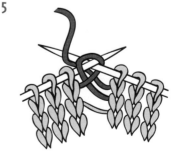

5

# Slimming Down: Basic Decreasing Stitches

When you want fewer stitches in your knitting, you'll need to know how to decrease. These different methods all reduce the number of stitches per row by one each time they are worked. As with increasing, the results are slightly different appearance-wise, so choose the technique that will achieve the look you require.

- ◆ **Knit 2 together (k2tog)** The easiest and fastest way to turn two stitches into one is by working them together. If you are knitting, insert the point of your right needle into the front legs of the second and first stitches on the left needle and knit them as if they were a single stitch, as that is what they will become. (See figure 1.)

1

- ◆ **Purl 2 together (p2tog)** Just like k2tog, except you will be purling into the first two stitches on the left needle to make a brand new one. (See figure 2.)

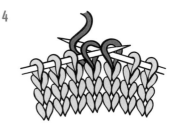

2

- ◆ **Slip one, knit one, pass slip stitch over (s1, k1, psso or skp)** Slip the next stitch knitwise from the left needle to the right needle without knitting it. Knit the next stitch as normal, then with the point of your left needle, lift the slipped stitch over the last knitted stitch and off the needle. This can also be done with a purl stitch and would be written "s1, p1, psso." (See figure 3.)

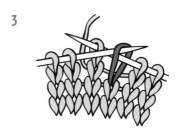

3

- ◆ **Slip, slip, knit (ssk)** As simple as it sounds, slip the next two stitches from the left needle, one at a time, to the right needle without knitting them, then insert the point of the left needle back through the front legs of these two stitches and knit them together. If you really want your stitches to lay perfectly when doing this decrease, try slipping the first stitch knitwise, then the second stitch purlwise before knitting them together. (See figure 4.)

4

## A Match Made in Heaven: How to Knit Perfectly Matching Right and Left Slants

When knitting a sweater with raglan armholes, or any piece that needs to get narrower on the left and right sides at the same rate, you will need nicely matched decreases. You can do all your decreasing at the edges of your work, but it looks fancier and more professional if you decrease one or two stitches in from the sides. This also helps when sewing the edges together.

It's most likely that you'll be working your decreases on the right side (front) of your knitting. (This would be a good time to explain that pieces of knitting have a right and a wrong side. The right side of the knitting will be the outside of the item when it is finished. The wrong side isn't "wrong," it's just what will be on the inside.) If you are to decrease on the right side of your knitting, you will need a left-slanting decrease at the beginning of the row and a right-slanting decrease at the end. To achieve a matching pair of slanting decreases, a pattern could say "K1, ssk, k to last 3 sts, k2tog, k1," which means that you will knit the first stitch, then do a left slanting decrease (slip, slip, knit) over the next two stitches, knit all but the last three stitches from your right needle, do a right slanting decrease (knit the next two stitches together), and finally knit the last stitch. You will probably have to repeat this row a number of times, but only on the right side of the knitting, while purling, knitting, or whatever on the wrong side, without making any decreases. The instructions for this are likely to be something like "Dec as set on next and foll 3 alt rows until 10 sts rem." This means that you will decrease as you did before only on every following right side row, working without decreasing on the wrong side until you have a total of 10 stitches remaining.

## Vertical Double Decrease

If you need two decrease stitches that slant in toward each other to make a single central stitch, here's an attractive little move. Sl2tog kwise, k1, p2sso, which in longhand is "Slip the next two stitches knitwise, knit one, use the point of your left needle to lift the two slipped stitches over the last stitch and off the needle."

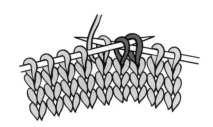

## A Hole in One: Knitting Lace and Pointelle Patterns

These increase and decrease methods aren't just for shaping your knitting; they are also used to make intentional holes and ridges for creating fancy lace and pointelle patterns. To make sure that the piece has the same number of stitches at the end of a row as it does at the beginning, there must be an equal number of increases as there are decreases.

Instructions for these designs will tell you the number of stitches you need to cast on to complete a single repeat of the pattern, which is useful if you want to knit a wide piece. It will say something like "worked over a multiple of 8 sts plus 1," which means that you will need to decide how many repeats you want to knit, multiply this number by eight, then add one. Let's say you want to knit four repeats. Then you will need to cast on 33 stitches = $4 \times 8 + 1$.

A good tip here is to place markers after each pattern repeat; that way, if you make a mistake, you won't have to go all the way back to the beginning of the row to fix it!

Take a peek at the abbreviations in the appendix to help you understand the shorthand used in the following patterns.

Let's first look at one of my all-time favorite fancy stitches, Feather and Fan.

## The Secrets of Short-Row Knitting

To make curved shapes without increasing, decreasing, and sewing together, there's a neat little trick called short-row knitting. This is often done for the heels of socks and can be used to knit a nice smooth shoulder shape.

Working a short row means that you will knit a number of stitches but before reaching the end of the row, you will turn your work to the other side, leaving the unknitted stitches on the end of the needle and work back on the stitches you have just knitted. An unwanted hole can appear at the turning point, so to avoid this it may be necessary to wrap the last stitch. Wrapping the stitch is very simple. When working the knit stitch, before you knit the stitch that is to be wrapped, move the yarn from the back to the front, between the needles and slip the chosen stitch. Then turn the work and move the yarn from the front to the back, and you will have wrapped your first stitch! When working the purl stitch, you will need to move your yarn from the front to the back before slipping it, then from the back to the front to continue. When it is time to work this stitch again, you will pick up its wrap with the point of your right needle and work it together with the stitch. This can be made a little less fiddly if you slip both the stitch and its wrap onto the right needle, then back to the left needle before working together.

You can use short rows to create a curve at the edge of your knitting. To achieve a nice smooth curve, it's important to work your short rows at regular intervals, usually an even number of rows.

## Feather and Fan

This four-row pattern is a great introduction to lace, as the fiddly stuff is all in the third row; the other three rows are plain old knit or purl. Multiple of 18 sts + 2. (Let's cast on 38 stitches for this trial run.)

**Row 1 (RS):** K. (Simple enough, right? This will be the right side of the work and you will be knitting every stitch.)

**Row 2:** P. (Just purl all the way across.)

**Row 3:** K1, *(k2tog) 3 times, (yf,k1) 6 times, (k2tog) 3 times: rep from * to last st, k1. (So

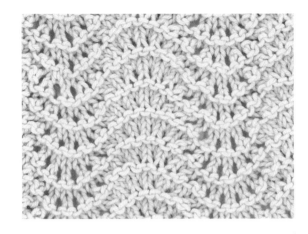

this is where you have to concentrate. Knit your first stitch, place a marker, knit two stitches together three times, then bring your yarn forward and knit one stitch six times, knit two stitches together three times and place another marker, then repeat the section between the asterisks again. You should be left with one stitch on your right needle; knit this last stitch.)

**Row 4:** K. (Knit every stitch.)

Rep these 4 rows. (Keep repeating the last four rows until your work is as long as you want it.)

Feather and Fan can also look really good in a stripe—just work four rows in one color, then four rows in another color, and keep repeating the stripe.

## Allover Lace and Lace Panels: Gallery of Stitch Patterns *2

### Tulip Lace

Multiple of 8 + 7

**Row 1 (RS):** K.

**Row 2 and every alt row:** P.

**Row 3:** K3, *yf, s1, k1, psso, k6; rep from * to last 4 sts, yf, s1, k1, psso, k2.

**Row 5:** K1, *k2tog, yf, k1, yf, s1, k1, psso, k3; rep from* to last 6 sts, k2tog, yf, k1, yf, sl, k1, psso, k1.

**Row 7:** As row 3.

**Row 9:** K.

**Row 11:** K7, * yf, s1, k1, psso, k6; rep from * to end.

**Row 13:** K5, * k2tog, yf, k1, yf, s1, k1, psso, k3; rep from * to last 2 sts, k2.

**Row 15:** As row 11.

**Row 16:** P.

Rep rows 1–16.

## Wave Stitch

Multiple of 6 +1.

Special abbreviations:

**Kw2:** Knit next stitch, wrapping yarn twice around needle.

**Kw3:** Knit next stitch, wrapping yarn three times around needle.

**Row 1 (RS):** K1, *kw2, (kw3) twice, kw2, k2; rep from * to end.

**Row 2:** K, dropping all extra loops from previous row.

**Row 3:** Kw3, kw2, k2, kw2, * (kw3) twice, kw2, k2, kw2; rep from * to last 2 sts. kw3, k1.

**Row 4:** As row 2.

Rep rows 1–4.

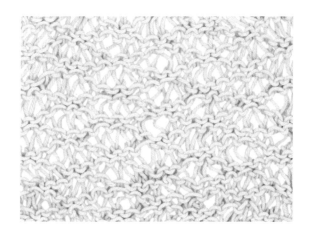

## Lacy Lattice Stitch

Multiple of 6 +1.

**Row 1 (RS):** K1, * yfrn, p1, p3tog, p1, yon, k1; rep from * to end.

**Row 2 and every alt row:** P.

**Row 3:** K2, yf, s1, k2tog, psso, yf, * k3, yf, s1, k2tog, psso, yf; rep from * to last 2 sts, k2.

**Row 5:** P2tog, p1, yon, k1, yfrn, p1, * p3tog, p1, yon, k1, yfrn, p1; rep from * to last 2 sts, p2tog.

**Row 7:** K2tog, yf, k3, yf, * s1, k2tog, psso, yf, k3, yf; rep from * to last 2 sts, s1, k1, psso.

**Row 8:** P.

Rep rows 1–8.

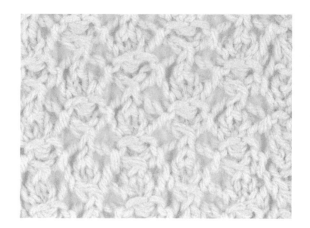

## Ridged Eyelet Border

Multiple of 2 +1.

**Rows 1, 2, and 3:** K.

**Row 4 (WS):** * P2tog, yrn; rep from * to last st, p1.

**Rows 5, 6, and 7:** K.

**Row 8:** P.

Rep rows 1–8.

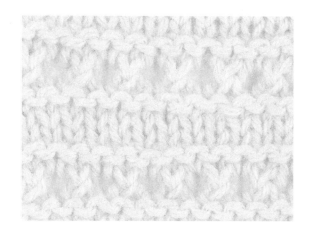

## Cascading Leaves

Worked over 16 sts on a background of reverse St st.

**Row 1 (RS):** P1, k3, k2tog, k1, yrn, p2, yon, k1, s1, k1, psso, k3, p1.

**Row 2 and every alt row:** K1, p6, k2, p6, k1.

**Row 3:** P1, k2, k2tog, k1, yf, k1, p2, k1, yf, k1, s1, k1, psso, k2, p1.

**Row 5:** P1, k1, k2tog, k1, yf, k2, p2, k2, yf, k1, s1, k1, psso, k1, p1.

**Row 7:** P1, k2tog, k1, yf, k3, p2, k3, yf, k1, s1, k1, psso, p1.

**Row 8:** K1, p6, k2, p6, k1.

Rep rows 1–8.

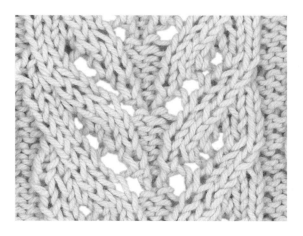

# Chapter **Five**

◆◆

# Twist and Shout: Knitting Cables and Bobbles

I had an Aran cardigan when I was around 4 or 5 years old, made from itchy cream-colored wool and finished with real leather buttons. I would stick my little fingers into the wooly twists and pull on the bobbles, wondering how they got there. My grandmother knitted that cardi for me, and it was from that same wrinkled pattern that I had my first cabling and bobble-making experience.

## Switch-a-Roo: How to Knit Cables

Not only do cables look attractive (if you like that sort of thing), they also add interest to an otherwise monotonous and flat piece of knitting. As small sections of stitches are pulled and twisted, the knitting becomes denser and a lot less elastic, which is great if you want to add bulk and warmth, but not so good if you need a stretchy fabric. Always knit your gauge swatch to include the cables you will be using and remember that adding cables to a plain garment will make it quite a bit skinnier. Measure and calculate accordingly!

After working the first twist of a cable, my reaction was similar to that of many knitters trying it out for the first time: "Oh, is that all there is to it, I thought it would be a lot more complicated!" Now, don't get me wrong, cables *can* be very complicated and get you all tied up in knots, but a simple six-stitch single-twist cable is far from rocket science.

You will be sliding three stitches, purlwise, onto a cable needle, which is then left to hang at the front of the work (for a left-twisting cable) or at the back of the work (if you want your cable to twist toward the right). Continue to knit the next three stitches from your left needle before knitting the three stitches from the cable needle.

These last six stitches have just switched positions. For the simplest of cables—that's all there is to it!

Using the following patterns, and with the help of the abbreviations listed in the appendix, go right ahead and knit your own practice swatches.

The most common type of cable is knitted in stockinette stitch (St st) on a background of reverse stockinette stitch.

So get yourself some yarn, needles, and a cable needle that's a similar size to your needles. (If you use a cable needle that's too big, you could stretch your stitches; if you use one that's too small, it could slip out of the stitches and become lost forever under the couch!)

## Simple Six-Stitch Cable

Worked over 6 sts on a background of reverse St st.
Cast on 20 sts.
**Rows 1, 3, and 7:** P4, k6, p4.
**Row 2 (WS):** K4, p6, k4.
**Row 4:** P4, c6f (which means slip the next three stitches purlwise onto your cable needle and let them hang to the front of your work, knit the next three stitches from your left needle, then knit the three stitches from your cable needle, being careful not to twist them), p4.
**Rows 6 and 8:** As row 2.
Rep rows 1–8.
    Easy, right?
    This will give you a cable that twists to the left. To make a cable twist to the right, simply hold the stitches on the cable needle to the back of the work instead of the front. (Row 4 will be written like this: P4, c6b, p4.)

## Goodness, Gracious, Great Balls of Yarn: How to Knit Bobbles

Bobbles are fabulous little balls in knitting whose only purpose is decoration. They are created by increasing a number of times into a single stitch, and can differ in size from a baby bobble to a big fat mama bobble!

## Baby Bobble

Here's how to knit a small bobble into a piece of stockinette stitch:

1. On the right side, knit to where you want your bobble to sit.
2. Keeping the next stitch on your left needle, knit into the front, and then into back, three times, so that you have made six stitches out of one.
3. With the point of your left needle, take the second stitch closest to the right needle point over the first stitch and off the needle.
4. Take the third stitch over the first and off, and so on, until all five stitches have been passed over the first stitch and off the left needle.

Carry on knitting until the mood strikes you to knit another, or you could have a go at a bigger one.

## Mama Bobble

Here's how to knit a larger bobble into a piece of stockinette stitch:

1. On the right side, knit to the stitch where you want the bobble to be.
2. Keeping the next stitch on your left needle, knit into the front, and then into the back, twice, then into the front again.
3. Turn your knitting so the wrong side is facing you.
4. Knit the five stitches, turn; do this twice, so that the wrong side is facing you again.
5. K1, sl, k2tog, psso, k1, turn.
6. Now the right side is facing you, k3tog and carry on knitting until you want to pop in another bobble.

# Reading a Chart *1

There is more than one way to write out knitting stitch pattern instructions. In my knitting life-time I have seen more patterns written out with abbreviations, but some people find it easier to follow a chart where each stitch is represented by a single square and each row of the chart represents a row of knitting.

Charts are usually read from the bottom up and from right to left on right-side rows and from left to right on wrong-side rows. When working in the round, every row will be read from right to left. The chart will usually show one repeat of the pattern and indicate where the different stitches should be by using symbols.

The chart on the next page shows some of the most commonly used symbols. They may vary from pattern to pattern, so a key to the symbols to show what each squiggle represents is also included.

Not only are stitch patterns worked in repeats, but also a series of rows can be a repeat. Some knitting patterns include a stitch pattern chart that covers the entire sweater (particularly those that involve intarsia), with lines drawn indicating size, sleeve, front, back, etc., so that all parts of the item can be worked from a single chart.

It is recommended that you make an enlarged copy of the chart and mark off each row as you knit it. Some knitters use a board and a magnetic straight line to keep track of where they are in the pattern; others use sticky notes placed directly above the row they are working on. This means that as well as being able to see the current row, you can see where the new stitches will be in relation to those you are working over.

If you don't want to work from the chart, you can follow it to write out the instructions so they will be easier for you to follow, and vice versa, as you can draw your own chart from written instructions if you prefer that method.

| | | |
|---|---|---|
| ☐ | = | Knit on right side, purl on wrong side |
| • | = | Purl on right side, knit on wrong side |
| ○ | = | Yarn over (yo) |
| ⧗ | = | Make 1 increase (m1) |
| ⧹ | = | Knit 2 stitches together (k2tog) |
| ⧸ | = | Slip 2 stitches, then knit them together (ssk) |
| ⧸ | = | Slip 1, knit 1, pass slipped stitch over (s1, k1, psso) |
| ● | = | Make bobble (mb) |
| ⧄ | = | Cable 4 stitches to the right (c4b) |
| ⧅ | = | Cable 4 stitches to the left (c4f) |

← Start here

# Cables and Bobbles: Gallery of Stitch Patterns *3

Put your cabling skills into practice by working the following stitch patterns. The first three give directions for the cable section only—cast on a few extra stitches (for a swatch, six extra stitches either side of the cable should be enough). Work these extra stitches in purl on the right side and knit on the wrong side—this will be your background of reverse stockinette stitch. In the fourth pattern, you'll get to practice both cabling and bobbles in the same swatch!

You may need to check out the abbreviations listed in the appendix to help decipher the shorthand.

## Nine-Stitch Plait

Worked over 9 sts on a background of reverse St st.
**Row 1 (RS):** K.
**Row 2 and every alt row:** P.
**Row 3:** C6f, k3.
**Row 5:** K.
**Row 7:** K3, c6b.
**Row 8:** P.
Rep rows 1–8.

## Double Cable

Worked over 12 sts on a background of reverse St st.
**Row 1 (RS):** K.
**Rows 2, 4, and 6:** P.
**Row 3:** C6b, c6f.
**Rows 5 and 7:** K.
**Row 8:** P.
Rep rows 1–8.

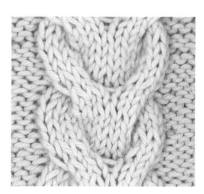

## Hugs and Kisses Cable

Worked over 8 sts on a background of reverse St st.

**Row 1 (RS):** K.
**Row 2 and all alt rows:** P.
**Row 3:** C4b, c4f.
**Row 5:** K.
**Row 7:** As row 3.
**Row 9:** K.
**Row 11:** C4f, c4b.
**Row 13:** K.
**Row 15:** As row 11.
**Row 16:** P.
Rep rows 1–16.

## Bobbles and Waves

Special abbreviations:

**C6b (cable 6 back):** Slip the next three stitches onto a cable needle and hold at the back; knit the next three stitches on the left needle; knit the three stitches from the cable needle.

**Mb (make bobble):** Knit into the front, back, and front of next stitch (turn and knit these three stitches) three times, then turn and s1, k2tog, psso).

**T3b (twist 3 back):** Slip next stitch onto cable needle and hold at back of work, knit next two stitches from left needle, then purl stitch from cable needle.

**T5b (twist 5 back):** Slip next two stitches onto cable needle and hold at back of work, knit next three stitches from left needle, then purl two stitches from cable needle.

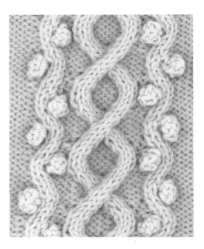

**T3f (twist 3 front):** Slip next two stitches onto cable needle and hold at front of work, purl next stitch from left needle, then knit two stitches from cable needle.

**T5f (twist 5 front):** Slip next three stitches onto cable needle and hold at front of work, purl next two stitches from left needle, then knit three stitches from cable needle.

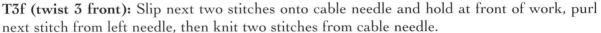

Worked over 26 sts on a background of reverse St st.

**Row 1 (RS):** P2, t3b, p5, c6b, p5, t3f, p2.

**Row 2:** K2, p2, k6, p6, k6, p2, k2.

**Row 3:** P1, t3b, p4, t5b, t5f, p4, t3f, p1.

**Row 4:** K1, p2, k5, p3, k4, p3, k5, p2, k1.

**Row 5:** T3b, p3, t5b, p4, t5f, p3, t3f.

**Row 6:** P2, k1, mb, k2, p3, k8, p3, k2, mb, k1, p2.

**Row 7:** T3f, p3, k3, p8, k3, p3, t3b.

**Row 8:** K1, p2, k3, p3, k8, p3, k3, p2, k1.

**Row 9:** P1, t3f, p2, t5f, p4, t5b, p2,t3b, p1.

**Row 10:** K2, p2, (k4, p3) twice, k4, p2, k2.

**Row 11:** P2, t3f, p3, t5f, t5b, p3, t3b, p2.

**Row 12:** K1, mb, k1, p2, k5, p6, k5, p2, k1, mb, k1.

Rep rows 1–12.

# Chapter Six

◆◆

# Painting by Stitches: How to Knit with Different Colors

For some people it's knitting instinct; they understand how stitches are formed, how the yarn loops into a stitch to create a new stitch, how all the stitches are joined in one continuous length of twisted fiber. But what happens if you run out of your yarn? What if you need to join a new ball or if you want to change color? Sooner or later you're gonna want to knit some stripes!

## Starting a New Ball of Yarn

Like just about every aspect of knitting, there are many different ways to begin knitting with a new yarn. I'll start with the most simple. This can be done anywhere along your row, but for less risk of the join showing, I highly recommend starting a new yarn right at the beginning of your row. Simply drop your old yarn and pick up the end of your new one, leaving a tail of around 6 inches, so the first stitch won't come undone. Now carry on knitting as normal with this new yarn, but you will have to anchor and tidy away those ends before too much longer.

Here are a few methods to join a new yarn, which will help give you a safer and neater finish.

## Easy Does It

Twist the end of the new yarn around the old one right at the base of the *first* stitch. Then weave in the ends as you knit them by picking up each strand of yarn alternately and twisting it behind the work before you knit a new stitch (just for around six stitches). This anchors the ends and tidies them away at the same time.

## More Advanced

Insert the point of your right needle into the first stitch as if you were to work it, then, leaving a tail end of around 6 inches, lay the new yarn between the needles as if you were to knit with it. Twist the new yarn around the old yarn and wrap the new yarn between the needles ready to make a new stitch. Take the tail end of the yarn that you put between the needles over this and off the needles as you make a new stitch.

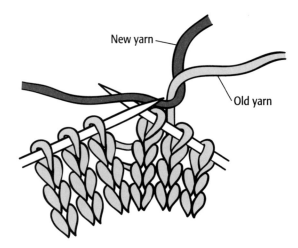

The smart way to join a new yarn

## The Spit Splice

I get strange looks when I do this on the subway but it makes an almost invisible join of two yarns. This method will only join yarns made from animal fibers, as it's a way of felting them together.

Fray the ends of your old and new yarns by pulling the fibers apart, just one half to three quarters of an inch. Lay them overlapped top to tail in your palm, then spit on them and vigorously roll them together. Voilà! A join you will not have to tidy up after! The four elements of felting are all working together here—animal hair, heat, moisture, and agitation—witness a tiny joining miracle!

---

### Is My End Long Enough? How to Tell if You'll Have Enough Yarn to Finish a Row

A nifty little trick to see if you'll have enough yarn to finish a row is to keep your eye on your ever-decreasing ball. When it gets a bit on the small side and you are at the end of a row, unravel your little ball and find the end. Hold the end together with the yarn next to your last stitch and find the mid-point of your remaining yarn. Tie a slip knot at this point, then carry on knitting. If you complete a row before reaching the slip knot, you will have enough yarn to knit another row. If you still have quite a bit of yarn to go before the slip knot, you can repeat the process.

Another way to tell if you have enough yarn for one more row is to see if the yarn remaining is four times the width of your knitting.

---

## A Stripe of a Different Color

The easiest introduction to multicolor knitting is the good old stripe. Stripes can be knitted vertically, but it's way easier and quicker to knit them horizontally—just knitting one color per row.

At the beginning of a new row, just start with a new color as I explained earlier, then knit away until you need to change color again.

If you don't want to deal with a lot of loose ends later, try carrying your yarns up the side. Your stripes will have to consist of an even number of rows so that the yarns always begin and end at the same side of your knitting. If your stripes are just two rows long, you don't need to twist the yarns together when changing colors. Just drop the old color, pick up the new color, and begin another stripe. Don't pull up too much on the new yarn; make sure you leave enough slack so that your edge will lay flat.

If your stripes are made from any odd-numbered rows and the yarn you need is at the other edge of your work, you can slip all the stitches from the left needle to the right needle without knitting them, thus enabling you to strand your yarn up to its new starting place.

## Two Techniques for Multicolor Knitting

There are two different techniques you can use for knitting colored patterns: Fair Isle and intarsia. Let's take a closer look at each.

## Fair Isle

With Fair Isle, small repeats of pattern are worked in stockinette stitch across the knitting using two or more colors. When switching colors, the yarns are twisted around one another to keep holes from appearing at the joins.

To prevent holes when you change colors, you'll be twisting your yarns around one another as you go along your row. A clever tip for keeping them untangled is to twist them all the same way going across your row, then twist them in the opposite direction coming back. When worked properly, you should end up with your yarns untwisted at the end of every row. The yarns not in work are stranded or woven in on the wrong side as you knit. It's important to keep the fabric elastic by not pulling the yarns across the back of the knitting too tightly, otherwise the pattern will be distorted and look ugly.

Stranding involves carrying the yarn not in use at the back of the work. You need to keep your strands, or floats, short (as you can get caught up in a large loop!). So, depending on gauge, you don't want to strand over more than three to five stitches. If you have to strand your yarn in the center of a color, just twist the yarns around each other once—(don't do this at the same point on each row as it might show through on the right side), alternating the strand length by a stitch or two.

There are different ways of holding your yarn when stranding—you can hold each yarn as you use it, then twist

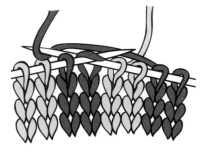

To prevent gaps, take new yarn over old yarn

it with the next yarn, drop it and pick up the new one; or you can hold a separate yarn in each hand, using the Continental method for the yarn in your left hand and the English method for the yarn in your right hand. Spread the stitches out along the needles as you knit to help keep you from pulling the yarns too tightly.

## Intarsia

You'll be using this method to knit isolated motifs using a different ball of yarn for each segment of the pattern. Again, it's important to twist the two strands of yarns around one another once at the join of two colors to stop holes from forming.

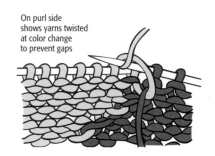

On purl side shows yarns twisted at color change to prevent gaps

New and old yarns twisted on the wrong side

# Twisted Up in Knots: Tips for Yarn Tangle Management

When working with different colors, it's likely that you'll have several balls of yarn hanging from your knitting just waiting to become a tangled and torturous mess. Here are several handy hints to prevent this:

♦ **Bobbins** Wind small amounts of all the different colors of yarn you'll be using onto separate bobbins. You can buy specially made bobbins that have a narrow, flat middle and wider ends to stop the yarn from unraveling too easily, or you could make your own bobbins from pieces of cardboard.

♦ **Baggies** Pop each different ball of yarn into a separate zip-top bag, leaving just a small opening for the yarn to be pulled from, or turn the bag upside down and snip off one corner and have the yarn come out from the hole.

♦ **Take-out drink containers** Drop your little ball of yarn in the bottom of the clean cup, thread the end through the hole in the lid and knit away!

♦ **Drinking straws** Threading the end of your yarn through a drinking straw will help keep it organized. Drinking straws can be used with all of the above methods, too.

# Reading a Chart #2

Some Fair Isle and intarsia patterns are written out in words telling you how many stitches to knit in a certain color, but most will give you a chart to follow, which is a very simple way to follow your progress.

Each stitch is represented by a square containing a symbol and will usually be in black and white. So how do you know which colors go where? There will also be a key to the chart, which tells you which color each symbol represents. It's a very good idea to photocopy your chart, enlarging it if necessary, then color in each square in the colors you will be using.

Charts are read as they will be knitted, starting at the bottom right-hand square, showing the right side of the pattern, working from right to left on the first and every odd-numbered row, and from left to right on the second and every even-numbered row.

Start second row here →

← Start first row here

Color key

☐ = A

☒ = B

◯ = C

# Fair Isle and Intarsia: Gallery of Stitch Patterns *4

Try your hand at knitting color patterns by working from the following charts. The Fair Isle charts show just one repeat of the pattern and can be worked over any multiple of the chart's total stitches. The intarsia charts show the single pattern, which can be worked into a background of any number of stitches.

## Simple 2-Color Fair Isle 8-Stitch Repeat

This stitch can also be worked as a stitch pattern by following the stitch key:

    A = Knit on right side, purl on wrong side.
    B = Purl on right side, knit on wrong side.

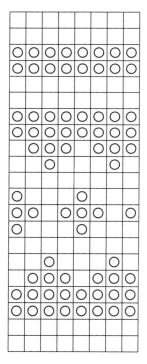

## 5-Color Fair Isle 14-Stitch Repeat

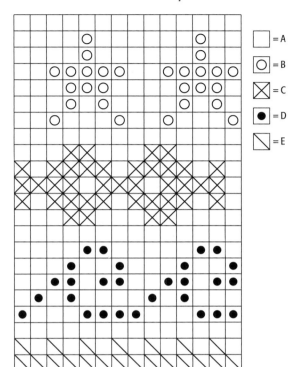

□ = A
○ = B
⊠ = C
● = D
◿ = E

## 2-Color Intarsia

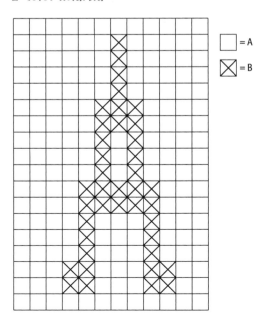

□ = A
⊠ = B

## 5-Color Intarsia

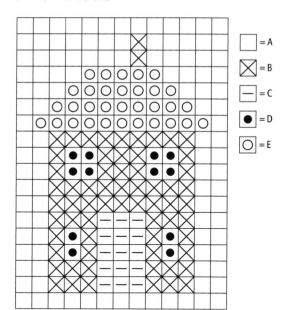

- □ = A
- ☒ = B
- ⊟ = C
- ● = D
- ○ = E

# Chapter Seven

◆◆◆

# It Ain't Over 'til the Fat Lady Pins: Finishing and Blocking

You've come a long way, baby, spending many hours carefully working away on your knitting, dreaming about the final result. Maybe you've had to frog (which I'll discuss in Chapter 9, "Oops, I Made a Big Booboo! Fixing Mistakes") and re-knit areas, perhaps dropped a stitch or two along the way, but you've managed to pick them back up and now have several pieces that need to be put together to complete your project.

The finishing stage is the least liked part of the process and many knitters downright despise it, leaving bags full of UFOs (unfinished objects), in their knitting stashes. But don't despair—done properly, finishing can be enjoyable and will make all the difference in the finished look of your work. Follow the methods shown here and complete your project in the correct way, ensuring that your work of art can be shown off with pride.

## Seams Like a Nice Girl: The Correct Stitching Method for the Job

Different sections of your knitting will require a different type of seam. If you are new to sewing, it wouldn't be a bad idea to practice on your gauge swatch before tackling the main job at hand.

Start by laying your pieces side by side on a nice flat surface. (Scrunched up in your lap may be the comfiest position, but you want this to look good, right?) Pin them in place.

Get yourself a blunt tapestry needle and thread it with a length of yarn to match your knitting (for multicolored knitting, go with the most prominent color).

## Mattress Stitch

This stitch creates an almost invisible seam on the right side of the fabric by working either a half or a whole stitch in from the edge (depending on yarn thickness or neatness of edge stitches).

## Joining Stockinette Stitch

Gently pull apart the first and second edge stitches of your knitting and look for the little bars that join the columns of stitches—they look a bit like ladders. This is where you will be making your seam, taking your needle and thread from right piece to left piece and back again, picking up these running bars as you work upward.

1. With right sides facing toward you, start at the bottom of your work and insert your needle between the first and second stitches of the right piece.
2. Do the same in the left piece and pull tight, leaving a tail of about 6 inches to weave in later.
3. Pick up the first two running bars on the right piece.
4. Do the same on the left piece.
5. Go back to the right piece and insert the needle into the same place where it came out and pick up the next two yarn bars.
6. Do the same on the left piece.

Repeat the last two steps, pulling the yarn firmly but not too tightly every couple of inches, and watch how the pieces magically join to become one with no trace of a seam on the right side.

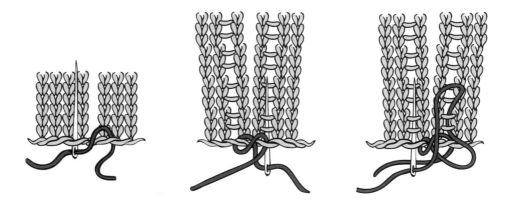

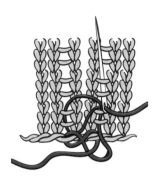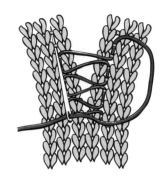

## Joining Reverse Stockinette Stitch or Garter Stitch

This is very similar to the method used to join two pieces of stockinette stitch, but you will only be working through one stitch each side at a time.

Take a good look at your edge stitches and notice that instead of the little Vs of stockinette stitch you will see that the stitches look like little bumps—some arching upward and some arching downward. You'll be stitching alternately into the upward-arching bumps on the right piece and the downward-arching bumps on the left piece.

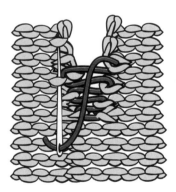

## Joining Ribs

When sewing seams of ribbed pieces together, work half a stitch in from the edge. A complete stitch will then be formed by joining two half stitches.

## Joining Stitches to Rows

You'll need this method for sewing sleeves into place. It's not a true mattress stitch, as you will be attaching a bound-off edge (the top of your sleeve) to the edge of your body from shoulder seam to underarm.

Keeping your body piece to your right and your sleeve to the left, pin the pieces in place, matching the center of the sleeve cap to the shoulder seam.

1. Insert the needle into the stitches of your right piece as in mattress stitch, picking up one or two bars, then insert the needle into the left piece, picking up a whole stitch.
2. Now back over on the right side, insert your needle into the same place it came out and pick up the next one or two bars.
3. Back to the left piece, insert your needle back into the spot where it exited and pick up the next stitch.

Repeat the last two steps until you have stitched the two pieces together, pulling the yarn every inch or so to close the seam.

In most cases, the stitches and rows won't match up exactly, so you will have to pick up either one or two yarn bars along the way to equal them out.

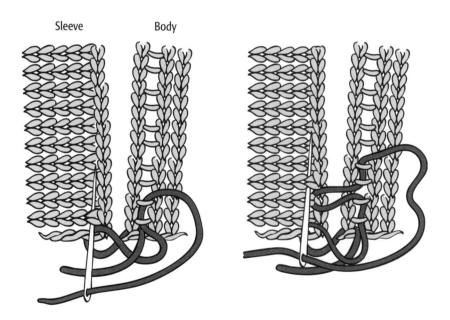

Sleeve　　　　Body

## Joining Stitches to Stitches

This method is also called fake grafting, as you will be imitating the shape of a knit stitch, passing from stitch to stitch with your needle and yarn. This method can be used to sew bound-off shoulder seams together. It works best on pieces knitted in stockinette stitch.

Lay your pieces right side up on a flat surface with the bound-off edges facing one another, top to top.

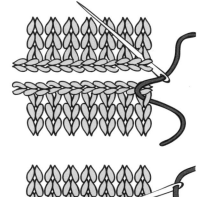

1. Insert your needle into the first piece, from the back into the center of the first stitch, just under the bound-off edge, leaving a tail of yarn to weave in later.

2. Insert your needle into the second piece, from the back into the space between the first and second stitches, just under the bound-off edge.

3. Back to the first piece, insert your needle into the spot where it exited and out of the middle of the next stitch just below the bound-off edge.

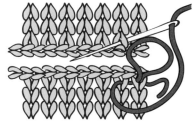

4. On the second piece, insert your needle into the spot where it exited and out of the space between that stitch and the next one just below the bound-off edge.

Repeat the last two steps until you have completed the seam, but do not pull the yarn too tightly, just enough to create fake stitches the same size as your original knitted stitches.

## Kitchener Stitch

Also known as grafting, this method creates completely invisible and flat seams by duplicating a row from stitches that have not been bound off (called live stitches). Kitchener stitch can also be used to graft two pieces of knitting together that have been altered to change the length after adding or taking away a number of rows.

This seaming method can be quite fiddly, so only attempt this seam when you are in a peaceful state of mind or you may end up tossing the whole thing out of the window. If this is your first attempt at Kitchener stitch, try it out on a light- or bright-colored, non-slipping yarn—nothing finer than worsted weight—with good lighting and a stiff drink on hand!

You will need two pieces of knitting with exactly the same number of stitches in each piece, such as an unshaped shoulder.

1. Lay your pieces on a flat surface right side up with the top edges facing one another.
2. Breathe.
3. I like to take the first two stitches off each knitting needle, but you can also leave them on if you prefer and insert your tapestry needle, from the back into the first stitch of the lower piece.
4. Take the tapestry needle and insert it from the back though the first stitch on the upper piece.
5. Back to the lower piece, insert your tapestry needle into the first stitch again, but this time from the front, then into the next stitch of the same piece from the back.
6. On the upper piece, insert your tapestry needle into the first stitch again, but this time from the front, then into the next stitch of the same piece from the back.

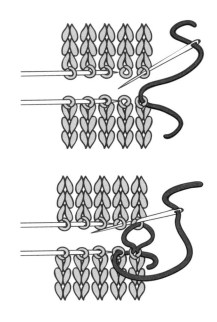

Repeat these last two stages, either taking two stitches off each knitting needle at a time, or leaving them on the needles until they have been worked, creating a row of fake stitches, making them the same size as your knitted stitches so they will become undetectable. Now take a big gulp of that drink—you deserve it!

## Backstitch

Unlike the magic created by the mattress stitch, backstitch is quick, but your seams will be bulky and quite visible, although strong and non-elastic. I'm embarrassed to admit it, but this was just about all I knew, seamwise, until my eyes were opened to discover mattress stitch quite recently.

I still use backstitch today for adding attention to seams—mainly on the outsides of accessories and where I want corners to be more pronounced. It is also good for sewing the seams of linings for bags.

1. Pin pieces to be seamed together with right sides facing for seam on inside or wrong sides together for seam on outside.
2. Insert the needle from back into first stitch just below edges in the same place through both pieces, leaving a tail of yarn to weave in later.
3. Make a stitch from front to back. Reinsert the needle from back to front just to the right of the exit point of the first stitch.

Make all the stitches the same size until the seam is completed, being careful not to pull the yarn too tightly.

## Running Stitch

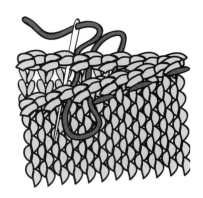

This is probably the simplest seam of all, but I would only recommend using running stitch for basting two pieces of knitting together.

It's useful for times when pins may slide out, for keeping pieces together to be seamed properly later, or when you want to see if your garment will be the right size before you tackle the seaming for real.

Start as you did for backstitch, but instead of going backward and forward with your stitches, just keep on going forward, making simple short stitches through both pieces.

## Slip Stitch

This stitch can be used for attaching one piece of knitting on top of another, like a pocket, or for sewing up a hem or attaching a zipper. It can be done on either the right or the wrong side of the knitting, depending on what you are seaming.

Where possible, it's best to match the pieces stitch for stitch to yield a flat seam.

When working on the wrong side, insert your tapestry needle only partway through the stitch, splitting it so that it won't show on the right side.

1. On a flat surface, pin the pieces into position.
2. Insert your needle into the first stitch (as close to the edge as possible) of the smaller piece, then into the larger piece.

Work all stitches this way, going through each of the two pieces with every stitch.

# Picking Up Stitches

Now that you're a seaming pro, I'll introduce you to a method of adding to your knitting that requires no sewing of seams whatsoever!

Picking up stitches is the carefree way to add a collar to the neckline of a sweater, or knit a fancy trim directly onto the edge of a garment. You can pick up stitches to add a pocket or knit down a sleeve directly from an armhole.

When making bags, I often work the base straight, then pick up stitches all around the edges and knit up the main part of the bag in the round. This saves a lot of time in the finishing stages when there are fewer seams to sew!

A lot of patterns use the term "pick up and knit" a certain amount of stitches, although you won't actually be picking up stitches. Rather, you'll be making new ones appear out of old ones. There really isn't any knitting involved; in fact, many people find it easier to pick up stitches with a crochet hook (as the action is very similar to a simple crochet stitch), then transfer the picked-up stitches to a knitting needle as they go along.

## Picking Up Stitches Horizontally

With the right side facing you, hold your knitting in your left hand and your knitting needle (or crochet hook) in your right hand.

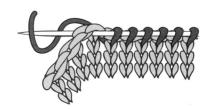

1. Holding the yarn at the back of your knitting and leaving a 6-inch or so tail to weave in later, insert your knitting needle (or crochet hook) into the center of your first stitch, wrapping your yarn around the needle.
2. Bring the new loop back though the stitch where it was entered, and voilà! You've picked up your first stitch!

Just carry on picking up stitches along your knitting in this way, transferring them as you go onto a knitting needle, if you are using a crochet hook.

## Picking Up Stitches Vertically

You'll want to turn your knitting so that the edge you need to pick up stitches along is now laying horizontally. Pick up stitches as you would horizontally, but insert your knitting needle (or crochet hook) between the stitches instead of through the centers.

What happens when the number of stitches to be picked up does not match the number of stitches along your edge? This happens fairly often, especially when picking up stitches at a neck edge. But not to worry, a little bit of simple division and multiplication is all that is needed.

Measure your edge and calculate how many stitches you will need to pick up per inch. Mark off the inches with pins and pick up the number of stitches you need between each pin. This will ensure you have the correct number of stitches that will be evenly spaced along the edge.

If you have too few stitches from which to pick up new ones, you can split the stitches by inserting your needle though the yarn of the stitch. You can also split the stitches to disguise holes that can occur, especially on a curved edge or after turning the heel of a sock.

If you have too many stitches from which to pick up new ones, just skip a stitch occasionally, but make sure you do this evenly along your edge.

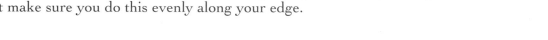

# Binding Off

Why bind off two pieces of knitting and then sew a seam at their bound-off edges when you can bind them off together? The following methods for finishing your knitting will give you neat, professional-looking seams.

## Three-Needle Bind-Off

Especially good for finishing a shoulder seam, the three-needle bind-off can feel a bit cumbersome at first, as you will have two needles full of stitches in one hand, but the results are worth a bit of fumbling.

You will need an equal number of stitches on each needle.

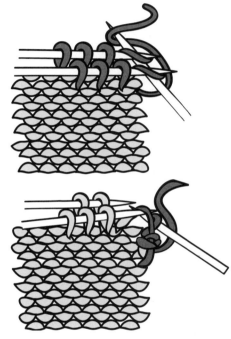

1.  With right sides together, hold both pieces in your left hand, both needles pointing to the right. Insert a third needle knitwise into the first stitch on the front needle, and knitwise into the first stitch on the back needle. Knit the two stitches at the same time.

2.  Do the same with the next set of stitches from each needle. You now have two stitches on the third needle. Pass the first stitch over the second and off, just like you do when binding off.

Repeat these two steps until all stitches have been bound off. This will leave you with a neat seam on the right side—and you didn't have to sew a stitch!

## Five-Needle Bind-Off

"Five needles?" you ask. "Surely this can't be done!" Have faith in yourself, my fine knitting friend, for this is just a simple method of binding off two ribbed pieces together.

Three needles was a piece of cake, right? Managing four needles in your left hand will be a walk in the park!

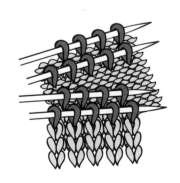

Again you will need to start with an equal number of stitches on two needles. Then simply divide the knits and purls from each needle onto two separate needles. (You may need some dpns, as the points at both ends will make this process much easier.)

Now working on the knit stitches only, continue as with the three-needle bind-off, then work the same way with the purl stitches, purling them instead of knitting. This will give you an almost invisible seam, which is otherwise hard to achieve when working with ribbed stitches.

## Buttonholes

Snaps and zippers are all well and good, but sooner or later you're going to have to learn how to knit buttonholes, and there's no time like the present. Once you've mastered casting on, binding off, knitting two stitches together, and yarn overs, making a tiny little buttonhole will be a breeze.

Like buttons, buttonholes come in different shapes and sizes. Be sure to match the type of buttonhole needed to the size of the button you will be using.

### Two-Row Buttonhole

This is the most versatile of the buttonhole methods. You will bind off and cast on the number of stitches to match the size of your button. As its name suggests, it is worked over two rows.

1. Work to the place where you need your buttonhole to begin, then work the next two stitches and bind off as many stitches as you will need for the width of your buttonhole.
2. Work the rest of the stitches to the end of the row.
3. On the next row, work up to the point of the last bound-off stitch, then turn your work around to cast on stitches on the other side. Using the cable method, start by inserting your right needle between the first and second stitches on your left needle.
4. Cast on the same number of stitches that you bound off on the previous row, but before putting the last cast-on stitch onto the left needle, take the yarn between the needles to the front of the work. This stops a loop from forming and messing up the beauty that is the two-row buttonhole.
5. Turn the work back to the other side again and continue working to the end of the row.

Carry on with your knitting until you need to make another buttonhole.

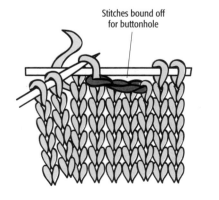
Stitches bound off for buttonhole

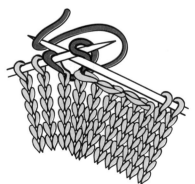

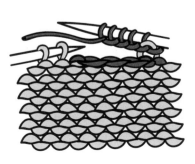

## Yarn Over or Eyelet Buttonhole

This is the easiest but not so versatile method of making a buttonhole. The size of your yarn and needles will determine the size of your buttonhole.

1. Work to the place where you need your buttonhole to begin. If your yarn needs to be at the back of your work for your next stitch, bring it to the front of your work between your needles (yarn forward).

2. If your yarn needs to be at the front of your work for the next stitch, take it to the back, over your right needle then to the front again between the needles (yarn forward over needle).

3. Depending on your pattern, work the next two stitches together either knitwise or purlwise.

4. Your buttonhole is now complete. Continue working to the end of your row.

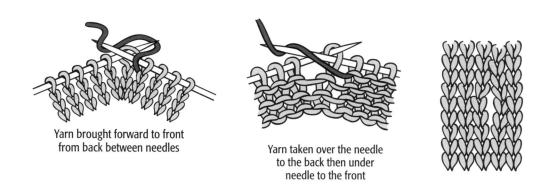

Yarn brought forward to front
from back between needles

Yarn taken over the needle
to the back then under
needle to the front

## How D'You Like My Weave? How to Weave in Your Loose Ends

Knitters use all sorts of different methods for tidying away their loose ends. I prefer to work them into my knitting as I go, but there are usually still a few strays left hanging when the knitting is completed. Take your time while sewing in your loose ends and hide them away as neatly as possible.

The easiest way to hide a loose end is to thread it through a tapestry needle and neatly sew it into a seam or through the bumps of the stitches on the wrong side of your work for 1 to 2 inches. If there are two loose ends hanging together (where a new ball of yarn has been started), sew them into your knitting so that they go off in opposite directions—this will close a possible hole and prevent them from creating too much bulk.

While you have your tapestry needle loaded with yarn, you can tidy up any messy seams or correct misshapen stitches by giving them and their neighbors gentle tweaks to help them back on the path of neatness and conformity.

You can also weave in your loose ends using a crochet hook. Choose a hook that's a size smaller than the needles you were using to knit the piece. Insert the hook through the stitches where you want your loose end to make its final resting place in reverse order, then loop the loose end around the hook and gently pull it back through the stitches.

You don't have to tie knots into your yarn—this will look messy and add unnecessary bulk. The ends should be safely anchored into your knitting by just hiding them through the back of a few stitches, but if your yarn is particularly slippery you may want to zigzag your stitches back and forth a few times to prevent them from coming undone.

## The End Is in Sight: Blocking Your Finished Item

You've knitted, you've seamed, you've woven in all your loose ends. Your precious item is finished, right? Wrong! Hold your horses, Bucko, you'll be wanting to block that sweater before it hits the catwalk!

Some knitters block their pieces to measurements separately before joining them, but I prefer to leave this chore until after the seaming is all done. Washing and blocking your newly finished sweater can make a world of difference in its look and feel. Follow these steps for successful blocking.

If your item is all or part animal or vegetable fiber, follow these steps:

1. Fill your sink with warm water (never hot, you don't want your sweater to shrink) and add some special detergent for your yarn type, or a little baby shampoo. Swish this around to work up the suds.

2. Place your item into the soapy water and very gently squeeze it to get the suds into it. Do not rub!

3. Do not leave it to soak for too long—five minutes should be enough.

4. Gently squeeze out the suds and remove from the sink.

5. Empty out the soapy water and refill with clean warm water. Add the item again and gently swish to rinse.

6. Repeat the last two steps until the water runs clear.

7. If your yarn is a bit on the scratchy side, you can add a little hair conditioner to the final rinse.

8. Use your hands to press out as much water as you can, without causing too much agitation.

9. Lay the item out on a large clean towel, then roll and squeeze to remove more of the water. Do not wring.

10. Get another large clean towel and place this on a flat surface (a table or the floor will do).

11. Place the washed item on the towel and lay it flat, gently patting, pulling, and pushing until it measures what it is supposed to. Your pattern should give you finished measurements or a schematic (sketch of pattern pieces including measurements). Be careful with ribs; you don't want to flatten out their lovely ribbiness!

12. Leave the item undisturbed to dry completely. Now and only now is it ready for its close-up!

If your item is made from a man-made fiber, you can skip the washing stage. Follow these steps:

1. Lay the item out on top of a clean, dry towel over a blocking board or large piece of thick cardboard on a flat surface.

2. Using rustproof pins, pin around the edges to the size required.

3. Set your iron to steam and hold it over your pinned item. Do not press.

4. Give your item a good old steam and leave it to dry thoroughly before unpinning.

Blocking is completed. Give yourself a well-deserved pat on the back and start thinking about what you're going to knit next!

# Chapter **Eight**

◆◆◆

# Everything but the Kitchen Sink: Embellishments

The time will come, my trusty knitting pal, when you will yearn for more than just knits and purls. Right about the time when your hands can work the stitches without engaging your brain, you'll be ready to teach them some new and exciting maneuvers. Hold onto your hats as we enter the crazy world of embellishments, some of them ridiculously easy and a few that require a little more manual dexterity. Add a flirtatious fringe to the ends of a scarf or a big fluffy pompom to the top of a hat. Work that tapestry needle for some colorful embroidery and appliqué, or learn the basics of crochet to liven up your seams.

A friendly little word of warning: Before we get totally carried away with the whole embellishment kick, remember that minimalism and subtlety are key, and although an artful bloom tastefully placed on your lapel can give you the whole Carrie from *Sex and the City* vibe, covering your sweater with tassels will add bulk to the whole silhouette and could make you look like a demented troll!

## Embroidery

With a tapestry needle loaded up with yarn, you can spice up your knitting, adding color and texture with some simple embroidery.

## Duplicate Stitch

This useful little stitch is also known as Swiss darning. It can be a quick and easy way to disguise mistakes made in Fair Isle or intarsia patterns, or create a new pattern over a plain piece of knitting. But work only small areas with this stitch, as it will create bulk. Using a yarn of similar thickness to that of your knitting will ensure proper coverage of the stitches.

1. Insert your needle from the back into the top of the loop below the stitch you want to work over (left illustration), then pass your needle behind the base of the stitch above your chosen stitch.

2. From the front of the work, insert your needle into the same point you came up from at the start to complete the stitch, then either come up into the next stitch to the left, if working horizontally (middle illustration), or in the stitch above if working vertically (right illustration).

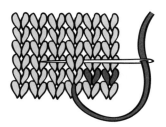
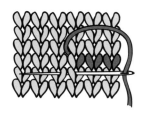
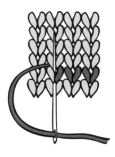

## Running Stitch

The easiest stitch known to man, the running stitch can add just a touch of color to a plain old piece of knitting. Try working it around a sweater close to the edges of side seams, collars, or pockets. Remember that most embroidery stitches don't stretch, unlike knitting, so be careful on areas like neck and sleeve openings, which need to be elastic to fit your body parts through.

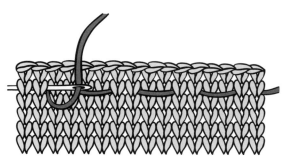

You can also use running stitch for a simple outline of a design in straight lines or curves. I love this stitch for its pure simplicity.

1. Take your trusty tapestry needle and start from the back of your knitting. Insert the needle where you want your stitch to start and stick it back through your knitting where you want your stitch to end.

2. Repeat this easy maneuver using the knit stitches as a guide to keep the lengths of your running stitches even. Keep a nice even tension; working this stitch too tightly will make your knitting bunch, and if your embroidery is too loose, it will form loops that could snag and look sloppy or break.

## Cross Stitch and Herringbone Stitch

Make little crosses by working a single stitch to form a diagonal line, then cross it with your second stitch, matching its length and mirroring its angle. Herringbone stitch is made from a series of elongated cross stitches, where the crosses occur close to the stitch ends.

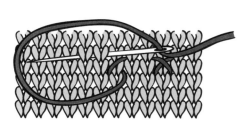
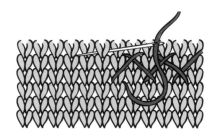

## Stem Stitch

Somewhat similar to backstitch, you can create thicker lines using this technique.

1. Begin as you would a straight stitch, then take your needle from the back of your work to the front overlapping it halfway along the first stitch.
2. Continue in this way, either keeping the stitches all the same size or varying the lengths to create a more organic look.

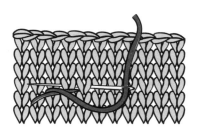
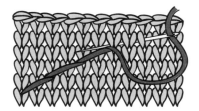

## Satin Stitch

This stitch is used to form a solid block of embroidery. It can be worked in a variety of shapes, covering the knitting below it completely.

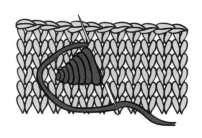

1. Start as with stem stitch, but instead of overlapping the second stitch over the first, take it back right next to the beginning of the first stitch.

2. Work the stitches to fill the space of the shape required.

## Chain Stitch and Lazy Daisy Stitch

Make a linked chain by placing these stitches one after the other or create a flower by arranging them in a circle.

1. Take your needle from back of work to front, then to the back again right next to the first point of entry. But before pulling the needle though your knitting, insert the needle through from the back once more at the place you want your chain to end, wrapping the yarn behind the needle.

2. Pull the yarn so that it lays flat against the knitting and finish the stitch with a small straight stitch over the loop.

3. The location of your next chain will depend on whether you are working a linked chain (middle illustration) or a lazy daisy (right illustration). Add a French knot (see the following section) to the center for a more finished look.

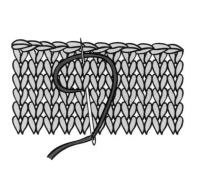
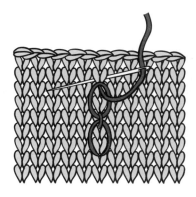
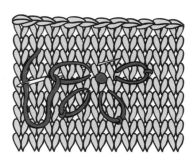

## French Knot

Like the full stop of embroidery, this stitch may be small, but put in the right place it can add so much more to your finished piece.

1. Insert the needle from the back of the knitting and then wrap the yarn two or three times around your needle.
2. Finish the stitch by returning the needle to the back next to the starting point and pulling the yarn through.

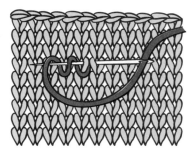 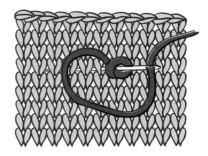

## Blanket Stitch

Believe it or not, some blankets have this stitch at their edges. It's a nice way to finish an otherwise boring edge with a contrasting color. It's good for neatening the edges of appliqué, but it can also be used on any flat part of your knitting.

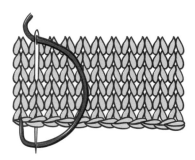

1. Make a tiny stitch to start at the lower left side edge then insert the needle from the front just above this stitch at the height you want your stitch to be. Point your needle to the edge of your knitting, then wrap the yarn behind your needle.
2. Keeping the loop of yarn close to the edge, pull your needle through and the stitch taut.
3. Keep your stitches evenly spaced along your edge using your knit stitches as a guide for width and height.

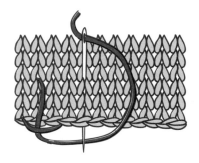

## Whipstitch or Overcast Stitch

Used over seams, whipstitch can strengthen the bond or add decoration. It's another simple in-out type of stitch, just taking the yarn over the seam between the stitches.

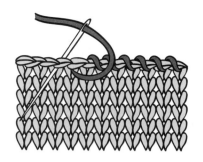

## Couching

Like a simple version of appliqué, couching is a means of sewing a length of yarn onto your knitting using little whip-stitches in sewing thread or fine yarn.

Lay the yarn onto your knitting and pin into place, then starting at the left from the back of your work, sew over your yarn to anchor it to your knitting.

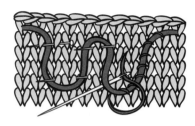

## Appliqué

Add a bit of va va voom! to your knitting by applying cut-out shapes. Less time consuming than knitting intarsia, appliqué adds color and texture by sewing on some funky designs. Choose fabrics that don't fray too easily—felt is a good option, as it doesn't fray, comes in loads of different colors, and is available to buy in squares from most craft stores.

1. Cut pieces into desired shapes and pin in place on your knitting. Work around edges in either running or blanket stitches.
2. Work other embroidery stitches onto appliqué to give it more definition.

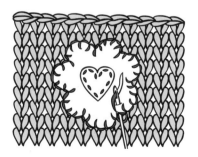

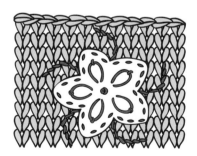

# Now in 3D!

Prepare to enter a new dimension as you discover the wonderful world of fringe, tassels, and pompoms! Whip up some of these beauties, then hang them from your knitting, serving no purpose except to twirl around and look pretty!

## Fringe

The quickest and easiest way to add life to a boring old scarf is to add fringe to the ends.

1. Find a sturdy rectangular object just a bit wider than you want for the length of your fringe, such as a book or DVD case (a knitting friend of mine uses the free packaging you can get from courier services!).

2. Wrap your yarn around the chosen template, then cut through all thicknesses at one end.

3. Take half as many strands as you want for the thicknesses of your fringe and fold in half.

4. Insert a crochet hook from the back to the front of your knitting in the position you want it to hang from, looping your strands into the hook.

5. Pull the top of the loop through the knitting, then place the bulk of the strands into the hook and pull through the loop.

6. Tighten and neaten the loop so that it sits nicely at the edge.

Carry on adding as much fringe as you like, then trim the edges so all strands are of equal length.

## Knotted Fringe

Fancy up your fringe by knotting the strands together, macramé style. This works best on the less chunky fringe.

1. Start as you would for regular fringe, making your strands a couple of inches longer than you will need.

2. Add an even number of strands to your knitted edge as normal, then take half the strands from one fringe and half from its neighbor and knot them together.

Carry on in this way until all fringe has been knotted. To add a second row of knots, repeat as before, alternating the placement of the knots.

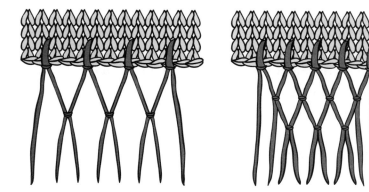

## Tassels

Like a more sophisticated big sister of fringe, a tassel can be added to the corners of a scarf or cushion, or the top of a hat or hood for that Moroccan feel. You can even attach them to the end of a tie-belt and twirl them around while you're waiting for the bus!

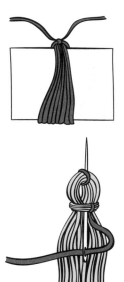

1. Start to make a tassel in the same way you would fringe, by wrapping yarn around a rectangular object. But before you take the scissors to it, get your tapestry needle threaded with 6 to 8 inches of the same yarn as your tassel and loop it through the top of your tassel-to-be, enclosing the number of strands to make a tassel of required thickness, and tie a really tight knot.

2. Cut the other end of the strands and take it off the template.

3. Drop the shorter end of the knotted yarn in to join the rest of the strands and wrap the longer end tightly around the strands about ½ inch from the top. Secure these wraps in place with a small stitch through some of the strands, then insert the needle up into the center of the tassel and out through the top. Use this yarn to sew the tassel into its new home.

## Pompoms

Not just for cheerleaders anymore, pompoms have made a comeback lately and can be spotted hanging from the unlikeliest of places! You can make tons of pompoms in solid or multicolors and liven up your accessories and your home!

1. Using compasses (or conveniently sized circular objects), draw a pair of circles the size you want your pompoms to be, with 1-inch diameter centers, onto a piece of card.

2. Cut out these two donut-shaped pieces of card and sandwich them together.

3. Cut approximately 4 yards of yarn and wind evenly around the cardboard-donut sandwich. (The amount of yarn required will vary depending on the thickness of your yarn and the required density of your pompom. I usually keep winding lengths of yarn around the donuts until the center hole is filled.)

4. Tuck in ends of yarn.

5. Insert the blade of your scissors through the yarn at the outside edge and between the two donuts. Cut evenly through the yarn all around the outside edge.

6. Loop a length of yarn around the center of the pompom between the two pieces of cardboard, pull tightly, and secure with a double knot, leaving an end long enough to sew into place. Pull the pieces of card apart and off.

7. Fluff the yarn and trim away any ends of yarn to make a perfectly round pompom.

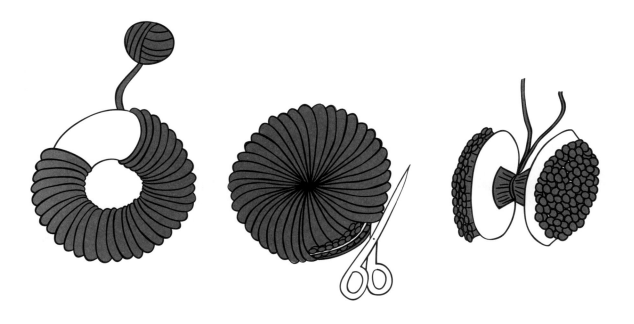

## Tie Me Up

Need something to hang your pompoms from? Here are a few methods to make a trusty tie. Use them for belts, laces, and drawstrings.

### Braided Tie

Measure out a multiple of three lengths of yarn 6 inches longer than you want your finished tie to be and knot them together at one end and secure. (Tie it to a door knob, loop it over a hook, pin it to a board, or if you're very nimble, hold it between your knees.)

Divide the strands into three groups and pass the group on the right over the center group, swapping their positions. Pass the group on the left over the center group, swapping their positions. Continue in this way until the braid is completed. Tie a knot in the end to secure.

### Twisted Tie

Quicker than braiding, twisting a tie is another option for a similar finished look. You will need to start with lengths of yarn cut two and a half to three times longer than your finished tie. Because it will be folded, you will need half the number of strands than the finished width.

Tie a knot in one end and secure as for the braided tie (although I wouldn't recommend holding it between your knees this time). Knot the other end and insert a knitting needle through the strands. Use the knitting needle to twist the strands counterclockwise until the entire length is fully twisted. Keeping the needle in place and the twisted strands taut, hold the center of the tie and fold one end to meet the other. Let go of the center and watch the two halves twist together. Smooth out any uneven areas, knot both ends together, and trim any loose ends.

# I-Cord

Back when I was a little girl my aunty gave me a Knitting Nancy as a Christmas present. It was a wooden tube shaped like the torso of a curvaceous woman with a painted face and a red dress. Knocked into her head was a crown of five or six small nails.

I spent days wrapping yarn around the nails, passing the loops over one another and letting them drop inside her head, until a type of knitted tube tail appeared from the hole in the bottom by her feet. I must've made miles of the stuff!

Nowadays you can buy a machine that, with the turn of a handle, cranks the stuff out much quicker than my young fingers ever could, but for shorter pieces you can knit cords with a couple of double-pointed needles or a short circular needle.

This technique was named by Elizabeth Zimmerman, who claimed that the "I" in I-cord stands for idiot, because any idiot can do it and you don't have to turn your work!

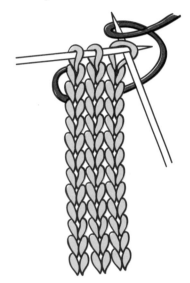

1. Cast on as many stitches as your pattern calls for, or three, just to practice.

2. Knit the first row normally, then without turning, slide the stitches along the needle from one end to the other and hold in your left hand.

3. Take the yarn that will be hanging from the left, pull it tightly, and knit the stitches normally.

4. Repeat this process, sliding stitches back to the other end of the needle instead of turning them, knitting every row (every round, actually) and keeping the first stitch tight to close the gap between the edges.

You will soon see that you are knitting a tube and not a flat fabric.

# Ha Hem!

You can create all types of edges when knitting, which can alter the look of an item. Bored with ribs, rolls, and seed stitch? Then choose a plain hem for a clean, flat finish or a picot edge for a touch of a scallop.

## Plain Hem

Best worked in stockinette stitch, a plain hem is very easy to make either flat or in the round. Work about ½ to 1 inch of stockinette stitch in the normal way (it's a good idea to work the part that will be turned under in a smaller needle size than the main part, so that it doesn't flare), then on a right-side row, purl all the stitches instead of knitting them. This will form a nice line to fold along and will be the finished edge of the piece.

Carry on in stockinette stitch as normal.

When you have finished knitting, fold up the hem along the row of purl stitches to the wrong side and slip stitch into place.

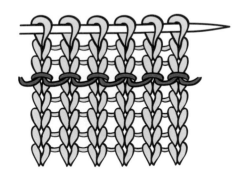

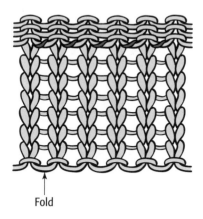

Fold

## Picot Edge

Using yarn overs, work a row of eyelets into your knitting, which when folded in half will give you a neat edge of tiny scallops. Work in stockinette stitch until you reach the right-side row where you want your edge to be, as for the plain hem.

K1, *yo, k2tog; rep from * to last 1 or 2 sts, k1 or 2 (this depends on whether you have an odd or even number of stitches).

Continue in stockinette stitch until all knitting is finished.

Fold up the hem to the wrong side along the row of eyelets and slip stitch into place.

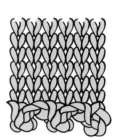

# Crochet

Every good knitter should learn at least the basics of crochet. Think about it...if you can work wonders with two pointy needles, just imagine how much easier it will be working with just one needle that even has a hook at the end to help make the stitches! If you knit using the Continental method (see Chapter 3, "Beginners, Start Your Engines: Basic Techniques"), you have no excuse not to crochet, as the yarn is held in a similar way.

Use crochet to close seams, add decorative trims, and make simple flowers to add to your knitting.

## Chain Stitch

Chain stitch is the beginning stage for most crochet stitches, and can be used as a provisional cast-on for knitting and for making button loops and ties. If nothing else, you must learn how to crochet a chain.

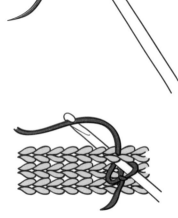

1. Make a slip knot as you would at the start of a knitted cast-on. Place the slip knot on the crochet hook held in your right hand.
2. Holding the yarn in your left hand, as if you were knitting the Continental way, wrap the yarn around the hook.
3. Slide the crochet hook though the slip knot, taking the wrapped yarn with it to form a new loop.

Continue making loops in this way, being careful not to pull them too tightly. It's better to start with your loops a little loose, as this will make it easier to slide the hook through.

## Slip Stitch Crochet Seam

Here's a nifty way to join two pieces of knitting by making a feature of the seam on the outside. Try using a contrast color yarn to add even more depth. If you can work a crochet chain, this stitch is the same motion, only here you are adding the edges of your knitting sandwiched between the stitches.

1. Pin the knitted pieces together with wrong sides facing one another.
2. Make a slip knot and place on your crochet hook.
3. Insert the hook into the knitting from front to back just below the edge at the far right side. Wrap the yarn around your hook.
4. Pull your hook through the knitting and the slip knot, bringing the wrapped yarn with it.

Continue in this way all along the seam.

## Single Crochet

This makes a good flat edge to a piece of knitting that may otherwise roll in on itself. It also looks rather nice, too!

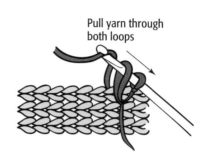

**Pull yarn through both loops**

1. Start with a slip knot on your crochet hook and insert into your knitting from front to back just below the edge at the far right side.
2. Wrap the yarn around the hook and bring it through to the front, but not through the slip knot. You will now have two loops on your needle.
3. Wrap the yarn around the hook once more and pull it though both loops. You have now made one stitch.

Continue in this way all along the seam.

## Simple Crochet Flowers

Start with a crochet chain of six loops. Insert your hook into the first loop and wrap the yarn around the hook.

Bring the yarn through both loops on the hook to join the circle. Insert your hook into the center of the circle and wrap the yarn around the hook. Slide your hook back through the circle. Wrap the yarn around the needle again and pull it through the two loops on your hook. You have just made one single crochet (sc) stitch.

Chain stitch 12 loops (ch 12).

Repeat the last two stages 11 more times, then finish the flower by making a slip stitch into the first single crochet: Insert your hook into the base of the first petal, wrap the yarn around the hook, and bring it through both loops.

Change the shape and size of your flowers by altering the lengths of the crochet chains and the number of petals worked into the center.

Sew a small flower in one color on top of a larger flower in another color. Try out different yarns to alter the textures. Fuzzy mohair flowers can be a fun little embellishment, or experiment with metallics and multicolored yarns.

# Chapter Nine

◆◆

# Oops, I Made a Big Booboo! Fixing Mistakes

Alas, we are only human and are bound to make our fair share of mistakes along the rocky path of life. Your knitting will be no exception, and no matter how much of a talented crafter you are, you will need to know how to fix those annoying little mishaps that test the patience of us all. In all my decades of knitting, I've hardly ever completed a project without having to fix some problem or other.

As you become more advanced, you'll be knitting away at lightning pace and may not notice the mistakes you are making. It's a good practice to stop and have a close look at your work every couple of rows to check that everything looks in order. It's easier and quicker to fix mistakes right after they have happened instead of several rows down.

This chapter outlines most of the mistakes knitters will fall prey to. With a bit of patience and a steady hand, I'll show you how to make that mistake disappear into thin air!

## Frogging

It seems as though everyone wants a piece of the knitting action, but what have frogs got to with any of this? Back in my homeland, frogs just hop about and croak, but here in the good old U.S. of A. the official language of the frog is "ribbit," which sounds a lot like "rip it." Therefore, the affectionate term for the annoying task of having to unravel your lovingly knitted stitches is "frogging."

Another imaginative phrase that has spun off from this term is "sending it to the frog pond," which translates as "My knitting needs to be unraveled, but I'm throwing it in a corner until I have the patience to tackle it."

If, heaven forbid, you find a mistake a few rows down in your knitting and none of the following methods will fix your booboo, you may have to frog all the way back to the row before your mistake.

Before you rush right in to ripping out your stitches with all your might, grab yourself a smaller-sized (so as not to stretch your stitches) circular needle (or dpn if your work is narrow—you can also use a tapestry needle and contrast color yarn), and pick up the front leg of every stitch on the row below your mistake. That way you will know exactly where to rip back to and you won't risk dropping stitches and leaving yourself with even more of a fixing job.

As an alternative to having to re-knit rows upon rows of a perfectly good piece of knitting after a mistake has been made, you can thread a needle through the row of stitches above the mistake as well as below it. Cut the yarn of a stitch below the top needle and with the help of a tapestry needle, carefully unpick that row, then rip back to the bottom needle. Re-knit only the section where the mistake was made—all but the last row, which can then be grafted to the row of stitches on the top needle—and the mistake will be all but a distant memory!

# Unknitting

If the stitch you need to fix is on the last or previous row, a bit of unknitting, or "tinking" as it is known by some knitters, is all that is needed to get back to the point where you can mend your mistake.

1. To unknit knit or purl stitches, insert your left needle into the front of the loop of the stitch below the first stitch on your right needle.

2. Keeping the loop on your left needle, drop that first stitch off your right needle and gently pull on your yarn to unravel the old stitch.

Repeat these last two steps until you have unknitted all stitches needed.

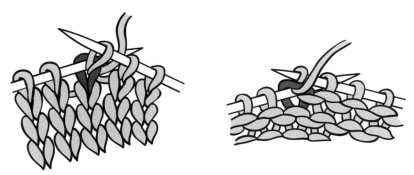

Unknitting knit stitches (left) and purl stitches (right)

# Reworking Stitches

It's very important to have your stitches all sitting correctly on your needles. A stitch that has been twisted, incompletely knitted, or put back onto your needle the wrong way will stand out like a sore thumb when your project is finished.

After fixing mistakes, be sure that your stitches have been properly replaced onto your needles.

Take a look at your stitches. They should all be little loops, sitting comfortably astride your needle. Knit and purl stitches should have their front leg slightly closer to the point of your needle than their back leg.

## Twisted Stitches

If your stitch has its back leg closer to the needle point than its front leg, it has been knitted or put back on the needle incorrectly—it is twisted. Twisted stitches will not have the elasticity of their sisters and brothers and will need to be untwisted. Simply take the naughty stitch off your needle and put it back on again so it is sitting properly.

Twisted knit stitch (left) and twisted purl stitch (right)

## Unfinished Stitches

Occasionally you will come across a stitch that has been incompletely knitted. Either you have not dropped the old stitch off the needle, have worked an unwanted yarn over, or have slipped the stitch and not knitted it at all.

Simply unknit this stitch and work it again. If you find an unfinished stitch several rows down in your knitting, you can locate the stitch on your needle that is directly above the unfinished stitch and drop it off your needle, causing a ladder to reach the stitch in question. The stitch can then be picked up as a dropped stitch and your knitting will look perfect once more.

# Dropped Stitches

In your knitting life you will drop more stitches than you will eat hot dinners. Those pesky loops just love to jump off your needles and create ladders many rows down into your knitting— I swear they have minds of their own!

## Dropped Stitches from Only One Row Down

If you have dropped a stitch one row down, there's no need to unknit back to it. Just keep it from laddering further with a safety pin until you reach it.

When you have dropped a knit stitch one row below:

1. Insert your right needle into the front of the loop, then pick up the bar of yarn behind it, being careful not to twist it.
2. Insert the point of your left needle into the dropped stitch and pass it over the bar.
3. Now put this stitch back on the left needle the correct way and knit it normally.

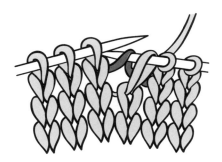 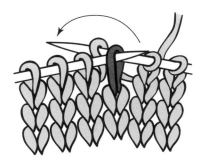

When you have dropped a purl stitch, take these steps to fix (see illustrations at the top of the next page):

1. Insert your right needle into the back of the loop, then pick up the bar of yarn in front of it, being careful not to twist it.
2. Insert the point of your left needle into the dropped stitch and pass it over the bar.
3. Now put this stitch back on the left needle the correct way and purl it normally.

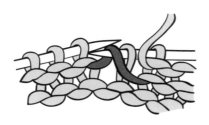 

## Dropped Stitches from Several Rows Down

Picking up dropped stitches several rows below is no big deal. You'll need a crochet hook of a similar size to the needles you are using.

1. If you have dropped more than one stitch, secure them with safety pins to keep them from unraveling any further while you pick them up one at a time.

2. For knit stitches, knit to the point in the row where the stitch was dropped. Insert your crochet hook into the top loop of the dropped stitch from front to back and pick up the lowest bar of the ladder.

3. Pull this bar through the stitch and continue picking up the bars though the loops, making sure you always pick up the lowest bar first.

4. For purl stitches, insert your crochet hook into the stitch from the back to the front.

5. Continue picking up the dropped stitches until all the ladder bars have been made into stitches. Then put the top stitch back onto your needle facing the correct way.

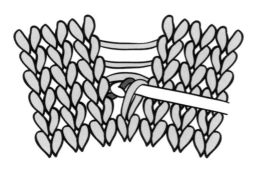 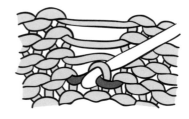

# Chapter Ten

◆◼◆

# 'Sall Greek to Me: How to Read a Knitting Pattern

If you haven't knitted from a pattern before, it can look a little daunting, to say the least. Some of it makes sense, like what types of yarns and needles to use, but to a beginner, the directions can look like the love child of a math equation and Egyptian hieroglyphics!

Designers use a special kind of shorthand and abbreviations, keeping directions tidy and manageable while offering bite-size chunks of information. This may seem like insanity at first, but with a little practice you too will be reeling off the knitters' mantra: "Knit one, slip one, pass slip stitch over," or "K1, s1, psso," as it is written.

You might want to make a copy of the abbreviations listed in the appendix to keep with your pattern for handy referral, but in no time at all the knitalogical fog will be lifted and you'll be able to read a pattern like a pro.

For now, hold my hand and I'll take you through making sense of a pattern step by step. Like recipes, knitting patterns are usually written out in a standard format, giving you a guide to size, yarn type and needle size, gauge needed, any special notes or abbreviations needed for the pattern, the actual knitting directions, and ending with finishing instructions.

## Patterns 101

Here's the standard information you'll find in most patterns:

♦ Size This tells you the size or sizes in which the pattern can be made. For a sweater, cardigan, or jacket, this will be the chest size; for skirts, it will be the waist size; for baby and children's items, size will be given for their age. For other items, such as accessories or home items, the finished size will be

93

given. Choose your size wisely and measure yourself properly. You don't want to spend hours, days, or even months knitting away at a sweater only to have it be embarrassingly tight or so roomy you could invite someone else in there with you!

Most patterns also include a schematic or sketch with actual measurements of the finished pieces—use this to guide you in which size to knit.

If you follow the pattern using the correct size yarn and in the correct gauge (I can't emphasize enough how import the gauge is—but more about that in the next section), then your finished item will be the size it was meant to be.

If the pattern offers multiple sizes, it will be written with the smallest size first, with larger sizes following in brackets in ascending order, like so: 32 [34, 36, 38, 40, 42]. Chose your size and highlight it. (You may want to make a copy of your pattern if you don't want to write all over the original—it also makes it more portable and handy for whipping out on the bus or at a boring meeting!) In the main pattern directions, instructions will be given for all sizes and always written in the same order as before; for example, K2 [2, 4, 4, 6, 6]...or continue working straight for 10 [12, 14, 16, 18, 20] rows...so it's very wise to mark off your size throughout the pattern before you begin. Many times I've had students come to me with a project they put down only to forget which size they were knitting. All this confusion can be avoided by taking a minute to highlight all the instructions for your size before you begin.

♦ **Materials** This is everything you'll need to make the item.

♦ **Yarn** This gives the yarn name, fiber content, color name and number, length or weight per skein or ball, and number of skeins or yards needed to knit your size (again in the same ascending order). As I mentioned earlier, you don't *have* to use the yarn the pattern calls for, but if you want your tea cozy to be just like the one in the photo, it's a good idea to use the correct yarn, at least until you're a little more experienced.

♦ **Needles** These are the suggested size or sizes of needles used to achieve the all-important gauge. Sometimes you will need a set of dpns or circulars in a particular length—this info will be here.

For most projects, you'll also need scissors and a tape measure, but some patterns need a little something else, like buttons, zippers, pins, or a crochet hook. Make sure you get everything together before you begin—it's very frustrating to be whizzing away on a fabby sweater and then have to put it down because you don't have a crucial item you need in order to continue!

## Size Is Important: Understanding Gauge (Tension)

Like many before me, I'm embarrassed to admit that I didn't understand what a gauge or tension square was until I had knitted up numerous sweaters that didn't come out looking anything like they were supposed to. Then I saw the light...I knitted a test swatch, measured it, and from that little piece of knitting managed to work out the correct size for a finished sweater. Never again will I blindly knit for days on end only to be miserable at the oddly sized garment I produce. You must *always* get your gauge correct before you start your knitting!

With your yarn and suggested needles, knit a swatch slightly larger than the one that is given in the pattern—usually 4 inches (10cm) square.

If the gauge says 16 stitches and 24 rows to 4 inches (10cm), measured over stockinette stitch using 7 US (4½mm) needles, I would cast on at least 20 stitches (an extra 2 on each side), and knit stockinette stitch for at least 28 rows, as the edge stitches aren't as easy to measure accurately.

Take a tape measure to your swatch and carefully measure how many stitches you have over 4 inches (10cm). If you have 16 stitches horizontally and 24 stitches vertically, then congratulations, you can now continue with your pattern.

If you have more than 16 stitches horizontally and 24 stitches vertically, then your knitting is tighter than the gauge needed. If you don't change your needle size you will end up with a finished piece that is far tighter than it's supposed to be. You need to go up a needle size and try again, repeating the process until your gauge is correct.

If you have fewer than 16 stitches horizontally and 24 stitches vertically, then your knitting is looser than the gauge needed. If you don't change your needle size, you will end up with a tent instead of a halter top. You need to go down a needle size and try again, repeating the process until your gauge is correct.

It may not seem like a big deal if you have 14 stitches instead of the required 16, but that is only in a tiny 4-inch square—imagine you're knitting a sweater where the chest measurement should be 36 inches. Your 2 little stitches multiplied by 9 will add on an extra 18 stitches—over 4 inches—to your finished size! Always, always, always knit with the correct gauge.

After knitting your gauge square you could rip it out and begin your pattern, but it's a good idea to hang onto it. You could put it in a notebook with the yarn band and any notes you might want to make, such as how you rate the yarn, whether you would knit with it again, and any other information that might be useful when starting similar projects.

If the swatch is in a pattern, you could stick it to the front of a homemade greeting card, or collect them as you go and sew them into a blanket for a pet or a baby. Just a thought....

## Special Notes or Instructions

Your pattern might have a cable or lace pattern that needs special instructions, or you may have to work two yarns together. Any additional information like this will be given here. Highlight it if necessary.

# What's with All the Stars and Squiggles?

Patterns use asterisks and parentheses as markers or to isolate a set of instructions. Here's what they mean:

| | | |
|---|---|---|
| * | = | A single asterisk shows starting and stopping points. Repeat all instructions between the asterisks for the specified amount of times. |
| ** ** | = | Double (or triple, or quadruple) sets of asterisks mark the starting and stopping points for longer repeats within a pattern. For example, where a front piece is the same as a back piece up to the neck shaping, there will be asterisks showing you where to knit up to before moving on to new instructions. |
| [ ] | = | Numbers given in brackets are for alternate sizes. Highlight your size throughout the pattern before you begin. |
| ( ) | = | Numbers given in parentheses indicate instructions to be worked as a group a specified number of times. |

## Following the Instructions

Now comes the fun part, the actual knitting! If your pattern is written for multiple sizes and you followed my earlier advice, you will have highlighted the number of stitches you need to cast on (let's say you're making the third size). Now's the time to whip out the abbreviations listed in the appendix. The instructions will be written something like this:

**Back**

With size 7 needles and MC, CO 60 [66, 70, 76, 82, 88] sts.

This means that you'll begin by knitting the back piece (the back usually comes first so that you can knit this piece again, just changing the neck shaping for the front). With size 7 needles and your main color yarn, you will cast on 70 stitches. Easy enough, right?

Then the first row might read:

**Row 1 (RS):** *K1, p1; rep from * to end.

Translation: Your first row will have the right side (RS) facing you as you knit. You will be working a repeat of knit one stitch, purl one stitch rib pattern (k1, p1) to the end of the row.

Instructions given following an asterisk need to be repeated by the number of times given—in this particular case all the way to the end of the row.

More complicated instructions might look like this:

**Row 1:** K2, *k2tog (k1, yf) twice, k1, sl 1, k1, psso, k3; rep from * to last 2 sts, k2.

Does it make any sense? Here's what it all means:

Knit the first two stitches (remember that there is an asterisk here, so you'll repeat from this point later), knit two stitches together (k2tog, a decrease). The next set of instructions are in parentheses followed by the number of times you have to repeat them—in this case, twice—so you knit one stitch (k1), bring your yarn forward (yf—this increase makes a loop of yarn over the needle, which will be knit on the next row), and then repeat the knit one and yarn forward, knit one (k1), slip the next st (sl 1—insert the right needle purlwise into the next stitch on the left needle and, without knitting or purling, slip it onto the right needle), knit one (k1), now pass slip stitch over (psso—decrease by using the point of your left needle to lift the slipped stitch over the last knit stitch and off the right needle), knit the next three stitches (k3). Now repeat the instructions following the asterisk until two stitches remain on your left needle, then knit these last two stitches (k2).

Seeing it all written like this, you can understand why we need to use abbreviations!

Your pattern will end with finishing instructions. These will tell you how to sew your knitting together. For more about this, see Chapter 7, "It Ain't Over 'til the Fat Lady Pins: Finishing and Blocking."

# • Part Two •

## ...And a Bag of Chips

# Chapter Eleven

◆◆◆

# Heads Up!

**Bean Beanie**

Take a plain old beanie pattern and with a few tweaks here and there, change its shape. Top-down-in-the-round pattern for two different hats: striped beanie and cabled earflap.

**Put-Your-Hair-Up Hat**

Want to wear a hat and have your hair up? Make these chunky striped hats with spaces for your 'do and say goodbye to a lumpy head!

**Cable Access**

Wanna try your hand at cables? Knit up a bag or a scarf from the same simple pattern.

**Bar Code**

Throw on this black-and-white knitted boa and bring out your inner diva.

**It's a Cinch**

Knit a simple rectangle to embellish with pompoms, ribbons, beads...too much is never enough.

**Bobbles and Balls**

Feel the love as you wrap yourself up in this lace shawl with optional knitted balls.

# Bean Beanie

By knitting your hat top-down-in-the-round you can try it on as you go, making sure the fit is perfect. Knit a basic striped beanie, or try out my variation: a cabled hat with flaps to keep your ears warm. These hats are quick to knit and don't take up too much yarn, which makes them great for giving as gifts!

**Project Rating:** Flirtation

**Cost:** $25

**Necessary Skills:** purl (page 30); decrease (page 40); increase (page 38); stripes (page 55); knitting in the round (page 55); optional: Magic Loop method (page 33)

## Finished Size

Fits an average adult head, approximately 21 to 22 inches in diameter

## Materials

- Debbie Bliss Cashmerino Aran (55% Merino Wool, 33% Microfiber, 12% Cashmere); 98 yd/89.61m, 1.75 oz/50g
- 1 ball each of: A = #617 Purple; B = #602 Pink; C = #601 Lilac
- 1 set of US 8 (5mm) double-pointed needles, or 1 long (over 24 in) US 8 (5mm) circular needle if using the Magic Loop method
- Stitch markers
- Tapestry needle

## Gauge

19 stitches and 27 rows = 4 in/10cm worked in stockinette stitch in the round using US 8 (5mm) knitting needles, or size needed to obtain gauge

## Instructions

Using US 8 (5mm) double-pointed needles or long circular needle (if using Magic Loop method), and color A, CO 6 sts.

Join in a rnd and place a marker between the first and last sts.

**Rnd 1:** K.

**Rnd 2 (inc):** Kfb all sts—12 sts.

**Rnd 3 (inc):** (K1, kfb) 6 times—18 sts.

**Rnd 4 (inc):** (K2, kfb) 6 times—24 sts.

**Rnd 5 (inc):** (K3, kfb) 6 times—30 sts.

**Rnd 6 (inc):** (K4, kfb) 6 times—36 sts.

**Rnd 7 (inc):** (K5, kfb) 6 times—42 sts.

**Rnd 8 (inc):** (K6, kfb) 6 times—48 sts.

**Rnd 9 (inc):** (K7, kfb) 6 times—54 sts.

**Rnd 10 (inc):** (K8, kfb) 6 times—60 sts.

**Rnd 11 (inc):** (K9, kfb) 6 times—66 sts.

**Rnd 12 (inc):** (K10, kfb) 6 times—72 sts.

**Rnd 13 (inc):** (K11, kfb) 6 times—78 sts.

**Rnd 14 (inc):** (K12, kfb) 6 times—84 sts.

**Rnds 15–20:** K without shaping.

**Rnds 21–22:** Using color B, k.

**Rnds 23–32:** Using color C, k.

**Rnds 33–34:** Using color B, k.

**Rnds 35–40:** Using color A, k.

**Rnd 41 (dec):** (K5, k2tog) 12 times—72 sts.

**Rnd 42:** * K2, p1; rep from * to end.

Rep rnd 42 9 more times.

Using color B, BO in rib.

### Finishing Instructions

Sew in all loose ends.

# Variation

Now that you have mastered knitting the top-down beanie, you can work out all kinds of variations. Why not try this pattern for a styling cabled hat with earflaps to show old man winter who's boss!

## Necessary Skills

Cables (page 46); pompoms (page 82); tassels (page 81), I-cord (page 84)

## Abbreviations

**t2:** Insert the right needle into second stitch on left needle, knit this stitch, but before taking it off the left needle, knit the first stitch, then slide them onto the right needle together.

**c4f:** Place next 2 stitches onto a cable needle and hold at front of work, knit the next 2 stitches, then knit the 2 stitches from the cable needle.

*continued*

*continued*

**c4b:** Place next 2 stitches onto a cable needle and hold at back of work, knit the next 2 stitches, then knit the 2 stitches from the cable needle.

**c6f:** Place next 3 stitches onto a cable needle and hold at front of work, knit the next 3 stitches, then knit the 3 stitches from the cable needle.

**c6b:** Place next 3 stitches onto a cable needle and hold at back of work, knit the next 3 stitches, then knit the 3 stitches from the cable needle.

## Materials

Blue Sky Alpacas Blue Sky Worsted (50% Alpaca, 50% Merino), 3.5 oz/100g, 109 yd/99.66m; 2 skeins of #2003 Ecru

## Gauge

22 stitches and 26 rows = 4 in/10cm worked in cable stitch in the round using US 8 (5mm) knitting needles, or size needed to obtain gauge

## Instructions

Using US 8 (5mm) double-pointed needles or long circular needle, CO 6 sts.

Join in a rnd and place a marker between the first and last sts.

**Rnd 1 (inc):** Kfb all sts–12 sts.
**Rnd 2 (inc):** (K1, kfb) 6 times–18 sts.
**Rnd 3 (inc):** (P2, kfb) 6 times–24 sts.
**Rnd 4 (inc):** (P2, k1, kfb) 6 times–30 sts.
**Rnd 5 (inc):** (P2, k2, kfb) 6 times–36 sts.
**Rnd 6 (twist & inc):** (P2, k1, t2, kfb) 6 times–42 sts.
**Rnd 7 (inc):** (P2, k4, kfb) 6 times–48 sts.
**Rnd 8 (cable & inc):** (P2, c4f, k1, kfb) 6 times–54 sts.

**Rnd 9 (inc):** (P2, k6, kfb) 6 times–60 sts.
**Rnd 10 (inc):** (P2, k7, kfb) 6 times–66 sts.
**Rnd 11 (cable & inc):** (P2, k2, c6f, kfb) 6 times–72 sts.
**Rnd 12 (inc):** (P2, k9, kfb) 6 times–78 sts.
**Rnd 13 (inc):** (P2, k10, kfb) 6 times–84 sts.
**Rnd 14:** (P2, k12) 6 times.
**Rnd 15 (cable):** (P2, c6f, c6b) 6 times.
**Rnd 16:** (P2, k12) 6 times.
Rep rnd 16 twice more.
**Rnd 19 (inc):** (P1, pfb, k12) 6 times–90 sts.
**Rnd 20:** (P3, k12) 6 times.
Rep rnd 20 twice more.
**Rnd 23 (cable):** (P3, c6f, c6b) 6 times.
**Rnd 24:** (P3, k12) 6 times.
Rep rnd 24 twice more.
**Rnd 27 (inc):** (P2, pfb, k12) 6 times–96 sts.
**Rnd 28:** (P4, k12) 6 times.
Rep rnd 28 twice more.
**Rnd 31 (cable):** (P4, c6f, c6b) 6 times.
**Rnd 32:** (P4, k12) 6 times.
Rep rnd 32 5 more times.
Rep rnds 20–32 3 more times.
**Rnd 59:** (P4, k12) 6 times.
Rep rnd 59 3 more times.
Divide for earflaps. You will stop working in the round at this point:
**Row 1:** P2, put next 32 sts on a holder, turn.
**Row 2:** Starting with the last 2 sts worked, k2 (p12, k4) 3 times, p12, k2.
**Row 3:** K14 (p4, k12) twice, p4, k14.
**Row 4:** K2, p12, k4, p2, put rem 44 sts on a holder, turn.
Working on first earflap only:
**Row 5 (cable)(RS):** K2, p4, c6f, c6b, k2–20 sts.

**Row 6:** K2, p12, k6.

**Row 7:** K2, p4, k14.

Rep rows 6–7 twice more.

**Row 12:** K2, p12, k6.

**Row 13 (cable & dec):** K2 (p2tog) twice, c6f, c6b, k2–18 sts.

**Row 14 (dec):** K2, p12, k2tog, k2–17 sts.

**Row 15 (dec):** K2, k2tog, k13–16 sts. \*\*\*\*

**Row 16:** K2, p12, k2.

**Row 17 (dec):** K2, k2tog, k8, k2tog, k2–14 sts.

**Row 18:** K2, p10, k2.

**Row 19 (dec):** K2, k2tog, k6, k2tog, k2–12 sts.

**Row 20:** K2, p8, k2.

**Row 21 (cable):** K2, c4f, c4b, k2.

**Row 22:** K2, p8, k2.

**Row 23 (dec):** K2, k3tog tbl, k2, k3tog, k2–8 sts.

**Row 24:** K2, p4, k2.

**Row 25 (dec):** K2, k2tog tbl, k2tog, k2–6 sts.

**Row 26:** K2, p2, k2.

**Row 27 (dec):** K1, k2togtbl, k2tog, k1–4 sts.

**Row 28 (dec):** K1, p2tog, k1–3 sts.

Continue on these 3 sts on one dpn to knit a 10-in I-cord.

Cut yarn and draw through sts to secure.

Work second earflap. Return to sts on holder and with WS facing work across first 20 sts as folls:

**Row 1 (WS):** K6, p12, k2, turn, leaving rem 24 sts on holder.

**Row 2 (cable):** K2, c6f, c6b, p4, k2.

**Row 3:** K6, p12, k2.

**Row 4:** K14, p4, k2.

Rep rows 3–4 twice more.

**Row 9:** K6, p12, k2.

**Row 10 (cable & dec):** K2, c6f, c6b (p2tog) twice, k2–18 sts.

**Row 11 (dec):** K2, k2tog, p12, k2–17 sts.

**Row 12 (dec):** K13, k2tog, k2–16 sts.

Work as first earflap from \*\*\*\* to end, finishing with another 10-in I-cord tie.

Return to 24 sts on holder; beg with a WS row, work 2 rows garter stitch.

BO.

Slip rem 32 sts from first holder to needle. Beg with a WS row, work 2 rows garter st.

BO.

## Finishing Instructions

Sew down front and back loose edges to sides of earflaps. Make a 2-in diameter pompom for the top of the hat and two 4-in tassels for the ends of the I-cords; sew on securely. Sew in all loose ends.

# Put-Your-Hair-Up Hat

*by Anna Sorrentino*

The idea for this hat came from my boyfriend, who's always coming up with wacky suggestions along the lines of "Why don't you knit this, why don't you knit that?", and once in a while he strikes it right. My hair is rather long and it's rare for me to wear it down; it's usually up in pigtails, less frequently in a single ponytail. So here's a solution for those of us who don't want to look like our heads have got weird growths ready to emerge from under our hats.

**Project Rating:** Flirtation

**Cost:** $23

**Necessary Skills:** purl (page 30); k2tog (page 40); knitting in the round (page 55); optional: sc (page 87); Magic Loop method (page 33)

## Finished Size

Adult size: circumference (unstretched) = 19¾ inches, height = 7½ inches; stretches up to 24 inches in width

## Materials

- Brown Sheep, Lamb's Pride Bulky (85% Wool/15% Mohair); 4 oz/113g, 125 yd/114m; 1 skein each:

  Carioca (one-hole hat): A = #165 Christmas Green; B = #120 Limeade; C = #155 Lemon Drop

  Raspberry sundae (two-hole hat): A = #22 Autumn Harvest; B = #145 Spice; C = #38 Lotus Pink

- 1 set of US 10½ (7mm) double-pointed needles and 1 10½ (7mm) 12-in or 14-in long circular needle, or 1 long (over 24 in) US 10½ (7mm) circular needle if using the Magic Loop method

- Stitch marker

- Tapestry needle
- Optional: J-10 (6mm) crochet hook

## Gauge

13 stitches and 18 rows = 4 in/10cm worked in stockinette stitch in the round using US 10½ (7mm) knitting needles, or size needed to obtain gauge

**Note:** This simple but effective hat is knitted in the round on a circular needle until there are too few stitches left on the needles, then you switch to dpns. Or work the whole hat on one long circular needle if using the Magic Loop method. The "holes" are created by binding off a number of stitches on one row and then casting them back on (thumb method) on the following row. An optional single crochet row is worked along the holes to give them more stability.

## Stripe Sequence

1 rnd A, 2 rnds B, 3 rnds A, 1 rnd B, 1 rnd C, 1 rnd A, 2 rnds C, 3 rnds B, 2 rnds C, 1 rnd B, 2 rnds A, 1 rnd B, 3 rnds C, 2 rnds B, 2 rnds A, 1 rnd B, 2 rnds C, 2 rnds A, 2 rnds C, 2 rnds B, 1 rnd A, 1 rnd B, 1 rnd A

## Instructions

### Both Hats

With size 10½ needle and color A, CO 64 sts.

Place marker between first and last st, and join the rnd, taking care not to twist sts.

Following stripe patt, k 6 rnds.

**Rnd 7:** Maintaining stripe patt, *k2, p2; rep from * to end.

Rep last rnd 5 times, maintaining stripe patt.

Maintaining stripe patt, k 9 rnds. **

### One-Hole Hat Only (Make Hole)

**Rnd 22:** K1, BO8, k to end of rnd.

**Rnd 23:** K1, CO8, k to end of rnd.

Knit 1 rnd.

### Two-Hole Hat Only

Knit 3 rnds.

### Both Hats

**Rnd 25 (dec):** *K6, k2tog; rep from * to end of rnd (56 sts).

### Two-Hole Hat Only (Make Holes)

**Rnd 26:** K10, BO8, k20, BO8, k10.

**Rnd 27:** K10, CO8, k20, CO8, k10.

Knit 1 rnd.

### One-Hole Hat Only

Knit 3 rnds.

### Both Hats (Shape Top)

***Rnd 29:** *K5, k2tog; rep from * to end of rnd—48 sts.

Knit 3 rnds.

**Rnd 30:** *K4, k2tog; rep from * to end of rnd—40 sts.

Knit 2 rnds.

**Rnd 31:** *K3, k2tog; rep from * to end of rnd.—32 sts.

**Rnd 32:** *K2, k2tog; rep from * to end of rnd—24 sts.

**Rnd 33:** *K1, k2tog; rep from * to end of rnd—16 sts.

**Rnd 34:** *K2tog; rep from * to end of rnd—8 sts.

Cut the yarn, leaving a 6-in tail. Using the tapestry needle, thread the tail through the rem 8 sts and pull to close the hole, ensuring the sts are secured tog. Thread the needle through the very top of the hat and bring the rem yarn to the inside of the hat. Weave in any ends.

### Finishing Instructions

Optional for hats with holes: Work a row of single crochet along the hole edgings to give them more stability.

# Variation

If you recently did a Natalie Portman and no longer have a ponytail to pull through the hat, make a hat without holes. I call this color combo Ocean Floor. I used A = #78 Aztec Turquoise; B = #62 Amethyst; and C = #59 Periwinkle.

Work as for one-hole hat to **.

Maintaining stripe patt, k 3 rnds.

**Rnd 25 (dec):** *K6, k2tog; rep from * to end of rnd–56 sts.

Maintaining stripe patt, k 3 rnds. Keep that stripe patt going and work as for both hats from *** to the end.

# Cable Access

### by Melissa Webster

One of my first knitting projects was a scarf using Lamb's Pride Bulky yarn, which I love. As I was knitting, I was concerned that it would be too itchy for my neck. My mentor, Heather, suggested that I make it into a small bag instead. When I got to the size I wanted, I lined the purse and finished it with an easy strap and button-loop closure. Voilà! Since then, I've made several of these bags as gifts for my friends and family. If you're itching to make a scarf using this stitch pattern, check out the variation.

**Project Rating:** Flirtation

**Cost:** $7.50

**Necessary Skills:** purl (page 30); cables (page 46); I-cord (page 84); mattress stitch (page 62); optional: fringe (page 80)

**Abbreviation: cf4:** Slip next 2 stitches onto cable needle and hold at front of work, knit next 2 stitches from left needle, then knit the 2 stitches from cable needle.

## Finished Size

Length: 8 inches; width: 6½ inches

## Materials

- Brown Sheep, Lamb's Pride Bulky (85% Wool/15% Mohair); 4 oz/113g, 125 yd/114m: 1 skein of #185 Aubergine
- 1 pair of US 10 (6 mm) knitting needles
- 1 set of US 10 (6 mm) double-pointed needles for working I-cord
- Cable needle
- Tapestry needle

### Bag Only

- Lining fabric (17 in x 7½ in)
- Button
- Sewing needle and thread

## Gauge

18 stitches and 20½ rows = 4 in/10cm worked in cable pattern, using US 10 (6mm) knitting needles, or size needed to obtain gauge

## Instructions

### Cable Pattern (32 sts)

**Row 1 (RS):** K2, (p4, k4) 3 times, p4, k2.

**Row 2:** P2, (k4, p4) 3 times, k4, p2.

**Row 3:** K2, p4 (cf4, p4) 3 times, k2.

**Row 4** As row 2.

**Row 5:** As row 1.

**Row 6:** As row 2.

**Rep rows 1–6.**

## Bag

Using US 10 (6mm) knitting needles, CO 32 sts.

**Foundation row 1 (RS):** K2, (p4, k4) 3 times, p4, k2.

**Foundation row 2:** P2, (k4, p4) 3 times, k4, p2.

Beg with row 1, work 6 repeats of the cable patt.

Rep rows 1 and 2 twice more. **

**Next row (fold line):** K.

Rep from ** to ** once more.

Bind off in patt.

## Strap

Using US 10 (6mm) double-pointed knitting needles, CO 4 sts.

Knit a 43-in I-cord.

Finish off I-cord by cutting yarn, thread tail through 4 sts, and pull to tighten.

## Button Loop

Using US 10 (6mm) double-pointed knitting needles, CO 2 sts.

Knit a 5½-in I-cord.

Finish off I-cord by cutting yarn, thread tail through 2 sts, and pull to tighten.

## Finishing Instructions

Fold bag in half along knit fold line and neatly sew up each side using mattress stitch. Using tapestry needle and a length of yarn, neatly sew one end of strap to each top side of the bag. Neatly sew ends of button loop to center back top side of the bag.

Using sewing needle and thread, neatly sew button to center front top side of the bag.

## Lining

Fold lining fabric in half with right sides of the lining fabric together. Sew up the long sides of the bag lining ½ inch in from the edges.

Fold over ¾ inch of the top edge of the bag lining to the wrong side and baste.

Place bag lining inside of bag and neatly slip stitch lining into bag just below the top edges.

## Scarf

Sew in all loose ends.

# Variation

To make a great (non-itchy!) scarf, pick up a soft, wearable bulky yarn like Morehouse Merino Variegated Bulky (100% Merino Wool). I used Indian Summer. You'll need three skeins with size 13 US (9mm) knitting needles. Or for the fringed version, I used four skeins of Tahki Yarns Bunny (50% Merino Wool, 25% Alpaca, 25% Acrylic), in color #045 Turquoise with size 9 US (5.5mm) knitting needles. You'll also need one skein of Tahki Yarns Jolie (70% French Angora, 30% Merino Wool) in color #5021 Light Blue for the fringe.

CO 32 sts and set up the scarf like this:

**\*\* Foundation row 1 (RS):** K2, (p4, k4) 3 times, p4, k2.

**Foundation row 2:** P2, (k4, p4) 3 times, k4, p2.

Beg with row 1, work as many repeats of the cable pattern until you reach your desired length.

Rep rows 2 and 1 twice more. \*\*

BO in patt.

If you like, add some long fringe to the short ends of the scarf.

# Bar Code

My wooly knitted version of a feather boa is quick and easy to knit. If you're a beginner, it's a perfect project to ease you into working with stripes. The fringe is knitted right in as you go along, meaning almost no finishing—fabulous!

**Project Rating:** Flirtation

**Cost:** $32

**Necessary Skills:** stripes (page 55); fringe (page 80)

## Finished Size

One size: length = 74 inches; width (not including fringe) = 2 inches (my scarf reached this length when I ran out of yarn!)

## Materials

- 1 skein each Tahki Yarns, Baby (100% Merino Wool); 3.5 oz/100g, 60 yd/55m in Black (A) and Ivory (B)
- 1 pair of US 15 (10mm) knitting needles
- Tape measure
- Scissors

## Gauge

10 stitches and 15 rows = 4 in/10cm worked in garter stitch (every row knit), using size US 15 (10mm) needles, or size needed to obtain gauge

## Instructions

Cast on 5 sts in A, leaving a 5-in tail.

**Row 1:** K.

Do not break yarn A.

**Row 2:** Using yarn B, leave a 5-in tail, then k to end.

**Row 3:** K.

Do not break yarn B.

**Row 4:** Using yarn A, leave a10-in loop, then k to end.

**Row 5:** K.

Do not break yarn A.

**Row 6:** Using yarn B, leave a10-in loop, then k to end.

**Row 7:** K.

Do not break yarn B.

Rep rows 4–7 until scarf is desired length and BO all sts.

### Finishing Instructions

For a loopy scarf, leave as is, pulling loops to full length. For a fringed scarf, cut all loops, then knot into pairs to avoid unraveling.

Block to shape and straighten any crumpled fringe.

# Variation

This scarf can be knitted in any type of yarn, using many color combinations. As an alternative to the tired old fuzzy scarf, try different stripe patterns and mixing yarn textures for an individual look.

To make this scarf date-night ready, knit two rows of Lion Brand Moonlight Mohair every 10 rows. This will add sparkle and flash without looking like your great Aunt Gertrude at the over-60s singles mixer.

For the most basic of striped scarves, I worked up a little tonal number using one skein each Tahki Yarns, Alpaca Soft (100% Alpaca), 1.75 oz/50g, 43 yd/40m in #002 Brown (A) and Fawn #001 (B), omitting the fringe.

# It's a Cinch

Want an extremely simple knitting project? Then this one's for you! The beauty of this baby is all in the embellishment. You'll be knitting a plain old rectangle—no tricky shaping here—to make either a neck warmer or a waist clincher, and then decorating it with pompoms, ribbons, beads, or all three!

**Project Rating:** Flirtation

**Cost:** $31 will make at least two neck warmers!

**Necessary Skills:** purl (page 30); pompoms (page 82)

## Finished Size

Neck warmer is one size: height = 4¼ inches; length = 16½ inches

Waist clincher: small = 24–28 inches [medium = 29–33 inches, large 34–38 inches]

## Materials

### For Neck Warmer with Pompoms

- A: 1 skein of Morehouse Merino Bulky (100% Merino); 102 yd/4 oz; with plenty left over for a second neck warmer. I used shade Fuchsia.
- 19 yd of each contrast yarn for pompoms and ties. I used Brown Sheep, Lamb's Pride Bulky (85% Wool/15% Mohair), 125 yd/100g; 19 yd each of: B, #M155 Lemon Drop; C, #M105 RPM Pink; A, same yarn as neck warmer
- Cardboard (an empty cereal box will do)
- Compasses for drawing circles
- Ruler or tape measure
- Tapestry needle

### For Waist Clincher

- 1 skein of Morehouse Merino Bulky (100% Merino); 102 yd/4 oz; with plenty left over for a second waist clincher. I used shade Cardinal.
- Tapestry needle
- 2 [2½, 3] yards ribbon for ties (I used ½-in-wide black satin ribbon)
- Decorative beads
- 1 pair of US 15 (10mm) knitting needles

## Gauge

8½ stitches and 14 rows = 4 in/10cm over stockinette stitch using US 15 (10mm) knitting needles, or size required to obtain gauge

## Instructions

### Neck Warmer

Using US 15 (10mm) knitting needles and yarn A, CO 35 sts.

**Note:** K first and last sts of every row to give a nice edge.

Beg with a k row, work in St st for 13 rows.

Row 14 (WS): K to end.

Beg with a k row, work in St st for 14 rows.

Bind off.

With wrong sides facing one another, fold neck warmer along line created in center of work.

Pin CO and BO edges together and sides together, then using tapestry needle threaded with a length of yarn A, sew along three open edges using a very neat running stitch about ¼ in from edge.

Weave in all loose ends.

## Ties (Make Two)

Cut 100 in of each yarn and hold them together. Fold in half and tie a knot at the folded end. (You now have a knot with six ends of yarns hanging from it.) Divide the six ends into three sets of two, with no two ends in a pair being the same color.

Braid to make a tie and knot at end to secure.

## Finishing Instructions

Using a large tapestry needle (or your fingers, if you are very dexterous), weave each tie (like a running stitch), through both thicknesses of the neck warmer close the edges of each long side.

Neatly sew a pompom to the end of each tie.

Place around your cold neck, being careful not to attract the attention of any nearby kitties who may wish to bat around those swinging pompoms!

## Waist Clincher

Using US 15 (10mm) knitting needles, CO 60 [70, 80] sts.
**Note:** K first and last st of every row to give a nice edge.

Beg with a k row, work 12 rows in St st.

Bind off.

Weave in all loose ends.

Thread tapestry needle with ribbon and knot at end.

Just above the CO edge of waist clincher, sew ribbon along neatly, trying not to let it twist too much.

When you get to the other end, even out stitching and adjust ribbon to look pretty.

Sew down beginning end neatly to inside of waist clincher.

Cut ribbon at second end and sew neatly to inside.

You are now left with a long length of ribbon—do not knot end, but leaving a few inches at the beginning, sew just under the CO edge as before.

Do not cut, but adjust ribbon so that the loose ends are of equal length.

Thread beads onto these long ends, then tie knots to secure.

Wrap around your midsection and lace beaded ribbon like a corset through the short edges of the waist clincher. Put on a circular skirt and go show off your curves!

# Variation

If you don't like natural fibers, you could make the neck warmer in fun fur, tied at the front with ribbons. I used one skein of Patons Cha Cha (100% Nylon, 77 yd/1¾ oz) shade Hippie–two strands held together for thickness; one yard of ribbon for ties, I used 1½-in wide white transparent ribbon.
CO 35 sts and follow directions for neck warmer with pompoms.

## Finishing Instructions

Take two pieces of ribbon, each 18 inches in length. Fold under one end about ½ inch and pin to inside of the neck warmer close to the top (the cast-on/cast-off edge). Neatly stitch the end of the ribbon to the neck warmer. Repeat, sewing the second piece to the other corner of the inside upper edge of the neck warmer. Trim loose ends of ribbon into points.

Tie a bow at the neck and parade around the room, smug in the knowledge that you made it yourself!

# Bobbles and Balls

Wrap yourself up in the warmth of buttery-soft alpaca. This pattern is a playful mix of lace and bobbles—add chunky balls to the edges to further enhance the three-dimensional feel. I wanted this wrap to be huge, as I'm on the tall side and like to wrap it around my neck and again over my shoulders and still have enough length to swing the ends dramatically as I strut around Central Park. If you are a little vertically challenged, or just want a shorter wrap, simply work to your required length then bind off after a bobble row.

**Project Rating:** Summer Fling

**Cost:** $102

**Necessary Skills:** purl (page 30); increase (page 38); decrease (page 40); lace (page 42); bobbles (page 47)

## Finished Size

23½ inches x 98 inches

## Materials

- Knit Picks, Decadence (100% Superfine Alpaca); 3.5 oz/100g, 121 yd/110m
- 15 skeins of color #6833 Brown (use two strands of yarn held together)
- 1 pair of US 13 (9mm) knitting needles
- Stitch markers (place them after each stitch repeat to help keep track of pattern)
- Tapestry needle
- Lightweight stuffing

## Gauge

8 stitches and 11 rows = 4 in/10cm worked in lace and bobble stitch using two strands Decadence and US 13 (9mm) knitting needles, or size needed to obtain gauge

## Instructions

### Make Bobble (MB)

(K1, yo, k1, yo, k1) into 1 st, turn, k5, turn, p5, turn, k1, s1, k2tog, psso, k1, turn, p3tog.

### Lace and Bobble Stitch (Multiple of 11 sts)

**Row 1 (RS):** *K1, MB, k2, yo, k1, yo, k4, k2tog; rep from * to end.

**Row 2:** *P2tog, p8, ptbl, p1; rep from * to end.

**Row 3:** *K5, yo, k1, yo, k3, k2tog; rep from * to end.

**Rows 4, 6, 8, and 10:** * P2tog, p10; rep from * to end.

**Row 5:** *K6, yo, k1, yo, k2, k2tog; rep from * to end.

**Row 7:** *K7, (yo, k1) twice, k2tog; rep from * to end.

**Row 9:** *K8, yo, k1, yo, k2tog; rep from * to end.

**ow 11:** *Ssk, k4, yo, k1, yo, k2, MB, k1; rep from * to end.

**ow 12:** *P1, ptbl, p8, p2togbl; rep from * to end.

**ow 13:** *Ssk, k3, yo, k1, yo, k5: rep from * to end.

**ows 14, 16, 18, and 20:** *P10, p2togtbl; rep from * to end.

**ow 15:** *Ssk, k2, yo, k1, yo, k6: rep from * to end.

**ow 17:** *Ssk, (k1, yo) twice, k7: rep from * to end.

**ow 19:** *Ssk, yo, k1, yo, k8: rep from * to end.

ep rows 1–20 for lace and bobble stitch.

## Wrap

sing US 13 (9mm) knitting needles and holding two strands of yarn together, CO 55 sts.

ork in lace and bobble stitch until work measures 98 in or length required, ending with a bobble row.

ind off loosely.

## Balls (Make 16)

sing US 13 (9mm) knitting needles and holding two strands of yarn together, CO 6 sts.

**ow 1 (RS):** Kfb into every st—12 sts.

**ows 2, 4, 6, and 8:** P.

**ows 3, 5, and 7:** K.

**ow 9:** K2tog 6 times—6 sts.

ut yarn, leaving an 8-in tail. Draw tail through rem sts to secure, then sew up side seam.

## Finishing Instructions

tuff all balls until they are nicely rounded. Sew cast-on end closed. Space balls evenly along cast-on and bound-off edges of wrap and sew in place. Sew in all loose ends.

## Variation

Experiment with different stitch patterns for your own wrap. Try out practice lace stitches or work an allover cable design. Use fringe, tassels, pompoms, or strings of beads to add your own twist on the edges. (Check out Chapter 8, "Everything But the Kitchen Sink: Embellishments," for embellishing techniques.)

# Chapter Twelve

◆◆◆

# Playing Footsie

## Pirate Socks

Don't fear the heel—knit these toe-up striped short or knee socks to bring out your inner Captain Hook.

## Toasty Tootsies

Cabling in the round has never looked so good! Stylish slipper socks for snuggling by the fire.

## Not-Quite-'70s Legwarmers

Big shoes and legwarmers can be worn together! Whip up some fabulous knits, wide enough to wear over your boots.

## Boot-i-licious

Boots feeling left out? Show them your love by giving them their own jewelry.

## PDA Mittens

One for you, one for your sweetheart, and one big enough to share. Embellish with duplicate stitch and hold on to the heat in the dead of winter.

## O Gloves

Sexy arm warmers are not just for the opera. Metallic-edged cables add just enough sparkle to light up the night.

# Pirate Socks

Even though the needles are small, I love knitting socks. They are the perfect project to take on the move—compact enough to fit in a handbag and easy to whip out when you find yourself with a couple of minutes on your hands. This toe-up pattern lets you try on the socks as you are knitting them to ensure the perfect fit. I was feeling the need for a bit of "yo-ho-ho-ing" when I dreamt up these pirate-inspired socks—and I had to get a skull and crossbones into this book somehow!

**Project Rating:** Summer Fling

**Cost:** $6

**Necessary Skills:** purl (page 30); crochet chain (page 86); pick up stitches (page 67); knitting in the round (page 55); increase (page 38); short-row knitting (page 42); Fair Isle (page 56); optional: Magic Loop method (page 33)

## Finished Size

To fit a women's shoe size 7–9

## Materials

- Knit Picks Palette (100% Peruvian Wool); 231 yd/50g
- 1 ball each: A = #23716 Red; B = #23728 White; C = #23729 Black
- 1 US 2 (2.75mm) circular needle at least 24 in long for Magic Loop method, or 1 set of US 2 (2.75mm) double-pointed needles
- C-2 (2.75mm) crochet hook
- Tapestry needle

## Gauge

34 stitches and 41 rows = 4 in/10cm worked in stockinette stitch, in the round, using US 2 (2.75mm) knitting needles, or size needed to obtain gauge

## Stripe Pattern

Repeat the foll 16 rnds for stripe pattern:
Using color B, knit 8 rnds.
Using color C, knit 8 rnds.

## Instructions

### Starting at the Toe

Using color A, make a crochet chain of 14 loops, pull the last loop so that it is large enough to pass the ball of yarn through it to secure, and pull tight.

Using US 2 knitting needles, pick up and k 14 sts through one side of the crochet loops, turn, and pick up and k 14 sts through the other side of the same 14 crochet loops—28 sts.

**Rnd 1:** K into the backs of all sts.

**Rnd 2:** (Pm, k14) twice.

**Rnd 3:** (K1, kfb, k to 2 sts before marker, kfb, k1) twice—32 sts.

**Rnd 4:** K.

Rep rnds 3–4 6 more times—56 sts.

Knit 4 rnds without shaping.

Cut yarn A.

Work 4 repeats of stripe patt for foot.

Using yarn B, knit 4 rnds.

## Divide for Heel

Row 1: Using yarn A, knit 27 sts, yf, sl 1, leave rem 28 sts on holder.

Returning to heel sts, work in short rows as follows:

Row 2: Yf, sl 1 pwise, p to last st, yb, sl 1 pwise.

Row 3: Yb, sl 1, k to st before the slipped st from the last row, yf, sl 1, turn.

Row 4: Yf, sl 1 pwise, p to st before the slipped st from the last row, yb, sl 1 pwise, turn.

Rep rows 3–4 6 times until 8 sts each side have been wrapped.

Row 17: Yb, sl 1, k12, k next st and its wrap tog, yf, sl 1 (this st will now be wrapped twice), turn.

Row 18: Yf, sl 1 pwise, p to next wrapped st, p this st and its wrap tog, yb, sl 1 pwise (this st will now be wrapped twice), turn.

Row 19: Yb, sl 1, k to next wrapped st, k this st and its two wraps tog, yf, sl 1 (this st will now be wrapped twice), turn.

Row 20: Yf, sl 1 pwise, p to next wrapped st, p this st and its two wraps tog, yb, sl 1 pwise (this st will now be wrapped twice), turn.

Rep rows 19–20 until all wrapped sts have been worked.

Break yarn A.

Using yarn B and with RS facing, pick up loop below first st on holder and k tog with first heel st, k to last st, pick up loop below last st on holder and k tog with last heel st.

Knit across 28 sts from holder—56 sts.

Knit 3 more rnds using yarn B.

Using yarn C, k 8 rnds.***

Work in stripe patt for 1 repeat.

Using yarn B, k 8 rnds.

Using yarn C, k 3 rnds.

### Left Sock Only

**N**ext rnd: K 37, turn, leaving rem 19 sts on holder. (You will be working back and forth in rows for the next bit.)

**W**ith WS facing, p across 19 sts, turn, leaving rem 18 sts on holder.

**W**ith RS facing and starting with a knit row, work in St st, following chart from row 1 to row 14.

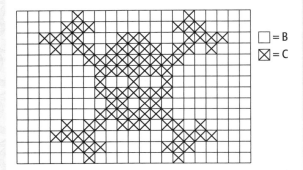

☐ = B
☒ = C

**P**ut these 19 sts on holder.

### Right Sock Only

**K**nit 1 rnd.

**N**ext rnd: K the first 8 sts, turn leaving 29 next sts on holder.

**N**ext rnd: P across 19 sts of first row of chart.

**W**ith RS facing and starting with a knit row, work in St st, following chart from row 1 to row 14.

**P**ut these 19 sts on holder.

### Both Socks

**R**eturn to 37 sts on holder, with RS facing work as folls:

**U**sing yarn C, kfb, k35, kfb—39 sts.

**W**ork in St st on these 39 sts. Beg with a purl row, work stripe patt as folls:
- ♦ 3 rows with yarn C.
- ♦ 8 rows with yarn B.
- ♦ 3 rows with yarn C.

**N**ext row: P2tog, p35, p2tog, p across 19 sts from holder—56 sts.

**W**orking in the rnd, k another 4 rnds with yarn C.

**K**nit 8 rows with yarn B.

**U**sing yarn C, work in k1, p1 rib for 10 rnds.

**B**ind off in rib.

### Finishing Instructions

**N**eatly sew seams of Fair Isle section to stripe section.

**S**ew in all loose ends.

# Variation

Everyone wears socks, so why not make everyone in your family a pair–changing the colors and patterns to match their different personalities?

Use this toe-up pattern as a base from which to design your own patterned socks. Try out different lace or stripe combinations. You can knit solid colored socks with a simple rib pattern on the leg, or try out some self-striping yarns like Lion Brand Magic Stripes. It's fun to watch the stripes evolve without having to switch yarns.

Not feeling so ambitious or sea-worthy? This pattern makes fetching striped knee socks:

Work as for shorter sock to ✻✻✻
Work in stripe patt for 4 repeats.
Using yarn B, k 7 rnds.
**Inc. rnd:** (K1, kfb, k24, kfb, k1), twice–60 sts.
Using yarn C, k 8 rnds.
Using yarn B, k 7 rnds.
**Inc. rnd:** (K1, kfb, k26, kfb, k1), twice–64 sts.
Using yarn C, k 8 rnds.
Using yarn B, k 7 rnds.
**Inc. rnd:** (K1, kfb, k28, kfb, k1), twice–68 sts.
Using yarn C, k 8 rnds.

Using yarn B, k 7 rnds.
**Inc. rnd:** (K1, kfb, k30, kfb, k1), twice–72 sts.
Using yarn C, k 8 rnds.
Using yarn B, k 7 rnds.
**Inc. rnd:** (K1, kfb, k32, kfb, k1), twice–76 sts.
Work in stripe patt for 1 more repeat.
Using yarn C work in K1, p1 rib for 10 rnds.
BO in rib.

## Finishing Instructions

Sew in all loose ends.

# Toasty Tootsies

Beat the winter chill by pulling on these chunky, cabled slipper socks—they are the cozy cure for a bad case of cold feet.

**Project Rating:** Summer Fling

**Cost:** $23

**Necessary Skills:** purl (page 30); crochet chain (page 86); increase (page 38); short-row knitting (page 42); cables (page 46); knitting in the round (page 55); slip stitch (page 67); optional: braided tie (page 83); pompoms (page 82); Magic Loop method (page 33)

**Abbreviations: t3f:** Slip next 2 stitches onto a cable needle and hold at front of work, purl next stitch from left needle, then knit 2 stitches from cable needle. **t3b:** Slip next stitch onto cable needle and hold at back of work, knit next 2 stitches from left needle, then purl stitch from the cable needle. **c4f:** Slip next 2 stitches onto a cable needle and hold at front of work, knit next 2 stitches from left needle, then knit 2 stitches from cable needle. **c4b:** Slip next 2 stitches onto a cable needle and hold at back of work, knit next 2 stitches from left needle, then knit 2 stitches from cable needle.

## Finished Size

Women's: Fits shoe size 6–9 [men's: shoe size 10–14]

## Materials

- Brown Sheep, Lamb's Pride Bulky (85% Wool/15% Mohair); 125 yd/114m per 4 oz/113g skein
- 1 skein A, 2 skeins B—I used A = #105 RPM Pink (#115 Oatmeal); B = #22 Autumn Harvest (#05 Onyx)

- 1 set of US 10½ (6.5mm) double-pointed needles, or 1 long (over 24 in) US 10½ (6.5mm) circular needle, if using the Magic Loop method
- Cable needle
- J-10 (6mm) crochet hook
- Stitch markers
- Tapestry needle
- 2 pieces of ½-in wide elastic, sewn into loop to fit around each calf

## Gauge

14½ stitches and 20 rows = 4 in/10cm worked in stockinette stitch using US 10½ (6.5mm) knitting needles, or size needed to obtain gauge

## Instructions

### Toe

Using color A and crochet hook, chain 5 [6] loops. Pull last loop big enough to pass skein through, then pass skein through loop and pull tight.

Using US 10½ (6.5mm) knitting needles, pick up and k 5 [6] sts along RS of crochet chain, turn and pick up and k 5 [6] sts on opposite edge of crochet chain—10 [12] sts.

Working in the rnd, and placing stitch markers after fifth [sixth] st and tenth [twelfth] st, k 1 rnd, knitting into the back of each st.

**Rnd 2:** (K1, kfb, k to 2 sts before st marker, kfb, k1) twice—14 [16] sts.

**Rep** last rnd to 30 [36] sts.

### Women's Size Only

**K**nit 1, kfb, k14, kfb, k to end of rnd—32 sts.

**Next 2 rnds:** K all sts.

**C**ut yarn A.

### Foot

**U**sing color B, work cable pattern as folls:

**Rnd 1:** K16, p1, t3f, t3b, p2, t3f, t3b, p1.

**Rnd 2:** K16, p2, k4, p4, k4, p2.

**Rnd 3:** K16, p2, c4f, p4, c4f, p2.

**Rnd 4:** As rnd 2.

**Rnd 5:** K16, p1, t3b, t3f, p2, t3b, t3f, p1.

**Rnd 6:** K16, p1, (k2, p2) 3 times, k2, p1.

**Rep** rnds 1–6 once more.

**Rnd 13:** K16, (t3b, p2, t3f) twice.

**Rnd 14:** K18, p4, k4, p4, k2.

**Rnd 15:** K18, p4, c4b, p4, k2.

**Rnd 16:** As rnd 14.

**Rnd 17:** K18, p3, t3b, t3f, p3, k2.

**Rnd 18:** K18, p3, k2, p2, k2, p3, k2.

**Rnd 19:** K18, p3, t3f, t3b, p3, k2.

**Rnd 20:** As rnd 14.

**Rnd 21:** As rnd 15.

**Rnd 22:** As rnd 14.

**Rnd 23:** K16, (t3f, p2, t3b) twice.

**Rnd 24:** As rnd 6.

**C**ut yarn B.

### Men's Size Only

**C**ut yarn A.

### Foot

**Next rnd:** Using color B, k20, (p2, k4) twice, p2, k2.

Rep last rnd 4 times.

Cable rnd: K20, (p2, k4) twice, p2, k2.

Next rnd: Using color B, k20, (p2, k4) twice, p2, k2.

Rep last rnd 4 times.

Rep last 6 rnds 4 times, then rep first 4 of these last 6 rnds again (or enough to fit top of foot/start of ankle).

Cut yarn B.

## Both Sizes

### Short-Row Heel

Using color A, k across 16 [18] sts—put rem 16 [18] sts on a holder. (You'll be working back and forth in rows for the heel.)

Row 1: P to last st, yb, sl pwise. (The last st is the first wrapped st, you will inc the number of wrapped sts at end of each row.) Turn.

Row 2: Yb, sl 1, k to last st, yf, sl 1, turn.

Row 3: Yf, sl 1 pwise, p to last st before wrapped st, yb, sl 1 pwise, turn.

Row 4: Yb, k to last st before wrapped st, yf, sl 1, turn.

Rep rows 3–4 4 more times.

Row 13: Yf, sl 1 pwise, p to next wrapped st, p this st and its wrap tog, yb, sl 1 pwise (this st is now wrapped twice), turn.

Row 14: Yb, sl 1, k to next wrapped st, k this stitch and its wrap tog, yf, sl 1, turn.

Row 15: Yf, sl 1 pwise, p to next wrapped st, p this st and its 2 wraps tog, yb, sl 1 pwise, turn.

Row 16: Yb, sl 1, k to next wrapped st, k this st and its 2 wraps tog, yf, sl 1, turn.

Rep these last 2 rows until 1 wrapped st rem on right side, pick up loop below first st on holder, and k tog with wrapped st and its wrap, k to last st, pick up loop below last st on holder and k tog with last st—16 [18] sts.

Break yarn A.

## Leg

### Women's Size Only

Using color B, start working in the rnd again, across all sts as folls:

Rnd 1: (Pfb, t3f, t3b, p2, t3f, t3b, p1) twice—36 sts.

Rnd 2: (P3, k4, p4, k4, p3) twice.

Rnd 3: (P3, c4f, p4, c4f, p3) twice.

Rnd 4: As rnd 2.

**Rnd 5:** (P2, t3b, t3f, p2, t3b, t3f, p2) twice.

**Rnd 6:** *P2, (k2, p2) 4 times; rep from * once more.

**Rnd 7:** *P2, (t3b, p2, t3f) twice, p1; rep from * once more.

**Rnd 8:** (P1, k2, p4,k4, p4, k2, p1) twice.

**Rnd 9:** (P1, k2, p4, c4b, p4, k2, p1) twice.

**Rnd 10:** As rnd 8.

**Rnd 11:** (P1, k2, p3, t3b, t3f, p3, k2, p1) twice.

**Rnd 12:** (P1, k2, p3, k2, p2, k2, p3, k2, p1) twice.

**Rnd 13:** (P1, k2, p3, t3f, t3b, p3, k2, p1) twice.

**Rnd 14:** As rnd 8.

**Rnd 15:** As rnd 9.

**Rnd 16:** As rnd 8.

**Rnd 17:** *P1, (t3f, p2, t3b) twice, p1; rep from * once more.

**Rnd 18:** As rnd 6.

**Rnd 19:** (P2, t3f, t3b, p2, t3f, t3b, p2) twice.

Rep rnds 2–6.

Rep rnd 19.

Rep rnds 2–6.

Rep rnds 7–19.

Rep rnds 2–6.

Rep rnd 19.

Rep rnds 2–6.

## Men's Size Only

Using color B, start working in the rnd again across all sts as folls:

**Rnd 1:** P1, k1, (p2, k4) twice, p2, k1, p1, then work sts from holder as folls: p1, k1, (p2, k4) twice, p2, k1, p1.

**Rnd 2:** P1, k1, (p2, k4) twice, (p2, k1) twice, (p2, k4) twice, p2, k1, p1.

**Rnd 3:** P1, k1, (p2, c4f) twice, (p2, k1) twice, (p2, c4f) twice, p2, k1, p1.

**Rnd 4:** P1, k1, (p2, k4) twice, (p2, k1) twice, (p2, k4) twice, p2, k1, p1.

Rep last rnd 4 times.

Rep last 6 rnds 5 times.

Then rep first 4 of these last rnds once more.

**Both Sizes**

**Next rnd:** *P1, k1; rep from * to end of rnd.

Rep last rnd 3 times more.

**Next rnd:** P to end.

**Next rnd:** *P1, k1; rep from * to end of rnd.

Rep last rnd 3 times more.

Bind off in rib.

## Finishing Instructions

Fold top of rib over at purl rnd to inside to form casing for elastic loop. Place elastic loop inside, and, using long end of yarn and tapestry needle, slip stitch neatly into place. Sew in all loose ends.

## Variation

Make a shorter, more elf-like sock by finishing with the rib a couple of inches up from the heel.

Instead of elastic, run a braided or twisted cord through the tops of your socks. Add a pompom to each end of your ties.

For more of a slipper-type sock, you can attach real or faux leather soles (available at craft stores). Using a strong thread, sew them onto the bottoms of your socks. Check with the manufacturer to see if they are washable before throwing them into your machine!

For a non-slip base, paint or spray the soles with special latex solution (also available at craft stores), to stop you from sliding into the furniture when you're running around on hardwood floors!

# Not-Quite-'70s Legwarmers

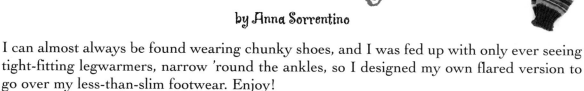

by Anna Sorrentino

I can almost always be found wearing chunky shoes, and I was fed up with only ever seeing tight-fitting legwarmers, narrow 'round the ankles, so I designed my own flared version to go over my less-than-slim footwear. Enjoy!

**Project Rating:** Summer Fling

**Cost:** $18

**Necessary Skills:** purl (page 30); k2tog (page 40); ssk (page 40); yo (page 39); knitting in the round (page 55); optional: Magic Loop method (page 33)

## Finished Size

Bottom circumference: 18 inches; cuff circumference (unstretched): 6¼ inches (stretches up to 10 inches); height:15 inches

## Materials

- ♦ MC = Regina sock yarn 6 ply (75% Wool, 25% Polyamide); 1.75 oz/50g, 136 yd/125m
- ♦ 2 balls of #5402 Passion
- ♦ CC = Debbie Bliss Merino DK (100% Merino Wool); 1.75 oz/50g, 120 yd/100m
- ♦ 1 ball of #608
- ♦ 1 set of US 5 (3.75mm) double-pointed needles
- ♦ Stitch markers (2)
- ♦ Tapestry needle
- ♦ Optional: E-4 (3.5mm) crochet hook (to bind off loosely); clear elastic thread (if you want to make the cuff a little firmer)

## Gauge

22 stitches and 28 rows = 4 in/10cm worked in stockinette stitch in the round using US 5 (3.75mm) knitting needles, or size needed to obtain gauge

**Note:** These legwarmers are knitted in the round on circulars until there are too few stitches left on the needles, then you will switch to dpns—or use the Magic Loop method, using one long circular needle. Decreases are done at sides (stitch markers are useful to help you keep track of the left and right folds).

## Instructions

Using the circular needles and CC, CO 104 sts.

Place marker after 52 sts twice to mark left and right folds.

Taking care not to twist the sts, join and work in the rnd.

**Rnds 1–5:** K.

**Rnd 6:** K1, *k2tog, yo; rep from * to last st, k1.

**Rnds 7–11:** K.

**Rnd 12:** Change to MC, fold hem at eyelet rnd, and join hem by knitting tog 1 st on the needle and the corresponding st on the cast-on row. To do this, insert the point of your left needle into the very first st of the cast-on, then k this tog with the first st on your left needle. Cont to pick up and k the cast-on sts tog with the sts on your left needle to the end of the rnd.

Rnds 13–14: K.

Rnd 15: Beg shaping: K1, k2tog, k to 3 sts before marker, ssk, k1, sl marker, k1, k2tog, k to 3 sts before marker, ssk, k1—100 sts.

Rnds 16–20: K.

Rnd 21: K1, k2tog, k to 3 sts before marker, ssk, k1, sl marker, k1, k2tog, k to 3 sts before marker, ssk, k1—96 sts.

Rnds 22–26: K.

Rnd 27: K1, k2tog, k to 3 sts before marker, ssk, k1, sl marker, k1, k2tog, k to 3 sts before marker, ssk, k1—92 sts.

Rnds 28–32: K.

Rnd 33: K1, k2tog, k to 3 sts before marker, ssk, k1, sl marker, k1, k2tog, k to 3 sts before marker, ssk, k1—88 sts.

Rnds 34–38: K.

Rnd 39: K1, k2tog, k to 3 sts before marker, ssk, k1, sl marker, k1, k2tog, k to 3 sts before marker, ssk, k1—84 sts.

Rnds 40–44: K.

Rnd 45: K1, k2tog, k to 3 sts before marker, ssk, k1, sl marker, k1, k2tog, k to 3 sts before marker, ssk, k1—80 sts.

Rnds 46–50: K.

Rnd 51: K1, k2tog, k to 3 sts before marker, ssk, k1, sl marker, k1, k2tog, k to 3 sts before marker, ssk, k1—76 sts.

Rnds 52–56: K.

Rnd 57: K1, k2tog, k to 3 sts before marker, ssk, k1, sl marker, k1, k2tog, k to 3 sts before marker, ssk, k1—72 sts.

Rnds 58–62: K.

Rnd 63: K1, k2tog, k to 3 sts before marker, ssk, k1, sl marker, k1, k2tog, k to 3 sts before marker, ssk, k1—68 sts.

Rnds 64–68: K.

Rnd 69: K1, k2tog, k to 3 sts before marker, ssk, k1, sl marker, k1, k2tog, k to 3 sts before marker, ssk, k1—64 sts.

Rnds 70–74: K.

Rnd 75: K1, k2tog, k to 3 sts before marker, ssk, k1, sl marker, k1, k2tog, k to 3 sts before marker, ssk, k1—60 sts.

**R**nds 76–80: K.

**R**nd 81: K1, k2tog, k to 3 sts before marker, ssk, k1, sl marker, k1, k2tog, k to 3 sts before marker, ssk, k1 — 56 sts.

**R**nds 82–96: K.

**S**witch to CC.

**R**nd 97: K.

**R**nds 98–118: * K2, p2; rep from * to end.

**B**ind off loosely; you may find that using a crochet hook to BO helps.

**Optional:** Thread clear elastic thread through the cuff ribbing to avoid the legwarmers loosening with wear.

### Finishing Instructions

**B**lock lightly to correct measurements. Sew in all loose ends.

## Variation

Feel that you need more flare to your wrists rather than your ankles? Why not knit up a sassy pair of armwarmers? Just follow the legwarmers pattern, but make the rib section longer to fit either just below or above your elbow.

Bring out your inner pixie by making a pointy hat! Follow the pattern for the legwarmers to the end of the dec, then cont dec until you are left with only 8 sts. Cut the yarn, leaving a tail of about 6 inches, and thread this through the rem sts. Pull yarn to close hole, thread tail through to inside, and sew in all ends.

# Boot-i-licious

## by Lynn Burdick

These little gems came about when I was looking through a fashion magazine and noticed all the embellishments on the boots. That's when it hit me—jewelry for boots! Now you can dress your boots up with a sleek knitted wire bracelet with beads. Once you have started making these bracelets you won't be able to knit fast enough to keep up with the ideas!

**Project Rating:** Flirtation

**Cost:** $10 will make around five bracelets

**Necessary Skills:** no special skills required

## Finished Size

Measure your boot at the ankle to determine your finished measurement. The one shown is for a 9-inch bracelet.

## Materials

- 26-gauge wire
- 1 pair of US 4 (3.5mm) knitting needles
- Headpins
- Jump rings
- Beads

## Gauge

Gauge is not important for these bracelets.

**Note:** Metal is not flexible, so knit it loosely. Don't worry about uneven stitches—when the work is done you can bend the knitting to neaten it up.

## Instructions

Loosely CO 6 sts.

Work in garter stitch until piece measures 9 in or the length needed to wrap around ankle of your boot.

Bind off.

### Finishing Instructions

Give the wire a twist at regular intervals to create the scallops. Sew the two ends securely together with your wire tail. Clip ends and secure. Take beads and put on headpins. Secure end of headpin with a loop. Cut off excess. Add jump ring to beaded headpin and attach at scallops.

# Variation

Knitting with wire is adaptable to any jewelry. Here are some ideas to get your creative juices flowing. Try the following techniques for more knitted boot or wrist bracelets, necklaces, or rings:

- CO 1½ in worth of sts. Leave a long tail to attach clasp. K in garter stitch for desired length then BO. Take a variety of novelty yarns and randomly weave in the wire knitting (horizontally or vertically). Leave ends as a decorative fringe.

- Before you start knitting, thread the wire with an assortment of beads. CO 2 in worth of sts. K in garter stitch, randomly knitting in the beads. Or use the same bead and knit them in a line.

- CO about 1 in worth of sts. K in garter stitch for about 2 in. BO. Wrap wire around a knitting needle and, using the tail from the cast-on, whip stitch the two ends together to form a wire-knitted bead. Thread a leather strap or purchased jewelry cord with clasp through the knitted bead. Put a large bead on a headpin and attach a jump ring and attach to the center of the knitted bead. Or do a whole row of beads, like fringe.

- CO 5 sts with silver wire and k in garter stitch for desired length. BO. Do the same thing with gold wire and brass wire. You will have three lengths of wire. Whip stitch the three tog with wire or novelty yarn. Attach clasp.

- For a unique pair of knitting earrings, CO 5 sts and k in garter stitch for about 3 in. BO. Wrap the wire knitting around a size-8 knitting needle to create a curlicue. Attach a jump ring at the top and attach to an earring post. Put beads on a headpin and attach to bottom of earring with a jump ring. You can add more beads on the sides. Make a second earring to match the first.

# PDA Mittens

Don't fear public displays of affection—hold your sweetheart's hand year-round. Knit a pair of mittens for yourself, a pair for your special someone, or share your body heat in a mitten made for two. Sizes and charts are given for women's and men's sizes, so whatever your sexual orientation, there's a PDA mitten for you.

**Project Rating:** Summer Fling

**Cost:** $30

**Necessary Skills:** purl (page 30); increase (page 38); decrease (page 40); knitting in the round (page 55); duplicate stitch (page 74); optional: Magic Loop method (page 33)

## Finished Size

For single mitten: woman's [man's]: to fit an average size adult hand

For double mitten: woman and man [woman and woman, man and man] to fit two hands

## Materials

- Brown Sheep, Lamb's Pride Bulky (85% Wool/15% Mohair); 4 oz/113g, 125 yd/114m
- 1 skein A, 2 skeins B, 1 skein C (I used A = #105 RPM Pink; B = #10 Crème; C = #52 Spruce)
- 1 set of US 10½ (6.5mm) double-pointed needles, or 1 long (over 24 in) US 10½ (6.5mm) circular needle if using the Magic Loop method
- Stitch markers (I used a loop of contrast color yarn)
- Tapestry needle

## Gauge

14½ stitches and 20 rows = 4 in/10cm worked in stockinette stitch using US 10½ (6.5mm) knitting needles, or size needed to obtain gauge

## Instructions

### Single Mitten

Using color A [C] and US 10½ (6.5mm) needles, CO 20 [24] sts.

Join into a rnd, placing marker between first and last st.

**Rnd 1:** *K1, p1; rep from * to end.

Rep last rnd 9 more times (or more if you prefer a longer cuff).

Cut yarn A [C].

**Next rnd:** Using yarn B, k.

✿ ✿

### Shape Thumb Gusset

**Next rnd (inc):** K8 [10], m1, k4, m1, k8 [10]—22 [26] sts.

**Next rnd:** K.

**Next rnd (inc):** K1, m1, k7 [9], m1, k6, m1, k7 [9], m1, k1—26 [30] sts.

**Next rnd:** K.

**Next rnd (inc):** K1, m1, k8 [10], m1, k8, m1, k8 [10], m1, k1—30 [34] sts.

Knit 8 [9] rnds even.

**Next rnd (inc):** K11 [13], m1, k8, m1, k11 [13]—32 [36] sts.

## Men's Size Only

Work two more rnds without shaping.

## Both Sizes

**Next rnd:** K20 [23], slip next 12 [13] sts onto a holder, then slip the first 12 [13] sts from the beg of the next rnd onto a holder.

Working on 8 [10] sts for thumb only, join into a rnd, placing marker between first and last st.

**Next rnd:** K. ***

Rep last rnd 9 [13] more times.

## Women's Size Only

**Next rnd (dec):** (K3tog) twice, k2tog—3 sts.

**Next rnd (dec):** K3tog—1 st.

## Men's Size Only

**Next rnd (dec):** (K3tog) 3 times, k1—4 sts.

**Next rnd (dec):** (K2tog) twice—2 sts.

## Both Sizes

Cut yarn, leaving a 6-in tail, and draw through rem 1 [2] st to secure.

****

Return to 24 [26] sts on holder.

**Next rnd:** Pick up 1 st from right side base of thumb, k24 [26], sts from holder, pick up 1 st from left side base of thumb. This st will be after the first picked-up st, twisting them to prevent a hole—26 [28] sts.

**Next rnd:** K2tog, k22 [23], k2tog—24 [26] sts.

**Next rnd:** K.

*****

Rep last rnd 11 [12] more times.

**Next rnd (dec):** *K2tog, k8 [9], k2tog tbl; rep from * once—20 [22] sts.

**Next rnd:** K to end.

**Next rnd (dec):** *K2tog, k6 [7], k2tog tbl; rep from * once—16 [18] sts.

**Next rnd:** K.

**N**ext rnd (dec): *K2tog, k4 [5], k2tog tbl; rep from * once—12 [14] sts.

**N**ext rnd: K.

**N**ext rnd (dec): *K2tog, k2 [3], k2tog tbl; rep from * once—8 [10] sts.

## Men's Size Only

**N**ext rnd: K.

**N**ext rnd (dec): (K2tog, k1, k2tog tbl) twice—6 sts.

## Both Sizes

**C**ut yarn, leaving a 6-in tail, and draw through rem sts to secure.

### Double Mitten

This double mitten will need two cuffs. Depending on which size you are making, make a cuff for each hand as the instructions for the single mitten. Leave the first cuff on a holder while you make the second cuff.

**U**sing yarn B, k across 22 [20, 24] sts from cuff just worked, then across 22 [20, 24] sts from cuff on holder—44 [40, 48] sts.

**J**oin into a rnd, placing marker between first and last st.

**N**ext rnd (inc): K1, m1, k20 [18, 22], m1, k2, m1, k20 [18, 22], m1, k1—48 [44, 52] sts.

**K**nit 20 rnds.

**N**ext rnd (dec): K1, k2tog, k6 [6, 8], k2tog, k2tog tbl, k6 [6, 8], k2tog tbl, k2, k2tog, k8 [6, 8], k2tog, k2tog tbl, k8 [6, 8], k2tog tbl, k1—40 [36, 44] sts.

**N**ext rnd: K.

**N**ext rnd (dec): K1, k2tog, k4 [4, 6], k2tog, k2tog tbl, k4 [4, 6], k2tog tbl, k2, k2tog, k6 [4, 6], k2tog, k2tog tbl, k6 [4, 6], k2tog tbl, k1—32 [28, 36] sts.

**N**ext rnd: K.

**N**ext rnd (dec): K1, k2tog, k2 [2, 4], k2tog, k2tog tbl, k2 [2, 4], k2tog tbl, k2, k2tog, k4 [2, 4], k2tog, k2tog tbl, k4 [2, 4], k2tog tbl, k1—24 [20, 28] sts.

**N**ext rnd: K.

**N**ext rnd (dec): K1, k2tog, k0 [0, 2], k2tog, k2tog tbl, k0 [0, 2], k2tog tbl, k2, k2tog, k2 [0, 2], k2tog, k2tog tbl, k2 [0, 2], k2tog tbl, k1—16 [12, 20] sts.

**N**ext rnd: K.

**C**ut yarn, leaving a 6-in-long tail, and draw through rem sts to secure.

### Finishing Instructions

**S**ew in all loose ends. Follow chart for duplicate stitch pattern.

Left: Bean Beanie (see page 102);
Right: Cabled Earflap Hat (variation
of Bean Beanie; see page 103)

Put-Your-Hair-Up Hats (see page 106)

From left to right: variation of Bar Code scarf (see page 113); variation of Cable Access (see page 111); Bar Code (see page 112); variation of Cable Access (see page 111)

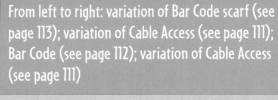

Cable Access (see page 109)

It's a Cinch (see page 114)

Neck Warmer (variation of It's a Cinch; see page 116)

Waist Clincher (variation of It's a Cinch; see page 115)

Bobbles and Balls
(see page 117)

Night Falls Scarf (to access this bonus pattern, go to www.wiley.com/go/NYMknitting)

From left to right: variation of Pirate Socks (see page 123); orange pair and cream pair of Toasty Tootsies (see page 124); Pirate Socks (see page 120); variation of Toasty Tootsies (see page 128)

Not-Quite-'70s Legwarmers (see page 129) and Boot-i-licious (see page 132)

O'Gloves (see page 138)

PDA Mittens
(see page 134)

Fingerless Mittens (variation of
PDA Mittens; see page 137)

Sweet and Seamless (see page 144)

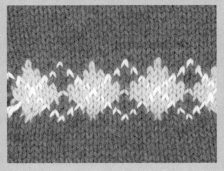

Motif variations for Sweet and Seamless (see page 147)

Fifi: Split Personality (see page 149)

Roxi: Split Personality (see page 149)

Barbi: Split Personality (see page 155)

Boudoir (see page 156)

Girly (see page 163)
Variation: dress (see page 167)

Frosty (see page 170)

V-neck sweater (variation
of Frosty; see page 174)

Wildflowers (see page 175)

Macho Picchu (see page 182)
Variation: pullover (see page 185)

Techno Bag (see page 188)

Shoulder Bag (variation of Techno Bag; see page 191)

Techno Junior with Front Flap
(variation of Techno Junior; see page 196)

Techno Junior (see page 194)

Left: Button Handbag (variation of Bandolero;
see page 201); Right: Bandolero (see page 197)

Little Boy Blue and Alpha Female
(see page 204)

Pampered Pooch Pullover
(see page 209)

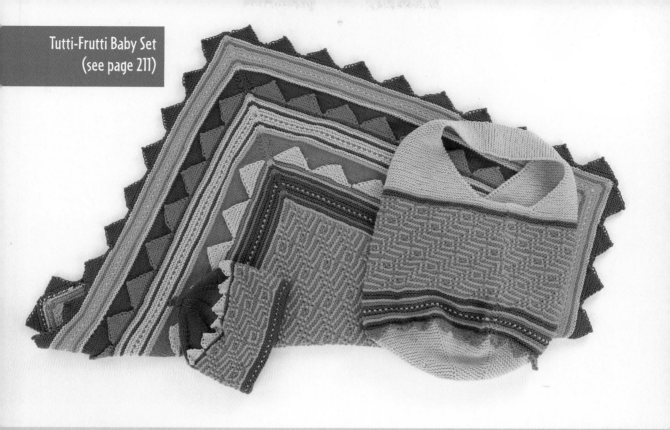

Tutti-Frutti Baby Set
(see page 211)

Hearts & Stars (see page 218)

Indulge (see page 225)

Loopy Landing (see page 223)

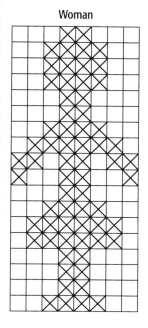

**Woman**            **Man**

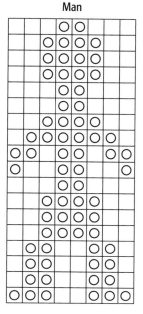

**Man**            **Woman**

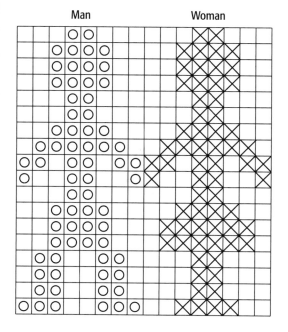

# Variation

Work out your own motifs for duplicate stitch or use stripes to add more color. Try using different yarns held together to create your own mélange of colors, making sure that your gauge is correct.

To create spaced-dyed fingerless mitts, I used four strands of sock yarn held together. The striped cuffs used one strand of bulky. Here's the recipe:

Brown Sheep, Lamb's Pride Bulky (85% Wool/15% Mohair), 4 oz/113g, 125 yd/114m
Small amounts of A = #22 Autumn Harvest
B = #155 Lemon Drop; Knit Picks Sock Garden (100% Merino Wool), 1.75 oz/50g, 220 yd
C = 2 balls of #23469 Zinnia–four strands held together!
*Starting with the cuff,* using color A, and US 10½ (6.5mm) needles, CO 20 [24] sts.
Join into a rnd, placing marker between first and last st.
**Rnd 1:** *K1, p1; rep from * to end.
Rep last rnd once more.
**Rnds 3–4:** Using color B, work in rib patt as set.
**Rnds 5–6:** Using color A, work in rib patt as set.
Rep rnds 3–6 once more.
Cut yarns A and B.
**Next rnd:** Using yarn C (remember–four strands held together!), k.
Work as single mitten from ** to ***.
**Next 7 rnds:** K.
BO.
Work as for single mitten from **** to *****.
**Next 8 rnds:** K.
BO and rep for second mitten.
Sew in all loose ends.

# O Gloves

### by Jennifer Wendell

I needed something to wear with that tiny black dress in the winter so I wouldn't freeze to death. Since the back of the dress is somewhat fancy, a shrug wasn't going to do it, so I settled on a pair of over-the-elbow gloves.

**Project Rating:** Love o' Your Life

**Cost:** $30

**Necessary Skills:** knitting in the round (page 55); yo (page 39); cables (page 46); intarsia (page 56); decrease (page 40); pick up stitches (page 67); sc (page 87); optional: Magic Loop method (page 33)

**Abbreviation: k3tog:** knit 3 stitches together, 2 stitches decreased; **sssk:** slip 3 stitches knitwise, one at a time to the right needle, then knit them through the back loops, 2 stitches decreased.

## Finished Size

Length: 18¾ inches; circumference at top: 8½ inches; circumference at wrist: 6 inches; fits most women

## Materials

- [MC] 3 balls of Jaeger Siena (100% Mercerized Cotton); 50 grams per 153 yd/140m; color: black
- [CC] 1 ball of Knit One Crochet Too 18 Karat (65% Viscose, 35% Metallized Polyester); 25g, 224 yd/205m; color: silver
- 1 set of US 2 (2.75mm) double-pointed needles, or 1 long (over 24 in) US 2 (2.75mm) circular needle if using the Magic Loop method
- 6 ¼-inch shank buttons
- Cable needle
- Stitch markers
- Row counters (2)
- D-3 (3.25mm) crochet hook
- Tapestry needle
- Sewing needle and thread in color to match yarn

## Gauge

28 stitches and 38 rows = 4 in/10cm worked in stockinette stitch in the round, using US 2 (2.75mm) needles, or size needed to obtain gauge

## Instructions

### Glove

You will begin at the upper arm, with a rolled and ribbed cuff, and work down toward the hand.

### Cuff

With MC, CO 64 sts, join in the rnd and place marker between first and last st.

Rnds 1–3: K.

Rnds 4–10: * K3, p1; rep from * to end.

Key:
- □ k on right side, p on wrong side
- > k2tog
- < ssk
- O yarn over
- ● p on right side, k on wrong side
- S k holding silver and black together
- c6b: knit the first stitch with silver and black, next two with just black, next three with silver and black
- c6f: knit the first three stitches with silver and black, next two with just black, next one with silver and black

## Begin Cable

You will need 2 lengths of CC, each approx 20 yd long; place each on a sep bobbin. Looking at the chart, you will see that the silver sts run in single st columns. Use one strand of CC for each of these and simply bring the yarn back behind the st to work the next rnd, being sure to twist MC and CC tog before and after working the CC st. When the cables are made, the left and right strands of CC will trade places.

**Note:** Over the following rnds, always work the cable eyelet pattern from the chart over the first 12 sts, and k the rest of the rnd in St st.

**Rnd 11:** Work row 1 of cable eyelet chart over first 12 sts of rnd, joining CC strands as specified, k to end.

Work the 16 rnds of the cable eyelet chart 4 times, then rnds 1–8 once more to rnd 82 (10 rnds for rolled and ribbed cuff; 72 rnds of cable pattern). On the last rnd, do not work the last st.

## Decreases

On dec rnds, you will be moving the rnd marker back one st and using the last st of the previous rnd to work the first dec. Dec on next and every fifth rnd 10 times as folls:

**Next rnd (rnd 9 of chart):** K3tog, using the last st of rnd 8 and first 2 sts of rnd 9, yo, k1 MC, c6f, k1 MC, yo, sssk, k to end of rnd—62 sts.

**Work rnds 10–13 from chart,** k to end of rnd, but do not work last st of rnd 13.

**Rnd 14:** K2tog, using last st previous rnd and first st of this rnd, p1, k1 MC, k1 CC, k4 MC, k1 CC, k1 MC, p1, ssk, k to end of rnd—60 sts.

Work rnds 15, 16, 1, and 2 from chart, k to end of rnd, but do not work the last st of rnd 2.

**Rnd 3:** K2tog using last st of previous rnd and first st of this rnd, k2 MC, k1 CC, k4 MC, k1 CC, k2 MC, ssk, k to end of rnd—58 sts.

**Rnds 4–7:** Work patt from chart, k to end of rnd, but do not work the last st of rnd 7.

**Rnd 8:** Work as for rnd 3 above—56 sts.

**Rnds 9–12:** Work patt from chart, k to end of rnd, but do not work the last stitch of rnd 12.

**Rnd 13:** K3tog using last st of previous rnd and first 2 sts of this rnd, yo, k1 MC, k1 CC, k4 MC, k1 CC, k1 MC, yo, sssk, k to end of rnd—54 sts.

**Rnds 14, 15, 16, and 1:** Work patt from chart, k to end of rnd, but do not work the last st of rnd 1.

**Rnd 2:** K2tog using last st of previous rnd and first st of this rnd, yo, k1 MC, k1 CC, k4 MC, k1 CC, yo, ssk, k to end of rnd—52 sts.

**Rnds 3–6:** Work patt from chart, k to end of rnd, but do not work the last st of rnd 6.

**Rnd 7:** Work as rnd 3 above—50 sts.

**Rnds 8–11:** Work patt from chart, k to end of rnd, but do not work the last st of rnd 11.

**Rnd 12:** Work as rnd 3 above—48 sts.

**Rnds 13–16:** Work patt as from chart, k to end of rnd, but do not work the last st of rnd 16.

**Rnd 1:** K3tog using last st of previous rnd and first 2 sts of this rnd, yo, k1 MC, c6b, k1 MC, yo, sssk, k to end of rnd—46 sts.

**Rnds 2–5:** Work patt from chart, k to end of rnd, but do not work the last st of rnd 5.

**Rnd 6:** Work as rnd 2 above—44 sts.

**Rnds 7–10:** Work patt from chart, k to end of rnd.

## Wrist

The wrist is worked back and forth, making a slit at the wrist where buttons will later be attached.

**Row 1:** Work row 11 of chart for first 12 sts, k16, pm. New marker is the new beg of row. Turn and begin working back and forth.

**Row 2:** P16, work row 12 of chart over next 12 sts, being sure to work it from the p side, p16. Turn.

Cont working back and forth, maintaining cable eyelet patt over center 12 sts for 14 more rows.

Row 17 (RS): Loosely BO first 10 sts. K6, work row 1 of chart over 12 sts and k 16 sts to end.

Row 18 (WS): Loosely BO first 10 sts. P6, work row 2 of chart for 12 sts, p6.

## Back of Hand

Row 19: K6, work chart over next 12 sts, k6.

Row 20: P6, work chart over next 12 sts, p6.

Rep rows 19–20 3 more times, ending with row 10 of chart.

Row 27: K1, k2tog, k3, work row 11 of chart over next 12 sts, k3, ssk, k1.

Row 28: P5, work row 12 of chart, p5.

Row 29: K5, work row 13 of chart, k5.

Row 30: P1, p2tog, p2, work row 14 of chart, p2, p2tog, p1.

Row 31: K4, work row 15 of chart, k4.

Row 32: P4, work row 16 of chart, p4.

Row 33: K1, k2tog, k1, work row 1 of chart, k1, ssk, k1.

Row 34: P3, work row 2 of chart, p3.

Row 35: K1, k2tog, work row 3 of chart, ssk, k1.

Row 36: P2, work row 4 of chart, p2.

You will now beg dec into the chart, but maintaining the cable as set.

Row 37: K1, k3tog, yo, k1 MC, k1 CC, k4 MC, k1 CC, k1 MC, yo, sssk, k1—14 sts.

Row 38: P2, k1, p1 MC, p1 CC, p4 MC, p1 CC, p1 MC, k1, p2.

Row 39: K1, k2tog, k1 MC, k1 CC, k4 MC, k1 CC, k1 MC, ssk, k1—12 sts.

Row 40: P3 MC, p1 CC, p4 MC, p1 CC, p3 MC.

Row 41: K1, k2tog, c6f, ssk, k1—10 sts.

Row 42: P2 MC, p1 CC, p4 MC, p1 CC, p2 MC.

Row 43: K1, k2tog with CC, k4 MC, ssk with CC, k1—8 sts.

Row 44: P1 MC, p1 CC, p4 MC, p1 CC, p1 MC.

Row 45: K2tog with CC, k4 MC, ssk with CC—6 sts.

Row 46: P1 CC, p4 MC, p1 CC.

## Ring

Holding both strands of silver together, k across the last 6 sts, and CO an additional 10 sts, join for working in the rnd, placing marker between the first and last st.

Knit 4 rnds.

Bind off loosely.

## Finishing Instructions

Single crochet three loops for buttons. Working from the right (public) side of the glove, attach CC to button slit near bound off edge and work 1 slip stitch. Ch 5, slip stitch to glove approx one-third of the way down the slit to create the first button loop. Ch 5 and slip stitch another third down glove slit to create second button loop. Ch 5 and slip stitch and secure end at bottom of button slit.

Sew buttons opposite the button loops with sewing needle and thread. Block and weave in ends.

You might want to use some clear nail polish or no-fray to make sure that the silver ends stay put.

## Variation

To make these gloves a bit funkier, try using a bulky yarn. CO 28 sts (with a gauge of about three sts per in). So the cable doesn't look ridiculously wide over your arm, you might want to work 4-stitch cable instead of the charted 6-stitch one in the pattern. Keep the funky vibe going with one large plastic button at the wrist opening and you'll be ready to strut the bohemian streets of Williamsburg!

Create a more casual style by using a brightly colored soft sock yarn (most sock yarns would probably get about the same gauge). Omit the silver traveling line and you'll be all set for a fun get-together!

If you have any scraps of eyelash or fluffy mohair yarn in your stash, you could glam it up by picking up stitches around the top of the gloves and knitting a couple of rows with it, giving the gloves a faux-fur trim to wear for a night on the town!

# Chapter **Thirteen**

◆◆◆

# Full Fluffy Jacket

**Sweet and Seamless**

A simple sweater for you to adapt. Try your hand at Fair Isle or work it in a solid color to make it individually yours.

**Split Personality**

The adaptation continues with this top-down pattern for three different cardis: Fifi, Roxi, and Barbi.

**Boudoir**

Dress up in lace and ruffles. Knit a sweet jacket that's too good for just bedtime!

**Girly**

Red hot lace says "va-va-voom" in this sexy cardi and dress.

**Frosty**

Subtle sparkles in simple stripes make a statement with a large cowl or plunging V-neck.

**Wildflowers**

A magic mixture of yarn, color, and texture in a gorgeous wrap cardi. Add buttons and embroidery to embellish as you please.

**Macho Picchu**

Is your man macho enough to wear this cozy zip-front cardi? If not, make one for yourself!

# Sweet and Seamless

## by Ruthie Nussbaum

Short-sleeve sweaters used to puzzle me. If it's cold enough to wear a wool sweater, why would you wear a short-sleeved one? This little beauty is form-fitting over tight long-sleeved t-shirts: a way to keep warm without sacrificing your style. Even better, it's quick to knit because the sleeves are virtually eliminated. This pattern presents a basic seamless crewneck sweater that requires minimal finishing. If you are ready for a bit more of a challenge, try knitting your own Fair Isle version, an homage to the sweater that first inspired me to write this pattern.

**Project Rating:** Summer Fling

**Cost:** Fair Isle sweater: $58; solid sweater: $21–$35

**Necessary Skills:** purl (page 30); increase (kfb) (page 38); decrease (k2tog and ssk; page 40); knitting in the round (page 55); Fair Isle (page 56); pick up stitches (page 67); Kitchener stitch (page 65)

## Finished Size

XS [S, M, L, XL]
To fit bust: 31 [33, 35, 37, 39] inches

## Materials

- (MC) 2 [2, 2, 2, 2] skeins Lion Brand Fishermen's Wool (100% Wool); 465 yd/425m per 8 oz/117g skein
- 1 skein each of the following colors for the Fair Isle section:

  Cascade 220 (100% wool; 220 yd/200m per 3.5 oz/100g skein)
  Green #620-175
  Colonial Blue #620-117
  Ranch Red #620-102
  Fuchsia #620-137
  Purple #620-147

### Solid Sweater Only

- (MC) 3 [4, 4, 4, 5] skeins Cascade 220 (100% wool); 220 yd/200m per 3.5 oz/100g skein
- 1 32-in US 7 (4.5mm) circular needle (use a 24-in circular needle if making size XS)
- 1 16-in US 7 (4.5mm) circular needle
- 1 set US 7 (4.5mm) double-pointed needles
- Stitch markers (4)
- Stitch holders (5)–in place of stitch holders you can use a tapestry needle to thread scrap yarn through stitches to keep them "live," or, for a larger number of stitches, a spare circular needle
- Tapestry needle

## Gauge

20 stitches and 28 rows = 4 inches in stockinette stitch, using US 7 (4.5mm) knitting needles, or size needed to obtain gauge

## Instructions

### Ribbing

Using longer circular needle, CO 156 [164, 176, 184, 196] sts. Join in the rnd, being careful not to twist. Place marker at beg of rnd and work in k2, p2 rib for 1½ in.

## Body Shaping

Switch to St st and place second marker 78 [82, 88, 92, 98] sts from beg of rnd. Work without shaping for 1 in.

**Note:** Check out the Fair Isle options in the Variation section if you want to work them into your sweater at this point.

**Next rnd:** K2tog, k to within 2 sts of marker, ssk, sl marker, k2tog, k to within 2 sts of next marker, ssk—152 [160, 172, 180, 192] sts.

Work 7 rnds without shaping.

Rep last 8 rnds 2 more times—144 [152, 164, 172, 184] sts.

Work 17 [17, 18, 18, 18] rnds without shaping.

**Next rnd:** Kfb, k to 1 st before marker, kfb, sl marker, kfb, k until 1 st rem, kfb.

Work 7 rnds without shaping.

Rep last 8 rnds 2 more times—156 [164, 176, 184, 196] sts.

Work without shaping until sweater meas 13½ [14, 14, 14½, 15] in from cast-on edge, stopping 6 [7, 7, 8, 8] sts before end of last rnd.

## Sleeves

Using double-pointed needles, CO 56 [60, 60, 64, 68] sts. Join in the rnd, being careful not to twist the sts, and place marker.

Work in k2, p2 rib for 1 in.

Switch to St st and k every rnd until sleeve meas 3 [3, 3½, 3½, 4] in from cast-on edge.

Place first 12 [13, 13, 15, 15] sts on a stitch holder. Leave the rest of the sleeve sts on the needles or on another stitch holder. Cut yarn.

Make second sleeve the same as the first.

## Attaching the Sleeves to the Sweater Body

You will now join the sleeves and body and begin working the yoke in the rnd, placing markers at four points where the sleeves and body meet for raglan shaping.

Place the next 12 [13, 13, 15, 15] sts of the body—the 6 [7, 7, 8, 8] from before the marker, and 6 [6, 6, 7, 7] after the marker—on a stitch holder for the underarm. Place marker.

Using the yarn attached to the sweater body, k the 44 [47, 47, 49, 53] sts from the first sleeve, making sure that sleeve is RS out. Place marker. This marks the left front raglan dec line and also indicates the beg of the rnd.

Knit across the front of the sweater body to 6 [7, 7, 8, 8] sts before the next marker. Place the next 12 [13, 13, 15, 15] body sts on a stitch holder for the second underarm.

Place marker and k the 44 [47, 47, 49, 53] sleeve sts from the second sleeve. Place marker and complete rnd. There are 44 [47, 47, 49, 53] sts on each sleeve, and 66 [69, 75, 77, 83] sts on the front and on the back, for a total of 220 [232, 244, 252, 272] sts. Work in St st without shaping for 1½ in.

## Raglan Shaping

Rnd 1 (dec rnd): Sl the left front (beg of rnd) marker, ssk, *k to within 2 sts of marker, k2tog, sl marker, ssk; rep from * 2 more times, k to last 2 sts of rnd, k2tog. (8 sts dec)

Rnd 2: K.

Rep rnds 1–2 7 [8, 8, 9, 11] times. There are 30 [31, 31, 31, 31] sts rem between each set of sleeve markers, and 52 [53, 59, 59, 61] sts on the front and the back—164 [168, 180, 180, 184] sts.

## Neck Shaping

As you shape the neck, you will be working back and forth rather than in the rnd. You will cont your raglan dec on the RS rows. There are no dec on the p rows.

Next row: Sl the first marker, k19, and place the next 14 [15, 21, 21, 23] sts on a stitch holder. Turn the work and beg working back and forth.

Row 2 (WS): Sl first st and p back across all sts.

Row 3 (RS): Sl first st, k2tog, work raglan dec as above, work to last 3 sts, ssk, k1.

Row 4 (WS): Sl first st, p across.

Rep rows 3–4 3 more times—110 [113, 119, 119, 121] sts.

Row 11: Sl first st, work raglan dec as established.

Row 12: Sl first st, p across.

Rep rows 11–12 9 times until only 2 [3, 3, 3, 3] sts rem bet the sleeve markers.

## Crewneck Ribbing

Transfer the rem 30 [33, 39, 39, 41] sts to the 16-in circular needle. With RS facing, pick up and k the 14 slipped sts along the neck edge, k across the 14 [15, 21, 21, 23] center front sts from holder, pick up and k the 14 slipped sts along the other side of the neck, place marker—72 [76, 88, 88, 92] sts.

Join rnd and work in k2, p2 rib for 1 in.

Bind off loosely in rib.

## Finishing Instructions

Graft underarm seams using Kitchener stitch.

Weave in ends.

Block.

# Variation

## Fair Isle

Choose some of the charted motifs or make up your own and to knit a super cute Fair Isle sweater. You could even use the alphabet chart from the Indulge pattern in Chapter 16, "Home Buddies," to "write" a message across your sweater!

Included here are the charts for some whimsical motifs that you can combine to create your own Fair Isle pattern (see next page). In the sweater pictured, the pattern begins 6½ inches from the cast-on edge.

Choose which motifs you want to include, or make up your own and draw them out onto graph paper. Use colored pencils to help keep track of which colors you will be knitting.

Note that because the number of stitches changes as the sweater is shaped, not all the motifs will always fit evenly into your sweater. All of the small filler patterns are multiples of 4 and can be used as is on any row of the sweater in any size. However, before knitting any of the larger motifs, you must divide the number of stitches of your knitting by the number of stitches in the motif pattern. Additional "plain" stitches can be worked on the sides near the two markers.

For example, to knit the heart on a section of the sweater with 78 sts on the front and 78 sts on the back, divide 78 by 8 (the number of sts in the motif). That's 9, with a remainder of 6. Nine hearts will fit across the front with 6 extra sts. Divide these on either side of the front, so work 3 plain sts before beginning the hearts, and 3 plain sts after the ninth heart. After the marker, do the same thing on the back. There will be 6 plain sts on each side.

## Pocket and Hood

Are you more of a jock and less of a prepster? Add a pocket and a hood to your sweater to give it a sportier vibe by following these directions.

### Front Pocket

Start working the front pocket on the row after the last decrease has been made in the sweater shaping. After this round, count 12 [14, 16, 18, 18] sts past the round marker. Then follow this st down to the first row of St st. Slip a circular needle into half of that st (one side of the "v") and slip the needle under half of the next 47 [47, 49, 49, 55] sts–48 [48, 50, 50, 56] sts on needle. The pocket will be worked back and forth on these sts. Attach yarn and k across on the RS. On the next row, k the first 4 sts, p to the last 4 sts, k the last 4 sts.

Start shaping the pocket as follows:
**Row 1:** K.
**Row 2:** K4, p to last 4 sts, k4.
**Row 3:** K4, k2tog, k to last 6 sts, ssk, k4.
**Row 4:** K4, p to last 4 sts, k4.
Rep rows 1–4 6 more times until pocket is height of sweater body. Now return to knitting the sweater body. K18 [20, 22, 24, 24] sts into rnd. Then hold up pocket sts in front of sweater body sts. On the next st insert the right needle into the first front pocket st *and* the next st on the sweater body and k these two together. Continue in this manner until all front pocket sts are attached to the sweater body. Continue with sweater patt.

*continued*

*continued*

## Hood

Follow patt until it is time to work the crewneck ribbing. Pick up the same number of sts as stated in patt, but start picking up sts from the center of the neck. Slip 7 [7, 10, 10, 11] of the held front neck sts to another holder. K7 [8, 11, 11, 12] from the holder, follow directions within crewneck patt to pick up sts around the sides and back of the neckline; finish with the 7 [7, 10, 10, 11] sts from holder–72 [76, 88, 88, 92] sts. Do not join.

**Next row (WS):** P.

**Next row (RS):** Inc 20 sts evenly across row–92 [96, 108, 108, 112] sts.

Work until hood meas 13 in from neck. Slip half the sts to a second needle and BO using three-needle bind-off.

If desired, pick up and k edge sts on hood and work k2, p2 rib for 1 in. Sew rib tabs down at center front neck.

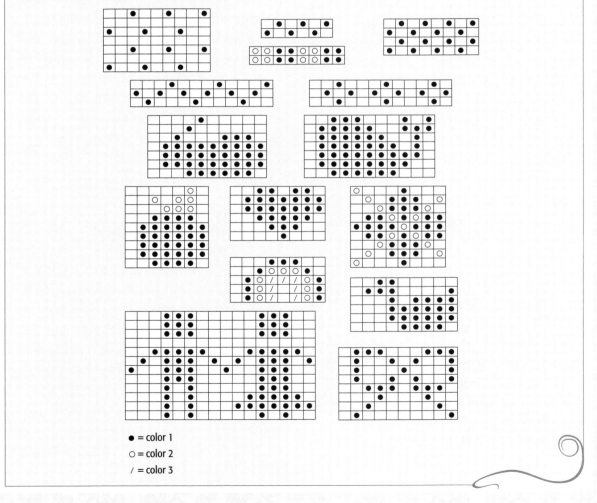

● = color 1
○ = color 2
／ = color 3

# Split Personality

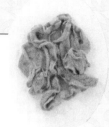

Cardi-tastic! Let your imagination run wild with this top-down raglan pattern. Cast on at the neck, for fronts, back and tops of sleeves all in one piece! The sleeve tops are put onto holders while the body is knitted, then the sleeves are continued one at a time in the round. Work your own cardi any which way you fancy. Here's my take on three different looks from one basic pattern: Fifi, romantic, soft, with lots of ruffles; Roxi, a figure-hugging, sassy blast of color; and the oh-so-simple Barbi variation, pink, sparkly, and hot to trot.

**Pattern Rating:** Summer Fling

**Cost:** Fifi: $96–$160; Roxi: $30–$50; Barbi: $37–$74

**Necessary Skills:** purl (page 30); increase (page 38); decrease (page 40); knitting in the round (page 55); optional: Magic Loop method (page 33); Fifi only: short-row knitting (page 42); I-cord (page 84); Roxi only: pick up stitches (page 67); buttonholes (page 70)

## Finished Size

XS [S, M, L, XL]
To fit bust: 32 [34, 36, 38, 40] inches

## Materials

- For Fifi: Tahki, Jolie (70% French Angora/30% Merino Wool); 0.87 oz/25g, 108 yd/100m; color #5016, Pale Green: 6 [7, 8, 9, 10] balls
- For Roxi: Lion Brand, Landscapes (50% Wool/50% Acrylic); 1.75 oz/50g, 55 yd/50m; color #277, Country Sunset: 6 [7, 8, 9, 10] balls
- 1 set of US 15 (10mm) double-pointed needles, or 1 long (at least 29 in) US 15 (10mm) circular needle, if using the Magic Loop method
- Roxi only: buttons (5)

### Fifi Only

- 1 pair of US 10½ (6.5mm) knitting needles

- Stitch markers
- Stitch holders
- Tapestry needle

## Gauge

**Fifi:** 10 stitches and 12½ rows = 4 in/10cm worked in stockinette stitch using US 15 (10mm) knitting needles, or size needed to obtain gauge

**Roxi:** 10 stitches and 14½ rows = 4 in/10cm worked in stockinette stitch using US 15 (10mm) knitting needles, or size needed to obtain gauge

## Instructions

### All Styles

Starting at neck and using US 15 (10mm) knitting needles, CO 19 [23, 27, 33, 39] sts.

Place stitch markers after st: 1 [1, 2, 2, 3], 6 [7, 8, 10, 12], 13 [16, 19, 23, 27], and 18 [22, 25, 31, 36].

**Row 1 (RS):** K0 [0, 1, 1, 2] *kfb, sl marker, kfb, k to next st before marker; rep from * to st before last marker, kfb, sl marker, kfb, k0 [0, 1, 1, 2]—27 [31, 35, 41, 47] sts.

**Row 2:** P.

**Row 3:** K1 [1, 2, 3, 3] *kfb, sl marker, kfb, k to next st before marker; rep from * to st before last marker, kfb, sl marker, kfb, k1 [1, 2, 2, 3]—35 [39, 43, 49, 55] sts.

**Row 4:** P.

**Row 5:** K1, kfb, k to st before next marker, *kfb, sl marker, kfb, k to st before next marker; rep from * to last 2 sts, kfb, k1—45 [49, 53, 59, 65] sts.

**Row 6:** P.

**Row 7:** K to 1 st before marker, *kfb, sl marker, kfb, k to next st before marker; rep from * to st before last marker, kfb, sl marker, kfb, k to end—53 [57, 61, 67, 73] sts.

**Row 8:** P.

Fifi Only

Rep last 4 rows 3 times—107 [111, 115, 121, 127] sts.

Rep last 2 rows once more—115 [119, 123, 129, 135] sts.

**Row 23:** K to first marker, turn, CO 2 [2, 2, 3, 3] sts, turn, pm, put next 27 [28, 28, 30, 31] sts for first sleeve on a holder, CO 2 [2, 2, 3, 3] sts, k across 29 [31, 33, 35, 37] sts for back, turn, pm, CO 2 [2, 2, 3, 3] sts, turn, put next 27 [28, 28, 30, 31] sts for second sleeve on a holder, CO 2 [2, 2, 3, 3] sts, k to end—69 [71, 75, 81, 85] sts.

**Row 24:** P.

**Row 25:** K.

**Row 26:** P.

**Row 27:** K1, kfb, k to last 2 sts, kfb, k1.

**Row 28:** P.

Rep rows 25–28—71 [73, 77, 83, 87] sts.

**Row 33:** (K to 2 sts before marker, ssk, sl marker, k2tog) twice, k to end.

**Row 34:** P.

Rep rows 33–34 twice more—59 [61, 65, 71, 75] sts.

Starting with a knit row, work 2 [2, 4, 6, 6] rows of St st.

**Next row (RS):** K1, k2tog, (k to 1 st before marker, kfb, sl marker, kfb) twice, k to last 3 sts, ssk, k1.

**Next row:** P.

**Rep** last 2 rows 4 more times—69 [71, 75, 81, 85] sts.

**Next row:** K1, k2tog, k to last 3 sts, ssk, k1—67 [69, 73, 79, 83] sts.

**Next row:** P.

**Next row:** K1, k2tog twice, k to last 5 sts, ssk twice, k1.

**Next row:** P.

**Rep** last 2 rows 4 more times—47 [51, 55, 61, 65] sts.

**Bind** off loosely.

## Roxi Only

**Rep** last 4 rows twice—89 [93, 97, 103, 109] sts.

**Rep** last 2 rows 3 times—113 [117, 121, 127, 133] sts.

**Row 23 (RS):** K to first marker, turn, CO 2 [2, 2, 3, 3] sts, turn, pm, put next 27 [28, 28, 30, 31] sts for first sleeve on a holder, CO 2 [2, 2, 3, 3] sts, k across 29 [31, 33, 35, 37] sts for back, turn, pm, CO 2 [2, 2, 3, 3] sts, turn, put next 27 [28, 28, 30, 31] sts for second sleeve on a holder, CO 2 [2, 2, 3, 3] sts, k to end—67 [69, 73, 79, 83] sts.

**Starting** with a purl row, work 5 rows of St st.

**Row 29 (RS):** (K to 2 sts before marker, ssk, sl marker, k2tog) twice, k to end—63 [65, 69, 75, 79] sts.

**Row 30:** P.

**Row 31:** K.

**Row 32:** P.

**Rep** rows 29–32 twice more—55 [57, 61, 67, 71] sts.

**Row 41 (RS):** *K1, p1; rep from * to last st, k1.

**Row 42:** K2, *p1, k1; rep from * to last st, k1.

**Rep** rows 41–42 10 [11, 12, 13, 14] more times.

**Bind** off loosely in rib.

## Sleeves

**Cast** on 2 sts, then k across 27 [28, 28, 30, 31] sts for sleeve from holder, CO 2 sts—31 [32, 32, 34, 35] sts.

**Rnd 1:** Pm, join rnd, and k to marker.

**Knit** 6 more rnds.

**Rnd 8:** K2tog, k to last 2 sts, ssk—29 [30, 30, 32, 33] sts.

### Fifi Only

Knit 4 [5, 5, 6, 6] rnds.

**Next rnd:** K2tog, k to last 2 sts, ssk—27 [28, 28, 30, 31] sts.

Rep last 5 [6, 6, 7, 7] rnds 4 times—19 [20, 20, 22, 23] sts.

Knit 20 rnds.

Bind off loosely. Rep for second sleeve.

### Roxi Only

#### XS and XL Sizes Only

Rnd 9: * K1, p1; rep from * to last st, k1.

#### S, M, and L Sizes Only

Rnd 9: * K1, p1; rep from * to end.

#### All Sizes

Rep the last rnd 4 [5, 5, 6, 6] times.

#### XS and XL Sizes Only

**Next rnd:** K2tog, *k1, p1; rep from * to last 3 sts, k1, ssk—27 [30, 30, 32, 31] sts.

#### S, M, and L Sizes Only

**Next rnd:** K2tog, *k1, p1; rep from * to last 2 sts, ssk—27 [28, 28, 30, 31] sts.

#### XS and XL Sizes Only

**Next rnd:** P1, *k1, p1; rep from * to end.

#### S, M, and L Sizes Only

**Next rnd:** *K1, p1; rep from * to end.

#### All Sizes

Rep the last rnd 4 [5, 5, 6, 6] times.

#### XS and XL Sizes Only

**Next rnd:** K2tog, *p1, k1; rep from * to last 3 sts, p1, ssk—25 [28, 28, 30, 29] sts.

#### S, M, and L Sizes Only

**Next rnd:** K2tog, *p1, k1; rep from * to last 2 sts, ssk—25 [26, 26, 28, 29] sts.

#### XS and XL Sizes Only

**Next rnd:** *K1, p1; rep from * to last st, k1.

#### S, M, and L Sizes Only

**Next rnd:** *K1, p1; rep from * to last end.

#### All Sizes

Rep the last rnd 4 [5, 5, 6, 6] times.

#### XS and XL Sizes Only

**Next rnd:** K2tog, *k1, p1; rep from * to last 3 sts, k1, ssk—23 [26, 26, 28, 27] sts.

## S, M, and L Sizes Only

**Next rnd:** K2tog, *k1, p1; rep from * to last 2 sts, ssk—23 [24, 24, 26, 27] sts.

## XS and XL Sizes Only

**Next rnd:** P1, *k1, p1; rep from * to end.

## S, M, and L Sizes Only

**Next rnd:** *K1, p1; rep from * to end.

## All Sizes

Rep the last rnd 4 [5, 5, 6, 6] times.

Bind off loosely in rib. Rep for second sleeve.

### Ruffles

### Fifi Only

Make 6 ruffles in total: 2 main ruffles and 4 sleeve ruffles.

### Main Ruffle

Using US 15 (10mm) knitting needles, CO 10 sts.

**Row 1 (RS):** K4, yf, sl 1, turn, leaving rem sts on needle.

**Row 2:** Yf, sl 1 pwise, p4.

**Row 3:** K4, k next st and its wrap tog, k2, yf, sl 1, turn, leaving rem sts on needle.

**Row 4:** Yf, sl 1 pwise, p7.

**Row 5:** K7, k next st and its wrap tog, k2.

**Row 6:** P.

Rep these 6 rows until ruffle's short edge fits (without stretching) all around neck, fronts, and back edges of cardigan.

Using US 10½ (6.5mm) knitting needles, work a second ruffle to match.

### Sleeve Ruffle

Work as for main ruffle until short edge fits (without stretching) all around the cuff edge.

Using US 10½ (6.5mm) knitting needles, work a second ruffle to match.

### Front Ties

### Fifi Only

Work 2 12-in long, 3-st I-cords by using a US 10½ (6.5mm) circular needle or same size dpns.

Sew cords to fronts of cardigan at bottom of neck shaping.

### Neck Band

### Roxi Only

Pick up and k 8 [9, 10, 10, 12] sts from right side of neck slope, 5 [6, 6, 8, 9] sts from top of right sleeve, 7 [9, 11, 13, 15] sts across back neck, 5 [6, 6, 8, 9] sts from top of left sleeve, and 8 [9, 10, 10, 12] sts from left side of neck slope—33 [37, 43, 49, 57] sts.

**Next row (WS):** *K1, p1; rep from * to last st, k1.

Rep last row twice more.

Bind off in rib.

## Button Band

### Roxi Only

Pick up and k 49 [51, 53, 55, 57] sts along left front edge from top of neck band to bottom edge of cardigan.

**Row 1 (WS):** *K1, p1; rep from * to last st, k1. ***

**Row 2:** K1, * k1, p1; rep from * to last st, k1.

**Row 3:** As row 1.

Bind off in rib.

Mark the positions of five buttons along buttonhole band with the first button placed 1 in above bottom edge and the fifth button placed ½ in down from top edge, and the remaining three buttons placed evenly in between.

## Buttonhole Band

### Roxi Only

Work as for button band to ***, picking up sts along right front edge from bottom edge of cardigan to top of neck band.

**Row 2:** K2, * yo, k2tog, p1, work to next buttonhole position, rep from * to last st, k1.

**Row 3:** As row 1.

Bind off in rib.

### Finishing Instructions

**Fifi only:** With the narrower ruffle placed on top of the wider ruffle, neatly sew in place.

**Roxi only:** Sew five buttons onto button band to match buttonholes.

**All styles:** Sew all ends in neatly.

# Variation

## Barbi

Need a little razzle-dazzle to throw on over a strappy dress or brighten up a plain t-shirt-and-jeans combo? Then knit up a carry-along sequined yarn, such as Berrocco Lazer FX, together with a brightly colored worsted weight yarn—I used Cascade 220, which is available in a gazillion colors!

For Barbi, my cap-sleeve shrug:

Cascade 220 (100% Peruvian Highland Wool), 3.5 oz/100g, 220 yd/201m; color #7805, Bright Pink: 1 [1, 1, 2, 2] skeins

Berroco Lazer FX (100% Polyester), 0.35 oz/10g, 70 yd/64m; color #6002, Silver: 2 [2, 3, 4, 4] skeins

**Note:** These two yarns are held together throughout the knitting of this style.

## Gauge

10 stitches and 14½ rows = 4 in/10cm worked in St st using a strand each of Cascade 220 and Lazer FX together and US 15 (10mm) knitting needles, or size needed to obtain gauge

## Starting at Neck

Holding a strand of sequin and worsted weight yarn together, work as for Fifi and Roxi to end of row 4.

**Row 5 (RS):** K1, kfb, k to st before next marker, *kfb, sl marker, kfb, k to st before next marker; rep from * to last 2 sts, kfb, k1–45 [49, 53, 59, 65] sts.

**Row 6:** P.

**Row 7:** K0 [0, 1, 1, 2], *kfb, sl marker, kfb, k to next st before marker; rep from * to st before last marker, kfb, sl marker, kfb, k0 [0, 1, 1, 2]–43 [47, 51, 57, 63] sts.

**Row 8:** P.

Rep rows 5–8 twice–89 [93, 97, 103, 109] sts.

Rep rows 7–8 three times–113 [117, 121, 127, 133] sts.

## Divide for Sleeve Openings

**Next row (RS):** K to first marker, turn, CO 2 [2, 2, 3, 3] sts, turn, pm, BO next 27 [28, 28, 30, 31] sts for first sleeve, CO 2 [2, 2, 3, 3] sts, k across 29 [31, 33, 35, 37] sts for back, turn, pm, CO 2 [2, 2, 3, 3] sts, turn, BO next 27 [28, 28, 30, 31] sts for second sleeve, CO 2 [2, 2, 3, 3] sts, k to end–67 [69, 73, 79, 83] sts.

**Next row:** P.

**Next row:** K1, ssk, k to last 3 sts, k2tog, k1–65 [67, 71, 77, 81] sts.

**Next row:** P.

**Next row:** K1, ssk (k to three sts before marker, k2tog, k1, sl marker, k1, ssk) twice, k to last 3 sts, k2tog, k1–59 [61, 65, 71, 75] sts.

**Next row:** P.

**Next row:** K1, ssk twice (k to three sts before marker, k2tog, k1, sl marker, k1, ssk) twice, k to last 5 sts, k2tog twice, k1–51 [53, 57, 63, 67] sts.

**Next row:** P.

Rep last 2 rows twice more–35 [37, 41, 47, 51] sts.

BO loosely. Sew in all loose ends.

# Boudoir

## by Katy Moore

This boxy lace jacket features ruffles at the sleeves and neck, and is tied with a ribbon or I-cord woven through eyelets at the neck and trimmed with crocheted shell stitches. It is designed to hit somewhere near your natural waist. I wanted a light, soft bed jacket to wear while I read in bed. This is the result.

**Project Rating:** Love o' Your Life

**Cost:** With recommended yarn, $30–$60

**Necessary Skills:** ssk (page 40); k2tog (page 40); p2tog (page 40); yo (page 39); kfb (page 39); sc (page 87)

**Abbreviations: sk2p:** slip 1, knit 2 together; **psso:** pass slip stitch over; **2yo:** double yarn over. **5 dc:** 5 double crochet.

## Finished Size

XS [S, M, L, XL]
To fit bust: 32 [36, 40, 44, 48] inches
(If you are going to increase beyond this, the repeat is based on 12 sts. The ease is approximately 4 inches.)

## Materials

- Knit Picks Shine (60% Pima Cotton/40% Modal); 1.75 oz/50g, 110 yd/100m
- (MC) #23615 Cream 9 [11, 14, 17, 19] skeins
- (CC) #23620 Sand 1 [1, 1, 2, 2] skeins
- 1 pair of US 5 (3.75mm) knitting needles
- E-4 (3.5mm) crochet hook
- Ribbon or I-cord for neck

## Gauge

22 stitches and 32 rows = 4 in/10cm worked in lace check pattern

**Note:** Stay in pattern through shaping when possible, but only if you can complete the entire four-hole lace section, as sewing holes together is difficult!

## Instructions

### Back

With CC, CO 89 [101, 113, 125, 137] sts.

**Foundation row 1:** Switch to MC and p.

**Foundation row 2:** K.

**Foundation row 3:** P.

### Lace Check Pattern

**Row 1 (RS):** K4, * yo, sk2p, yo, k3; rep from * to st, k1.

**Rows 2, 4, 6, 8, and 10:** P.

**Row 3:** Rep row 1.

**Row 5:** K.

**Row 7:** K7, * yo, sk2p, yo, k3; rep from * to last 4 sts, k4.

**Row 9:** Rep row 7.

**Row 11:** K.

**Row 12:** P.

Rep these 12 rows until back meas approx 10 [10½, 11, 11½, 12] in, ending with row 5 or row 11 of lace check pattern.

## Shape Armholes

Maintain the lace check pattern during dec. If there are not 3 or more sts before the first yo, k plain to the next patt rep.

Bind off 5 [5, 6, 6, 6] sts at the beg of the next two rows—79 [91, 101, 113, 125] sts.

Bind off 3 [3, 4, 4, 4] sts at the beg of the next two rows—73 [85, 93, 105, 117] sts.

Knit 1, ssk, cont in patt to last 3 sts, k2tog, k1 every RS row 3 [5, 6, 6, 7] times—67 [75, 81, 93, 103] sts.

Cont in patt until back meas approx 18½ [19, 19½, 19¾, 20] in, ending on row 5 or row 11 of lace check pattern.

## Shape Shoulders

Beg with a WS row and working in St st, BO 6 [7, 8, 9, 10] sts at the beg of the next 6 rows—29 [31, 31, 37, 41] sts.

**Next row (WS):** BO all sts pwise.

## Left Front

With CC, CO 47 [53, 59, 65, 71] sts.

**Foundation row 1:** Switch to MC and p.

**Foundation row 2:** K.

**Foundation row 3:** P.

## Lace Check Pattern for Left Front

**Row 1 (RS):** K4, * yo, sk2p, yo, k3; rep from * to last st, k1.

**Rows 2, 4, 6, 8, and 10:** P.

**Row 3:** Rep row 1.

**Row 5:** K.

**Row 7:** K7, * yo, sk2p, yo, k3; rep from * to last 4 sts, k4.

**Row 9:** Rep row 7.

**Row 11:** K.

**Row 12:** P.

Rep these 12 rows until front meas approx 10 [10½, 11, 11½, 12] in (or same as the back), ending with row 6 or row 12 of lace check pattern.

## Shape Armhole

**N**ext row (RS): BO 5 [5, 6, 6, 6] sts, work in patt to end—44 [50, 55, 61, 67] sts.

**N**ext row (WS): P.

**N**ext row (RS): BO 3 [3, 4, 4, 4] sts, maintain patt to end—41 [47, 51, 57, 63] sts.

**K**nit 1, ssk, at the beg every RS row 3 [5, 6, 6, 7] times—36 [40, 43, 49, 54] sts.

**C**ont in patt until front meas approx 17 [17½, 18, 18¼, 18½] in, ending with row 5 or row 11 of lace check pattern.

## Shape Neck

**B**eg working in St st.

**R**ow 1 (WS): BO 8 [8, 10, 10, 12] sts, p to end—28 [32, 33, 39, 42] sts.

**R**ow 2 (RS): K.

**R**ow 3: BO 3 [3, 3, 3, 3] sts, p to end—25 [29, 30, 36, 39] sts.

**R**ow 4: K.

**R**ow 5: BO 2 [2, 2, 2, 2] sts, p to end—23 [27, 28, 34, 37] sts.

**R**ow 6: K.

**R**ow 7: BO 0 [0, 0, 2, 2] sts, p to end—23 [27, 28, 32, 35] sts.

**R**ow 8: K across to last 3 sts, k2tog, k1—22 [26, 27, 31, 34] sts.

**R**ow 9: P.

**R**ow 10: K across to last 3 sts, k2tog, k1—21 [25, 26, 30, 33] sts.

**R**ow 11: P.

**R**ow 12: K across to last 3 sts, k2tog, k1—20 [24, 25, 29, 32] sts.

**C**ont in St st until left front meas the same as back to outside shoulder, ending with a WS row.

## Shape Shoulder

**R**ow 1 (RS): BO 6 [7, 8, 9, 10] sts.

**R**ow 2: P.

**R**ep rows 1–2 once more—8 [10, 9, 11, 12] sts.

**B**ind off rem sts kwise.

## Right Front

**W**ith CC, CO 47 [53, 59, 65, 71] sts.

**Foundation row 1:** Switch to MC and p.

**Foundation row 2:** K.

**Foundation row 3:** P.

Beg lace check pattern as folls:

### Lace Check Pattern for Right Front

**Row 1 (RS):** K4, * yo, sk2p, yo, k3; rep from * to last st, k1.

**Rows 2, 4, 6, 8, and 10:** P.

**Row 3:** Rep row 1.

**Row 5:** K.

**Row 7:** K7, * yo, sk2p, yo, k3; rep from * to 4 last sts, k4.

**Row 9:** Rep row 7.

**Row 11:** K.

**Row 12:** P.

Rep these 12 rows until right front meas approx 10 [10½, 11, 11½, 12] in (or same as the left front), ending with row 5 or row 11 of lace check pattern.

## Shape Armhole

**Next row (WS):** BO 5 [5, 6, 6, 6] sts, work in patt to end—44 [50, 55, 61, 67] sts.

**Next row (RS):** K.

**Next row (WS):** BO 3 [3, 4, 4, 4] sts, maintain patt to end—41 [47, 51, 57, 63] sts.

Purl 1, p2tog at beg of every WS row 3 [5, 6, 6, 7] times—36 [40, 43, 49, 54] sts.

Cont in patt until front meas approx 17 [17½, 18, 18¼, 18½] in, ending with row 6 or row 12 of lace check pattern.

## Shape Neck

Beg working in St st.

**Row 1 (RS):** BO 8 [8, 10, 10, 12] sts, k to end—28 [32, 33, 39, 42] sts.

**Row 2 (WS):** P.

**Row 3:** BO 3 [3, 3, 3, 3] sts, k to end—25 [29, 30, 36, 39] sts.

**Row 4:** P.

**Row 5:** BO 2 [2, 2, 2, 2] sts, k to end—23 [27, 28, 34, 37] sts.

**Row 6:** K.

**R**ow 7: BO 0 [0, 0, 2, 2] sts, k to end—23 [27, 28, 32, 35] sts.

**R**ow 8: P across to last 3 sts, p2tog, p1.

**R**ow 9: K1, k2tog, k to end.

**R**ow 10: P across to last 3 sts, p2tog, p1—20 [24, 25, 29, 32] sts.

**C**ont in St st until right front meas the same as left front to outside shoulder, ending with a RS row.

## Shape Shoulder

**R**ow 1 (WS): BO 6 [7, 8, 9, 10] sts.

**R**ow 2: K.

**R**ep rows 1–2 once more—8 [10, 9, 11, 12] sts.

**B**ind off rem sts pwise.

## Sleeves

### Cuff

**I**n CC, CO 158 [182, 206, 218, 230] sts.

**C**hange to MC and p 1 row.

Beg ruffle pattern.

### Ruffle Pattern

**Note:** For the 2yo (double yarn over), you will bring yarn to front between stitches, then around right needle once more before working next stitch. The 2yo will look like 2 stitches on the needle, lying diagonally. In this pattern, you will work 2 stitches in the 2yo in the next row, keeping the stitch count constant. (On WS rows, when you come to the stitches made from the previous row's 2yo, purl the first stitch and knit the second.)

**R**ow 1 (RS): K1, *ssk, 2yo, k2tog; rep from *, end k1.

**R**ow 2 (WS): P1 * p1 (p1, k1) in 2yo, p1; rep from *, end p1.

**R**ep rows 1–2 7 more times.

**N**ext row: K2tog across—[91, 103, 109, 115] sts.

**N**ext row: P.

### Lace Check Pattern for Sleeves

**R**ow 1 (RS): K3, *yo, sk2p, yo, k3; rep from * to last 4 sts, k4.

**R**ows 2, 4, 6, 8, and 10: P.

**R**ow 3: Rep row 1.

**R**ow 5: K.

**Row 7:** K6, *yo, sk2p, yo, k3; rep from * to last 1 st, k1.

**Row 9:** Rep row 7.

**Row 11:** K.

**Row 12:** P.

Cont until sleeve meas approx 10 in from CO edge, ending with row 6 or row 12 of lace check pattern.

## Shape Cap

Maintain the lace check pattern during dec. If there are not 3 or more sts before the first yo, k plain to the next patt rep.

**Row 1 (RS):** BO 5 [5, 6, 6, 6] sts, cont across in lace check pattern.

**Row 2 (WS):** BO 5 [5, 6, 6, 6] sts, cont across in lace check pattern—69 [81, 91, 97, 103] sts.

**Row 3:** BO 3 [3, 4, 4, 4] sts, cont across in lace check pattern.

**Row 4:** BO 3 [3, 4, 4, 4] sts, cont across in lace check pattern—63 [75, 83, 89, 95] sts.

Knit 1, ssk, cont across in lace check pattern to last 3 sts, k2tog, k1 every RS row 3 [5, 5, 6, 7] times—57 [65, 73, 77, 84] sts.

**For L and XL only:** K1, ssk, cont across in lace check pattern to last 3 sts, k2tog, k1 every fourth row 1 [4] times—57 [65, 73, 75, 76] sts.

**All sizes:** K1, ssk, cont across in lace check pattern to last 3 sts, k2tog, k1 every RS row 9 [9, 8, 8, 1] times—39 [47, 57, 59, 74] sts.

Switch to St st.

Bind off 2 sts beg next 4 [6, 10, 10, 4] rows—31 [35, 37, 39, 66] sts.

Bind off 3 sts beg next 4 [4, 4, 4, 12] rows—19 [23, 25, 27, 30] sts.

Bind off all sts purlwise.

## Collar

Sew both shoulder seams.

**Note:** The RS of the collar is on the WS of the sweater so that the RS is out when the sweater is worn.

**Row 1 (RS):** With the WS of the body facing you and beg at the left front neck shaping, pick up and k 87 [95, 103, 111, 119] sts evenly around neck.

**Row 2 (WS):** P.

## Eyelets

**Row 3:** K3 sts, *yo, k2tog, k2, rep from * across.

**R**ow 4: P.

**R**ow 5: Kfb into every st—174 [190, 206, 222, 238] sts.

**R**ow 6: P.

Beg ruffle pattern.

## Ruffle Pattern

**R**ow 1 (RS): K1, *ssk, 2yo twice, k2tog; rep from *, end k1.

**R**ow 2 (WS): P1 * p1 (p1, k1) in 2yo, p1; rep from *, end p1.

**R**ep rows 1–2 7 times more.

**S**witch to CC and BO all sts kwise.

## Finishing Instructions

**S**ew sleeve to body.

**S**ew sleeve and side seams in a continuous line.

## Edging

**F**or the 5 dc shell: *5 double crochet in the same stitch skip 2 sts, sc, skip 2 sts, repeat from *.

**W**ith CC and WS facing you, beg at left front where body and collar meet, and sc down left front, skipping every fourth row, around the bottom of the left front, the back and the right front working in each st, and up the right front, skipping every fourth row, ending at neck edge where the body and collar meet. Turn.

**W**ork 5 dc shell pattern down front as follows: *Work 5 dcs in the same stitch, skip 2 sts, sc in next st, skip 2 sts, rep from *. At bottom edge of right front, work 7 dcs in stitch rather than 5 to turn the corner. Cont with 5 dc shell pattern along bottom hem. Work 7 dcs at corner of left front and cont with 5 dc shell pattern up left front to collar.

**W**eave in loose ends.

**W**eave ribbon or I-cord through eyelets in neck.

**B**lock if desired.

## Variation

If you don't enjoy picking up stitches, you could work the collar separately and then sew it on afterward. For a different look, you could skip the collar completely and work the crochet shell around the neck instead. Try out different lace patterns or work in stockinette stitch if lace just isn't your thing. For a completely over-the-top boudoir look, use bright pink or hot red fluffy yarn for the trim!

# Girly

## by Jessamyn Lee

I'm a proud girly-girl, and I wanted to design a garment that would enhance the female form. By changing needle sizes instead of stitch count, this pattern makes lace knitting a more accessible challenge.

**Project Rating:** Love o' Your Life
**Cost:** $70–$100
**Necessary Skills:** purl (page 30); ssk (page 40); k2tog (page 40); yo (page 39)

## Finished Size

XS [S, M, L, XL]
To fit bust: 34 [36, 38, 40, 42] inches

## Materials

- Blue Sky Alpacas Alpaca & Silk (50% Alpaca, 50% Silk); 1.75 oz/50g, 146 yd/133.5m: 7 [8, 8, 9,10] skeins of #123 Ruby
- 15–20 yards of scrap yarn for provisional cast-on
- 1 pair US 7 (4.5mm), US 8 (5mm), and US 9 (5.5mm) circular or straight knitting needles (while this project may be worked on straight needles, circulars are recommended because of the size and weight of the garment)
- 1 US 9 (5.5mm) double-pointed needle
- J-9 (5.5mm) crochet hook
- Tapestry needle
- Stitch holders (2)
- Stitch markers
- 4–5 yards contrast color ribbon
- Optional: hooks and eyes

## Gauge

20 stitches and 24 rows = 4 in/10cm worked in blocked diamond eyelet lace pattern, using US 7 (4.5mm) knitting needles, or size needed to obtain gauge

**Note:** This cardigan is constructed in one piece from the provisional cast-on up until the armholes. The fronts and back are then worked separately. Once the body and sleeves are complete, the provisional cast-on is picked up and the edging is knitted on side to side.

## Stitch Patterns

### Vertical Eyelet Lace (5 st rep + 1):

**Row 1 and all RS rows:** K1, *yo, k2tog, ssk, yo, k1; rep from* to end.
**Row 2 and all WS rows:** P.

### Diamond Eyelet Lace (10 st rep + 1):

**Row 1 (RS):** *K1, yo, ssk, k2, yo, k2tog, k1, k2tog, yo; rep from * to last st, k1.
**Row 2 and all WS rows:** P.
**Row 3:** K2, *yo, ssk, k3, k2tog, yo, k3; rep from * to last 9 sts, yo, ssk, k3, k2tog, yo, k2.
**Row 5:** K3, *yo, ssk, k1, k2tog, yo, k1, ssk, yo, k2; rep from * to last 8 sts, yo, ssk, k1, k2tog, yo, k3.

**Row 7:** K4, *yo, sl1, k2tog, psso, yo, k2, yo, sl1, k2tog, psso, yo, k2; rep from * to last 7 sts, yo, sl1, k2tog, psso, yo, k4.

**Row 9:** K3, *k2tog, yo, k1, yo, ssk, k2, yo, k2tog, k1; rep from * to last 8 sts, k2tog, yo, k1, ssk, k3.

**Row 11:** K2, *k2tog, yo, k3, yo, ssk, k3; rep from * to last 9 sts, k2tog, yo, k3, yo, ssk, k2.

**Row 13:** *K1, k2tog, yo, k1, ssk, yo, k2, yo, ssk; rep from * to last st, k1.

**Row 15:** K4, *yo, sl1, k2tog, psso, yo, k2, yo, sl1, k2tog, psso, yo, k2; rep from * to last 7 sts, yo, sl1, k2tog, psso, yo, k4.

## Scalloped Diamond Trellis Edging

**Note:** This is worked side to side along bottom edge of body and sleeves.

CO 13 sts.

**Row 1 and all WS rows:** K2, p to last 2 sts, k1, k2tog.

Note: One of the two sts used in the k2tog is an edging st, the other is one of the body/sleeve sts.

**Row 2:** Sl1, k6, yo, ssk, yo, k4.
**Row 4:** Sl1, k5, (yo, ssk) twice, yo, k4.
**Row 6:** Sl1, k4, (yo, ssk) 3 times, yo, k4.
**Row 8:** Sl1, k3, (yo, ssk) 4 times, yo, k4.
**Row 10:** Sl1, k2, (yo, ssk) 5 times, yo, k4.
**Row 12:** Sl 1, k3, (yo, ssk) 5 times, k2tog, k2.
**Row 14:** Sl1, k4, (yo, ssk) 4 times, k2tog, k2.
**Row 16:** Sl1, k5, (yo, ssk) 3 times, k2tog, k2.
**Row 18:** Sl1, k6, (yo, ssk) twice, k2tog, k2.
**Row 20:** Sl1, k7, yo, ssk, k2tog, k2.
Rep rows 1–20 until desired length.

## Instructions

### Body

Using US size 9 needles and scrap yarn, CO 181 [191, 201, 211, 221] sts.

Cont with size 9 needles, switch to main yarn and p one row. With RS facing, beg vertical eyelet lace. K as directed until piece meas 4 in.

Switch to US size 8 needles. Cont with vertical eyelet lace until piece meas 8 in.

Switch to US size 7 needles. Cont with vertical eyelet lace until piece meas 11½ [12, 12, 12½, 13] in, ending with a WS row.

### Garter Stitch/Eyelet Empire Waist

Row 1 (RS): K.

Row 2 (WS): K.

Rows 3–4: P.

Row 5 (eyelet row): K1, *yo, k2tog; rep from * to end of row.

Rows 6–7: P.

Row 8: K45 [48, 50, 53, 55], place marker, k91 [95, 101, 105, 111], place marker, k45 [48, 50, 53, 55].

Note: The stitch markers are used to mark armhole placement, and will be referred to in the next section of the pattern.

## Bodice

Beg with row 1, work diamond eyelet lace pattern until piece meas 13 [13½, 14, 14½, 15] in from beg. Shape neck (RS): Maintaining lace pattern, dec 1 st at beg and end of every RS row 15 [15, 15, 17, 17] times. If maintaining the diamond eyelet lace pattern interferes with neck shaping, k those 2 or 3 sts in St st.

At the same time, when work meas 14 [14½, 15, 15½, 16] in, place the first and last 45 [48, 50, 53, 55] sts—these are the right and left fronts—each on stitch holders, and work the back as folls.

## Back

Shape armholes: Cont in diamond eyelet lace pattern, BO 3 [4, 5, 4, 5] sts at the beg of the next two rows—85 [87, 91, 97, 101] sts.

Dec 1 st at each end of every RS row 9 [10, 11, 13, 13] times—67 [67, 69, 71, 75] sts.

Cont working diamond eyelet lace pattern as established.

When armhole meas 7½ [7½, 7¾, 7¾, 8] in, dec for back neckline as folls.

## Shape Neck

Maintaining diamond eyelet lace pattern and RS facing, work across first 21 [21, 21, 22, 22] sts, BO 25 [25, 27, 27, 29] sts as you would in St st, work across rem 21 [21, 21, 22, 22] sts.

Attach a new ball of yarn and, working each side separately, dec 1 st at each neck edge on the next two rows until 19 [19, 19, 20, 20] sts remain on each side.

## Shape Shoulder

Bind off 10 [10, 10, 10, 10] sts at shoulder edge, work rem 9 [9, 9, 10, 10] sts.

Bind off all rem sts as you would in St st.

## Fronts

Work each front separately. Slip the 45 [48, 50, 53, 55] sts from first holder onto needle. Working in diamond eyelet lace, cont neckline shaping as established.

At the same time, shape armhole as directed for back. Shape shoulder and BO as directed for back when the piece meas same as back.

## Sleeves (Make Two)

Using scrap yarn and US size 9 needles, CO 51 [56, 61, 66, 71] sts. Cont with size 9 needles, switch to main yarn and p one row.

With RS facing, beg vertical eyelet lace. K as directed until piece meas 3 in.

Switch to US size 8 needles. Cont with vertical eyelet lace until piece meas 6 in.

Switch to US size 7 needles. Cont with vertical eyelet lace until piece meas 8½ [9, 9, 9½, 9½] in.

## Garter/Eyelet Arm Band

**Row 1 (RS):** K.

**Row 2 (WS):** K.

**Row 3:** P.

**Row 4:** P.

**Row 5 (eyelet row):** K1, *yo, k2tog; rep from * to end of row.

**Row 6:** P.

**Row 7:** P.

**Row 8:** K.

**Note:** For sizes S and L, inc 1 st in this row.

Beg diamond eyelet lace. You should have 52 [56, 61, 67, 71] sts.

**Note:** For sizes S and L, k 3 sts in St st at the beg and end of each row. This accounts for the 6 extra sts in these rows.

When work meas 13½ [13¾, 14, 14, 14] in from CO edge, shape sleeve cap as folls.

## Sleeve Cap Shaping

Cont in diamond eyelet lace, CO 3 [4, 5, 4, 5] sts at the beg of the next two rows—46 [48, 51, 59, 61] sts.

Dec 1 st at each end of every RS row 13 [15, 16, 20, 20] times—20 [18, 25, 19, 21] sts.

Cont working in diamond eyelet lace pattern until sleeve cap meas 7½, [7½, 7¾, 7¾, 8] in.

Bind off rem sts as you would in St st.

## Edging

Using US size 9 needle, pick up 181 [191, 201, 211, 221] sts. To pick up sts, insert your needle into each main yarn st.

**Note:** The picked-up sts are actually your first row of knitting. To avoid dropped sts, please do *not* remove contrast-colored scrap yarn until *all* sts are picked up. It may be helpful to use your crochet hook to pick up the sts and place them on the needle.

Remove scrap yarn.

With WS facing, CO 13 sts onto the circular needle, and beg diamond trellis edging. Use the US size 9 double-pointed needle to work the edging sts on and off the longer needle. It is perfectly acceptable to "fudge it" along the bottom edgings if it means the edging repeat ends in a more aesthetically pleasing place.

Rep edging along the bottom edges of both sleeves.

### Finishing Instructions

**W**eave in all loose ends before blocking. To block this project, give the unassembled pieces a good soak (20 to 30 minutes) either in lukewarm water, or in lukewarm water with a wool cleanser like Eucalan. This helps the fibers become as pliable as possible. Gently squeeze out water. On a flat surface, use your fingers to press into shape and get the lace as open as possible. Allow to dry fully before sewing the sleeves into the armholes.

**C**ut the contrast ribbon into two 1-yd pieces and one 2-yd piece, or longer if desired.

**A**fter assembly, use the yarn needle to thread the contrast ribbon through the eyelets around the empire waist and the arm bands. Trim the ribbons to the desired length. To help secure the front closure, you may want to sew hooks and eyes into the bodice edges at the ends of the eyelet rows.

**Note:** If rolling or curling is a problem along the neckline or cardigan front, work a simple crochet into the edge stitches.

# Variation

Using the same pattern, you could also make a Girly Camisole, a Girly Pullover, or a Girly Dress (described below)...use your creativity! Simply make some modifications.

Work in the round, varying the lace patterns in the following ways:

- ♦ Change all purl rows to knit rows.
- ♦ Reduce the total stitch count by one—the extra stitch is not needed in the round, only when worked flat.
- ♦ Lengthen the vertical eyelet lace section evenly among the three needle sizes by as much as desired.
- ♦ Start the neck shaping as high or low as desired to create a plunging or more modest V-shape.

## Girly Dress

This dress is constructed in one piece from the provisional cast-on up until the armholes. The front and back are then worked separately. Once the body is complete, the provisional cast-on is picked up and the edging is knitted on side to side. When working the lace patterns, change all purl rows to knit rows.

## Body

Using US size 9 needles and scrap yarn, CO 180 [190, 200, 210, 220] sts. Cont with size 9 needles, switch to main yarn and p 1 row. With RS facing, beg vertical eyelet lace. K as directed until piece meas 6 in. Switch to US size 8 needles. Cont with vertical eyelet lace until piece meas 12 in. Switch to US size 7 needles. Cont with vertical eyelet lace until piece meas 18 [18, 19, 19½, 20] in, ending with a WS row.

*continued*

continued

## Garter Stitch/Eyelet Empire Waist

**Row 1:** K.

**Row 2:** P.

**Row 3:** P.

**Row 4:** K.

**Row 5 (eyelet row):** K1, *yo, k2tog; rep from * to end of row.

**Row 6:** K.

**Row 7:** P.

**Row 8:** P90 [95, 100, 105, 110] sts, pm, p90 [95, 100, 105, 110] sts.

Note: The stitch markers are used to mark armhole placement, and will be referred to in the next section of the pattern.

### Bodice

Beg with row 1, work diamond eyelet lace pattern until piece meas 20½ [20½, 21½, 22, 22½] in, place 90 [95, 100, 105, 110] sts on a stitch holder, and work the back as follows.

### Back

Note: In this section, work the even rows of the diamond eyelet lace in p sts.

Shape armholes: Cont in diamond eyelet lace, BO 3 [4, 5, 4, 5] sts at the beg of the next two rows–84 [86, 90, 96, 100] sts.

Dec 1 st at each and every RS row 9 [10, 11, 13, 13] times–66 [66, 68, 70, 74] sts. If maintaining the diamond eyelet lace pattern interferes with neck shaping, k those 2 or 3 sts in St st.

Cont working diamond eyelet lace pattern as established until 9 [9, 9½, 10, 10, 10½] in from the beg of diamond eyelet lace.

BO all sts as you would in St st.

### Front

Note: In this section, work the even rows of the diamond eyelet lace in p sts.

Slip the 90 [95, 100, 105, 110] sts from the holder onto needle. Work 45 [47, 50, 52, 55] sts and attach a new ball of yarn. (For sizes M and XL, work the first 2 sts tog after attaching the new ball of yarn. You will have 47 and 52 sts rem, respectively.)

You now have two front pieces, which should be worked simultaneously.

Working in diamond eyelet lace, beg neckline and armhole shaping.

Dec 1 st on the neck and armhole edges on every RS row. If maintaining the diamond eyelet lace pattern interferes with neck shaping, k those 2 or 3 sts in St st. You will need to switch to St st near the top of each bodice piece when your stitch count falls below 10 sts. Cont in this manner until you have 3 [3, 2, 2, 3] sts remaining on each side.

BO.

### Edging

Using US size 9 needle, pick up 181 [191, 201, 211, 221] sts. To pick up sts, insert your needle into each main yarn st.

Note: The picked-up sts are actually your first row of knitting. To avoid dropped sts, please do *not* remove contrast-colored scrap yarn until *all* sts are picked up. It

may be helpful to use your crochet hook to pick up the sts and place them on the needle.

Remove scrap yarn.

With WS facing, CO 13 sts onto the circular needle and beg diamond trellis edging. Use the US size 9 double-pointed needle to work the edging sts on and off the longer needle. It is perfectly acceptable to "fudge it" along the bottom edgings if it means the edging repeat ends in a more aesthetically pleasing place.

## Finishing Instructions

Weave in all loose ends before blocking. To block this project, give the unassembled pieces a good soak (20 to 30 minutes) either in lukewarm water or in lukewarm water with a wool cleanser like Eucalan. This helps the fibers become as pliable as possible. Gently squeeze out water. On a flat surface, use your fingers to press into shape and get the lace as open as possible. Allow to dry fully before sewing the shoulder ties into place.

## Shoulder and Empire Waist Ties

For each shoulder tie, crochet a chain of at least 50 sts. For the empire waist tie, crochet a chain at least 2 yd long, or longer if desired. Sew the shoulder ties into place at the top points of each front and the top outer edges of the back.

## Another Option

Cut the contrast ribbon into four 18-in pieces and one 2-yd piece, or longer if desired. Sew the shoulder ties into place at the top points of each front and the top outer edges of the back.

Use the yarn needle to thread the contrast ribbon or crochet chain through the eyelets around the empire waist. Trim the ribbons to the desired length. If rolling or curling is a problem along front and back bodice edges, work a simple crochet into the edge stitches.

# Frosty

### by Jennifer Thurston

This fluffy, almost see-through sweater is sheer, silvery, and delicately sparkly, like a winter frost. Choose between long or shorter sleeves, and a giant neck that can be pulled up like a hood or a deep V-neck.

**Project Rating:** Summer Fling

**Cost:** $95–$110

**Necessary Skills:** purl (page 30); increase (page 38); decrease (page 40); stripes (page 55); pick up stitches (page 67)

## Finished Size
XS [S, M, L, XL]
To fit bust: 34 [36, 38, 40, 42] inches

## Materials
- Rowan Kidsilk Haze (70% Super Kid Mohair/ 30% Silk); 0.8 oz/25g, 229.6 yd/210m:
    - 5 [5, 5, 6, 6] balls of #589 Majestic
- Rowan Kidsilk Night (Mohair blends); 0.8 oz/25g, 227 yd/208m:
    - 1 ball of #608 Moonlight
    - 1 ball of #607 Starlight
- 1 pair of US 8 (5mm) knitting needles and 1 pair US 7 (4.55mm) knitting needles
- Tapestry needle

## Gauge
19 stitches and 26 rows = 4 in/10cm worked in stockinette stitch using US 8 (5mm) knitting needles or size needed to obtain gauge

## Stitch Pattern
Work 8 rows in Majestic.
Work 2 rows in Moonlight.
Work 2 rows in Starlight.
Rep last 12 rows.

## Instructions

### Back

Using US 7 (4.5mm) needles and the first yarn in your chosen stripe patt, CO 83 [87, 92, 97, 102] sts.

Work 4 rows in St st.

Change to US 8 (5mm) needles and start working in stripe patt. Cont in St st and stripe patt for rest of piece.

Work 4 rows.

**Row 9:** K2, k2tog tbl, k to last 4 sts, k2tog, k2.

Working all decs as set by previous row, dec 1 st at each end of every foll fourth row until 71 [75, 80, 85, 90] sts.

Work 11 more rows, ending with a WS row.

**Next row:** K2, m1, k to last 2 sts, m1, k2.

Working all incs as set by previous row, inc 1 st at each end of every foll eighth row until there are 83 [87, 92, 97, 102] sts.

Work 7 more rows, ending with a WS row.

Bind off 4 [5, 5, 6, 6] sts beg of next 2 rows—75 [77, 82, 85, 90] sts.

Dec 1 st at each end of next 3 [3, 5, 5, 7] rows, and on foll 1 [1, 1, 2, 2] alt rows—67 [69, 70, 71, 72] sts.

Cont straight for a further 51 [51, 49, 47, 45] rows, ending with a WS row.

## Shoulder Shaping

Bind off sts at the beg of next 2 rows—55 [57, 58, 59, 60] sts.

**ext row:** BO 6 sts, k until there are 10 [10, 10, 11, 11] sts on right needle and turn, leaving rem sts on a holder.

**ext row:** BO 4 sts.

**ext row:** BO rem 6 [6, 6, 7, 7] sts.

Rejoin yarn and BO center 23 [25, 26, 25, 26] sts, k to end.

Work to match opposite side, reversing shaping.

## Front (Large Neck Sweater Only)

Work as for back, until 20 rows before start of shoulder shaping.

**ext row:** Work until there are 26 [27, 27, 27, 27] sts on right needle.

Dec 1 st at neck edge on foll 3 rows, foll 2 [4, 4, 2, 2] alt rows, and foll 3 [2, 2, 3, 3] fourth rows—18 [18, 18, 19, 19] sts.

## Shape Shoulder

Bind off 6 sts at beg of next row.

Work 1 row.

Bind off rem 6 [6, 6, 7, 7] sts.

Rejoin yarn and BO center 15 [15, 16, 17, 18] sts, k to end.

Work to match opposite side, reversing shaping.

## Front (Deep V-Neck Sweater Only)

Work as for back until 11 [11, 10, 11, 10] rows before armhole shaping.

**ext row (XS, S, L sizes only):** P40 [42, 0, 47, 0] sts, p2tog, p to end—80 [84, 90, 94, 100] sts.

**ext row (all sizes):** K36 [38, 41, 43, 46] sts, k2tog, k1, pick up loop between sts (does not count as a st), slip next st kwise, and turn, leaving rem sts on a holder—39 [41, 44, 46, 49] sts.

**ext row:** P2 tog slipped st and the loop, p1, p2tog, p to end.

The last 2 rows set the patt for a slipped st edging on the neck edge. Cont working this edging for the rest of the front.

**Next row:** Inc 1 st at beg and dec 1 st at end of row—38 [40, 43, 45, 48] sts.

Work 1 row.

**S, M, L, and XL sizes:** Working decs as set in previous rows, dec 1 st at neck edge on foll row and foll 0 [1, 2, 1, 2] alt rows—0 [36, 40, 43, 45] sts.

**XS size:** Working decs as set in previous rows, dec 1 st at neck edge on foll third row—37 sts.

**All sizes:** Work 3 [3, 1, 3, 1] more rows, ending with a WS row.

## Shape Armholes

Bind off 4 [5, 5, 6, 6] sts beg of next row, dec 1 st at end of row.

Work 1 row.

Dec 1 st at armhole edge on foll 3 [3, 5, 5, 7] rows, and foll 1 [1, 1, 2, 2] alt rows, and *at same time* dec 1 st at neck edge on foll third row, and every foll fourth row until 18 [18, 18, 19, 19] sts rem.

Work 17 rows ending with a WS row.

## Shape Shoulders

Bind off 6 sts at beg of next row.

Work 1 row.

Rep last 2 rows.

Bind off rem 6 [6, 6, 7, 7] sts.

Rejoin yarn to sts on holder.

**Next row:** K2, k2tog tbl, k to end.

**Next row:** P to last 4 sts, p2tog tbl, p1, pick up loop between sts (does not count as a st), and slip last st pwise.

**Next row:** K2tog tbl slipped st and loop, k1, k2tog tbl, k to end.

The last 2 rows set the patt for a slipped st edging on the neck edge. Cont working this edging for the rest of front. They also set the patt for how to work decs—now work to match opposite side, reversing shaping.

## Long Sleeves

Using US 7 (4.5mm) needles and the first yarn in your chosen stripe patt, CO57 [61, 63, 65, 67] sts.

Work 4 rows in St st.

Change to US 8 (5mm) needles and start working in stripe patt. Cont in St st and stripe patt for rest of piece.

Work 4 rows.

**Row 9:** K2, k2tog tbl, k to last 4 sts, k2tog, k2.

Working all decs as set by previous row, dec 1 st at each end of foll sixth row—53 [57, 59, 61, 63] sts.

Work 19 rows ending with a WS row.

**Next row:** K2, m1, k to last 2 sts, m1, k2—55 [59, 61, 63, 65] sts.

Working incs as set by previous row, inc 1 st at each end of foll 3 twentieth rows—61 [65, 67, 69, 71] sts.

Work 29 more rows, ending with a WS row.

## Shape Sleeve Cap

Bind off 4 [5, 5, 6, 6] sts at beg of next 2 rows—53 [55, 57, 57, 59] sts.

Dec 1 st at each end of next 3 [5, 5, 5, 5] rows, then on foll 2 [1, 3, 1, 3] alt rows, then on foll 6 [6, 5, 6, 5] fourth rows, then on foll alt row, then on foll 3 rows—23 [23, 23, 25, 25] sts.

Bind off 3 sts at beg of next 2 rows.

Bind off rem 17 [17, 17, 19, 19] sts.

## Shorter Sleeves

Using US 7 (4.5mm) needles and the first yarn in your chosen stripe patt, CO 57 [61, 63, 65, 67] sts.

Work 4 rows in St st.

Change to US 8 (5mm) needles and start working in stripe patt. Cont in St st and stripe patt for rest of piece.

Work 22 rows.

**Row 27:** K2, m1, k to last 2 sts, m1, k2.

Working incs as set by previous row, inc 1 st at each end of foll twentieth row—61 [65, 67, 69, 71] sts.

Work 29 more rows, ending with a WS row.

Work sleeve cap as described for longer sleeves.

## Finishing Instructions

### V-Neck Sweater Only

Using US 8 (4.5mm) needles and first color in stripe patt, pick up and k sts evenly around neck edge of back piece.

Bind off.

Sew shoulder seams together, then side seams.

Sew sleeve seams together.

Sew sleeves into armholes.

## Large Neck Sweater Only

**J**oin one shoulder seam.

**U**sing US 8 (4.5mm) needles and first color in stripe patt, pick up and k sts evenly around neck edge.

**B**eg working the stripe patt, working in St st and changing to US 8 (5mm) needles after 4 rows, work straight until neck meas 11 in from pick-up row (should be 6 reps of stripe patt).

**B**ind off.

**J**oin neck seam and other shoulder seam.

**J**oin side seams.

**S**ew sleeve seams together.

**S**ew sleeves into sleeve holes.

## Variation

The easiest way to make this sweater your own is to mix and match the different options; for example, making a sweater with a deep V-neck and longer sleeves, or one with a big neck but shorter sleeves, or swapping the stripe patterns. Also, there are a lot of shades of this yarn, so making up your own stripe pattern could be fun and simple.

For a dramatically different, richly striped cardigan, follow this alternative stripe pattern:

Stripe pattern 2. Rich purples and gold:
Work 4 rows in Splendour.
Work 2 rows in Swish.
Work 4 rows in Dewberry.
Work 2 rows in Grace.
Rep last 12 rows.

# Wildflowers

### by Jeanette Sherritze

Wrap yourself in a field of late summer flowers. These beautiful wildflower landscapes were the subject of many Impressionists' masterworks. The fields' naturally rhythmic colors and textures inspire the harmony and flow of this simple sweater.

**Project Rating:** Summer Fling

**Cost:** $130–$140

**Necessary Skills:** purl (page 30); k2tog (page 40); p2tog (page 40); ssk (page 40); yo (page 39); stripes (page 55)

**Abbreviation: sk2p:** slip 1, knit 2 together, pass slipped stitch over.

## Finished Size

XS [S-M]
To fit bust: 32 [37] inches
Length: 20 inches

## Materials

- A: 2 skeins Araucania nature wool (100% Wool, 242 yd per 100g); #14AM0300 Variegated Brown
- B: 1 skein Araucania nature wool; #12VE0400 Brown
- C:1 skein Araucania nature wool; #04R00200 Pink
- D: 2 skeins Trendsetter Dune (41% Mohair/30% Acrylic/29% Nylon); #45 Brown/Olive/Mink
- E: 1 skein Mango Moon Recycled Sari Silk yarn (100% Silk or Silk/Rayon blend); 80 yd per skein
- F: 1 skein Plymouth Baby Alpaca Brush (80% Baby Alpaca/20% Acrylic), 110 yd per 50g; #1477 Beige
- G: 2 skeins Blue Sky Alpaca Silk (50% Alpaca/50% Silk); 146 yd to 50g; #i10 Natural
- Louet Sales Euroflax (100% Linen); 135 yd per 50g (knit two strands together to make more like a worsted weight); Pink
- 1 set US 7 (4.5mm) circular needles, 24 in or longer
- Stitch holders (4)
- Stitch markers
- H-8 (5 mm) crochet hook
- Tapestry needle
- Buttons in various sizes that complement your color scheme

## Gauge

16 stitches and 24 rows = 4 inches in stockinette stitch
20 stitches and 20 rows = 4 inches over chevron stitch

**Note:** There is hardly a way to go wrong with the stripes on this sweater, but you'll want to alternate yarns every 1 to 5 rows over the sleeves and body of the sweater, making contrasts between light, dark, and medium values. Resist making your striping pattern too regular.

## Instructions

Cast on 167 [191] sts, placing markers 10 sts in from either end. You will begin working the body in chevron pattern, with the first and last 10 sts worked as a plain garter st band on either side. This creates a nicely finished edge without a lot of finishing work.

## Chevron Pattern

Row 1 (RS): K5, sl 1 pwise wyib, k4; sl marker, k2; *yo, k4, sk2p, k4, yo, k1, rep from * 11 [13] times; end yo, k4, sk2p, k4, yo, k2, sl marker, k4, sl 1 pwise wyib, k5.

Row 2 (WS): K5, p1, k4; sl marker, p to next marker, sl marker, k4, p1, k5.

Rep these two rows for approx 9½ in or 48 rows.

## Slip Stitch Pattern

**Note:** On the RS, you will always sl the st just before the marker. On the WS, always p the first st after the marker through the back loop.

Row 1 (RS): K5, sl 1 pwise wyib, k4, sl band marker; k2, sl 1 pwise wyib, place marker, k10, sl 1 pwise wyib, place marker, *k11, sl 1 pwise wyib, place marker, rep from * 10 [12] times, k10, sl 1 pwise wyib, place marker, k2; sl band marker, k4, sl 1 pwise wyib, k5.

Row 2 (WS): K5, p1, k4, sl band marker, p2, sl marker, p1 tbl, p10, sl marker, p1 tbl, *p11, sl marker, p1 tbl, rep from * 10 [12] times, p10, sl marker, p1 tbl, p2, sl band marker, k4, p1, k5.

Rep these 2 rows for 8 times more, or until slip stitch section meas approx 3 in, ending with a WS row.

## Divide Front and Back

You will now divide the left front, back, and right front as folls and begin working pieces separately.

Next row (RS): Work 40 [45] sts maintaining slip stitch patt as set, BO 8 [10] sts for underarm, work 70 [80] sts maintaining slip stitch patt for back, BO 8 [10] sts for second underarm, work rem 41 [46] sts in patt.

Place all sts for back on a stitch holder.

Place all sts for right front on a stitch holder.

## Left Front

Row 1 (WS): Cont band and slip stitch patt as set to last 2 sts; p2tog—1 st dec.

Row 2 (RS): K1, k2tog, work to end of row maintaining slip stitch patt as set—1 st dec.

Rep rows 1–2 twice, then row 1 again—34 [39] sts.

Place sts on holder.

## Back

Transfer 70 [80] back sts to needle. Attach yarn on left side.

Row 1 (WS): P2tog, maintain slip stitch patt to last 2 sts, p2tog—1 st dec at each side.

**ow 2 (RS):** K1, k2tog, maintain slip stitch patt to last 3 sts, ssk, k1—1 st dec at each side.

**ep rows 1–2 twice, then row 1 again—** 56 [66] sts.

**lace sts on holder.**

## Right Front

**ransfer sts to needle. Attach yarn at** sleeve edge.

**ow 1 (WS):** P2tog, maintain slip stitch and band patt as set—55 [65] sts.

**ow 2 (RS):** Maintain band patt and slip stitch as set to last 3 sts, ssk, k1— 54 [64] sts.

**ep rows 1–2 twice, then row 1 again—** 33 [38] sts.

**lace sts on holder.**

## Sleeves

Since the sleeves are longer than the body, the first 5 in can be striped as you desire. After 5 in, begin following the same striping sequence used on the body of the sweater so that the body and sleeves will match up.

**ast on 63 [75] sts on larger needle using** long-tail method.

## Sleeve Chevron Pattern

**ow 1 and all RS rows:** K2, *yo, k4, sk2p, k4, yo, k1, rep from * 5 [6] times, k1.

**ow 2 and all WS rows:** k1, p across, k1.

**ont in sleeve chevron patt for 14½ in.**

## Slip Stitch Pattern

**ow 1 and all RS rows:** K1, sl 1 pwise wyib, place marker (or sl marker on following rows), *k11, sl 1 pwise wyib, place marker, rep from * 5 [6] times, k1.

**ow 2 and all WS rows:** P1, p1 tbl, *p11, sl marker, p1 tbl, rep from * 5 [6] times, k1.

**aintaining slip stitch patt as set, make** 2 inc on third, ninth, and thirteenth slip stitch rows as follows: Kfb, work in patt to last st, kfb. After row 13, there are 69 [81] sts.

**ont in patt as set for 4 more rows. At** this point you should be on the same row in your color pattern as you were on the body when you bound off the underarms and divided for front and back. Work more or fewer rows if this is not the case in order to match the pattern.

**ow 18:** BO 4 [5] sts at start of row, cont in patt.

**ow 19:** BO 4 [5] sts at start of row, cont in patt.

**ow 20 (RS):** K1, k2tog, maintain patt to last 3 sts, ssk, k1.

**ow 21:** P1, p2tog tbl, maintain patt to last 3 sts, p2tog, p1.

Rep rows 20–21 2 times more—57 [69] sts. Sleeve and body striping sequences should be matched.

Place sleeve sts on stitch holder and make second sleeve the same.

## Joining Body and Sleeves

Transfer all the pieces of the sweater together to the circular needle, being sure that right sides are all facing the same direction. Transfer 33 [38] right front sts, place marker; 57 [69] sleeve sts, place marker; 56 [66] back sts, place marker; 57 [69] sleeve sts, place marker; and 34 [39] left front sts. There are 227 [281] sts.

Beginning on right front (RS), attach yarn. Maintain slip stitch patt as set in each section, working fewer sts bet slipped sts as necessary, and work raglan decs as follows:

**Row 1:** Work right band and front sts as set to 3 sts before first marker, ssk, k1, sl marker, k1, k2tog; work sleeve sts as set to 3 sts before next marker, ssk, k1, sl marker, k1, k2tog; work back as set to 3 sts before next marker, ssk, k1, sl marker, k1, k2tog; work sleeve as set to 3 sts before last marker, ssk, k1, sl marker, k1, k2tog; work left front and band as set.

**Row 2 and following WS rows:** Work WS row of bands and slip stitch patt as set with no decs.

**Row 3:** Decs are made on sleeves only. Work right band and front sts as set to marker, sl marker, k1, k2tog; work sleeve sts as set to 3 sts before next marker, ssk, k1, sl marker; work back sts as set to marker, sl marker, k1, k2tog; work sleeve sts as set to 3 sts before marker, ssk, k1, sl marker; work left front and band as set.

**Row 5:** Rep row 1.

**Row 7:** You will be continuing with the raglan decs as set, and, at the same time, dec 1 st per each full rep of the slip stitch patt.

On right front, work 10 band sts as set, work next 10 sts in patt, on following reps of the slip stitch patt *work to 2 sts before next slipped st, ssk, sl 1 pwise wyib, rep from * to last 3 sts before raglan marker, ssk, k1, sl marker. On sleeve, k1, k2tog, k4, ssk, sl 1 pwise wyib, *k to 2 sts before next slipped st, ssk, sl 1 pwise wyib, rep from * to 3 sts before next raglan marker, ssk, k1, sl marker. On back, k1, k2tog, k2, sl 1 pwise wyib, *k to 2 sts before the next slipped st, ssk, sl 1 pwise wyib, rep from * to 3 sts before raglan marker, ssk, k1. On sleeve, k1, k2tog, k4, ssk, sl 1 pwise wyib, *k to 2 sts before next slipped st, ssk, sl 1 pwise wyib, rep from * to 3 sts before next raglan marker, ssk, k1, sl marker. On left front, k1, k2tog, k5, ssk, sl 1 pwise wyib, *k to 2 sts before next slipped st, ssk, sl 1 pwise wyib, work to end of row in patt.

**Row 9:** Rep row 1.

## Rib Section

**Row 1 (RS):** Work 10 band sts as set, *k2, p2, rep from * to last 10 sts, work 10 band sts as set.

**Note:** Continue to sl markers at sleeve placements as you get to them.

**R**ow 2 (WS): Work 10 band sts as set; k the knit sts, p the purl sts to last 10; work 10 band sts as set.

**R**ep these 2 rows 5 times more, or until rib section measures 1⅞ in.

**N**ext row (WS): BO first 5 sts; p1, *k2, p2, rep from * across, maintaining rib as set, to last 6 sts: p1, k5.

**N**ext row (RS): BO first 5 sts; k tbl of all sts, creating a turning ridge.

**N**ext row (WS): Sl 1 pwise wyib, *p2, k2; rep from * to last st, k1.

**A**ll following rows: Sl 1pwise wyib; k the knits, p the purls, to last st, k1.

**C**ont in rib for approximately 4 in, ending with a RS row.

**B**ind off.

## Finishing Instructions

**S**ew up sleeve seams and weave in all loose ends.

## Crochet Edging

**F**old right front band in half along the slipped stitch. Attach yarn at the bottom hem of the sweater at the outside edge of the band, which is now folded over to the WS of the sweater. Fix the band in place by crocheting a seam as follows: Insert hook into edge stitch of band and into back loop of tenth stitch of band, wrap yarn around hook and draw through both loops, 2 loops on hook; wrap yarn around hook again and draw through both loops so only one loop rems on hook. Rep process of inserting hook into next rows until you reach the top of the band. At top of band in corner, ch 1 extra st, then cont seaming along top edge of band by slip stitching into each st taking care that seam does not show above turning ridge sts). Do not break yarn.

**C**ont crocheting 1 st in every other row on collar. When you reach the corner of collar, turn. Ch 4. Sl st into third ch from hook 3 times. Ch 4, sl st into first crochet stitch at band edge, ch 4, sl st into third sl st of band 4 times—8 scallops. Fold collar so 4 scallops are on top with 4 scallops directly underneath them (each pair of scallops will make one buttonhole). Turn. Sl st the scallops tog along their top loops to join them on outside edge—4 buttonholes made. At top edge, break yarn, leaving an 8-in tail. With tapestry needle, sew other edge of buttonholes along collar edge.

**S**ew buttons in place on left side so that collar fits snug across shoulders. Embellish collar with other vintage buttons and knit flowers (the crowning glory, below) as desired, sewing through both thicknesses of collar to tack in place.

## Crowning Glory Flower

### Materials
- For flower center: Trendsetter Dune (as main pattern)
- For petals: ColorMart (100% Cashmere); fingering weight, 2 oz (50g), 250 yd, 1 skein light pink

- ◆ 1 set US 3 (3.25 mm) double-pointed needles
- ◆ Austrian crystal bicone or round beads (12)
- ◆ Flat coin pearl or other flat bead (1)
- ◆ Tapestry needle
- ◆ Beading needle and thread to match color of flower center
- ◆ Optional: pinback

## Center

With yarn for center of flower, CO 3.

**Row 1:** K 3 sts into each st (k1, k1 tbl, k1)—9 sts.

Divide so that there are 3 sts on each of 3 needles.

**Row 2:** K 2 into each st—18 total sts.

## Petals

Move sts so that there are 2 sts on the first needle.

Petals are worked back and forth. With yarn for flower petals, cut 76-in length of yarn; find midpoint. Attach midpoint of petal yarn on first st by drawing through and placing loop on right needle, then k the 2 sts on needle with a single strand of yarn, carrying the second strand across the back of this row only so that it will be correctly positioned—3 sts.

**Row 1:** K3.

**Row 2 (RS):** K1, k3 into next st, k1; turn—5 sts on needle.

**Row 3:** K1, p3, k1.

**Row 4:** K2 into first st, k3, k2 into last st—7 sts.

**Row 5:** K2, p3, k2.

**Row 6:** K7.

**Row 7:** K2, p3, k2.

**Row 8:** K2, k3tog, k2.

**Row 9:** K5.

**Row 10:** K2tog, k1, k2tog.

**Row 11:** K3.

**Row 12:** K2tog, k1. Pass first st over the second and draw yarn through to secure.

Go to rem sts on left needle. With other half of attached yarn, CO 1 (counts as first st). K 2 sts. Rep rows 1–12 for next petal.

Rep process until only 2 sts rem on flower center.

Cut a 38-in piece of petal yarn and attach on first st. CO 1 and k all 3 sts. Rep rows 1–12.

Weave in all loose yarns with tapestry needle.

With beading needle, sew coin pearl in center of flower and sew crystals around its circumference.

Sew pinback to back of flower, if desired, or sew directly onto garment.

## Variation

Almost any combination of yarns of approximately worsted weight will work for this garment. Consider using different textures, colors, fibers, even "carry alongs" to add interest to your work. For color inspirations, look at the great Impressionists' paintings. As you stroll through a museum or thumb through a book on Monet or van Gogh, notice what paintings you are drawn to. Let that artist's palette become your yarns!

# Macho Picchu

Zip him up in a big cozy cardi with stripes that highlight his broad shoulders and chest. You won't be able to resist cuddling into the soft alpaca yarn that will keep him warm as toast.

**Project Rating:** Love o' Your Life

**Cost:** $120–$144

**Necessary Skills:** purl (page 30); increase (page 38); decrease (page 40); stripes (page 55); knitting in the round (page 55); optional: Magic Loop method (page 33)

## Finished Size

S [M, L, XL]

To fit chest: 34–36 [38–40, 42–44, 46–48] inches

## Materials

- Kraemer Alpaca (100% Superfine Alpaca); 3.5 oz/100g, 110 yd/100.5m
    - A = 8 [9, 9, 10] skeins of Fawn
    - B = 1 skein of Black
    - C = 1 skein of White
- 1 set of US 10 (6mm) double-pointed needles, or 1 long (over 24 in) US 10 (6mm) circular needle, if using the Magic Loop method
- 1 set of US 10½ (6.5mm) double-pointed needles, or 1 long (over 24 in) US 10½ (6.5mm) circular needle, if using the Magic Loop method
- Stitch markers
- Stitch holders
- Tapestry needle
- 2-way zip to fit 22-inch front opening

## Gauge

14 stitches and 20 rows = 4 in/10cm worked in stockinette stitch in the round, using US 10½ (6.5mm) knitting needles, or size needed to obtain gauge

## Stripe Pattern

2 rows color B
2 rows color A
2 rows color B
2 rows color A
2 rows color B
2 rows color A
2 rows color C
2 rows color B
2 rows color C
2 rows color A
2 rows color C
2 rows color B
2 rows color C
2 rows color A
2 rows color B
2 rows color A
2 rows color B
2 rows color A

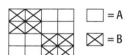

□ = A
⊠ = B

## Instructions

### Body

The body for this pattern is worked back and forth in rows.

Using US 10 (6mm) circular or double-pointed needles and yarn A, CO 164 [172, 180, 188] sts.

**Row 1 (RS):** K2, * k1, p1; rep from * to last 2 sts, k2.

Rep row 1 11 more times.

Change to larger needles.

**Row 13 (RS):** K.

**Row 14:** K2, p to last 2 sts, k2.

Keeping the k2, in color A, at beg and end of each row, follow 4 rows of graph with colors A and B.

Cut color B. Work with color A as folls:

**Row 19 (RS):** K.

**Row 20:** K2, p to last 2 sts, k2.

Rep rows 19–20 until work meas 17 [17, 18, 18] in, ending with a WS row.

Place sts on a holder.

### Sleeves

The sleeves for this pattern are worked in the round.

Using US 10 (6mm) circular or double-pointed needles, CO 36 [36, 40, 40] sts.

Place marker and join into a rnd.

**Rnd 1 (RS):** * K1, p1; rep from * to end.

Rep rnd 1 11 more times.

Change to larger circular needle.

**Rnds 13–14:** K.

Follow 4 rows of graph with colors A and B.

Cut color B. Work with color A as folls:

**Rnds 19–20:** K.

**Rnd 21:** Kfb, k to last st, kfb—38 [38, 42, 42] sts.

**Rnds 22–28:** K.

**Rnd 29:** Kfb, k to last st, kfb.

Rep rnds 22–29 7 times—54 [54, 58, 58] sts.

Knit every rnd without shaping until sleeve meas 19 [20, 21, 21] in from cast-on edge.

Place sleeve sts on holder.

Rep for second sleeve.

## Join Sleeves to Body

Put first 4 and last 4 sts of sleeves onto separate holders.

Row 1 (RS): Returning to body piece and with RS facing, k37 [39, 41, 43] sts for right front, put next 8 sts on a holder, k across 46 [46, 50, 50] sts of first sleeve, k across next 74 [78, 82, 86] sts for back, then put next 8 sts on a holder, k across 46 [46, 50, 50] sts of second sleeve, then across rem 37 [39, 41, 43] sts for left front—240 [248, 264, 272] sts.

Row 2: K2, p34 [36, 38, 40], pm, p2, pm, p44 [44, 48, 48], pm, p2, pm, p72 [76, 80, 84], pm, p2, pm, p44 [44, 48, 48], pm, p2, pm, p34 [36, 38, 40], k2.

Row 3 (dec): *K to 2 sts before first marker, ssk, sl marker, k2, sl marker, k2tog; rep from * 3 times, k to end—232 [240, 256, 264] sts.

Row 4: K2, p to last 2 sts, k2.

Cont to k first 2 and last 2 sts of every row in color A, follow stripe patt for 26 rows, at the same time dec 8 sts as established above on every RS row until 128

[136, 152, 160] sts rem, ending with a WS row.

## Neck Shaping

Maintaining stripe patt, BO 6 [6, 7, 7] sts at the beg of next 2 rows; at the same time dec 8 sts on the first of these 2 rows as set and cont with stripe patt—114 [122, 137, 145] sts.

Knit 2 tog at the beg and end of next 3 rows; at the same time dec 8 sts on the first and foll RS row as set and cont with stripe patt—92 [100, 115, 123] sts.

Next row (WS): P.

Knit 2 tog at the beg and end of next and foll 1 [1, 2, 2] alt rows; at the same time dec 8 sts on the first and every foll RS row as set and cont with stripe patt—66 [74, 84, 92] sts.

Next row: P.

Bind off.

## Collar

Using US 10 (6mm) knitting needles and color A, CO 2 sts.

Row 1 (RS): K.

Row 2: As row 1.

Row 3 (inc): Kfb, k to end.

Rep rows 2–3 until there are 24 sts.

Work in garter stitch (every row knit), without shaping until work meas 17½ [18, 18½, 19] in, ending with a WS row.

Next row (RS): K2tog, k to end.

Next row: K.

Rep last 2 rows until 2 sts rem.

Bind off.

## Finishing Instructions

Pin and sew shaped edge of collar to neck edge. Carefully graft together underarm sts. Pin zip in place to center fronts, being careful not to stretch your knitting. Baste down the center of the zip tape, then oversew neatly down tape edges. Sew in all loose ends.

# Variation

Don't fancy tackling a zip just yet? Then pull the wool (or in this case, alpaca!), over his eyes with this simple sweater.

## Body

Using US 10 (6mm) circular or double-pointed needles and yarn A, CO 164 [172, 180, 188] sts.
**Rnd 1 (RS):** * K1, p1; rep from * to end.
**Rnd 2:** * P1, k1; rep from * to end.
Rep rnds 1–2 3 more times.
Change to US 10½ (6.5mm) circular needle.
**Rnd 9:** K to end.
Rep rnd 9 until work meas 17 [17, 18, 18] in.
Place sts on a holder.

## Sleeve Stripe Pattern

Rnds 1–6 in color A.
Rnds 7–12 in color B.
Rep the last 12 rows.

## Sleeves

Using US 10 (6mm) circular or double-pointed needles and yarn A, CO 36 [36, 40, 40] sts.
Place marker and join into a round.
**Rnd 1 (RS):** * K1, p1; rep from * to end.
**Rnd 2:** * P1, k1; rep from * to end.
Rep rnds 1–2 3 more times.
Change to larger circular needle.
Work in stripe patt, at the same time work inc by kfb into first and last st of ninth and every following eighth rnd to 52 [52, 56, 56] sts.
Cut yarn B.
Continue working with yarn A, k 6 rnds.
**Next rnd:** Kfb, k to last st, kfb–54 [54, 58, 58] sts.
K every rnd without shaping until sleeve meas 19 [20, 21, 21] in.
Place sleeve sts on holder.
Rep for second sleeve.

*continued*

*continued*

## Join Sleeves to Body

Put first 4 and last 4 sts of sleeves onto separate holders.

**Rnd 1:** Returning to body piece and with RS facing, put first 4 sts onto a holder, k74 [78, 82, 86] sts for front; put next 8 sts on a holder, k across 46 [46, 50, 50] sts of first sleeve, k across next 74 (78, 82, 86) sts for back; then put next 4 sts on a holder, k across 46 [46, 50, 50] sts of second sleeve–240 [248, 264, 272] sts.

**Rnd 2:** K1, pm, k72 [76, 80, 84], pm, k2, pm, k44 [44, 48, 48], pm, p2, pm, k72 [76, 80, 84], pm, k2, pm, k44 [44, 48, 48], pm, k1.

**Rnd 3 (dec):** K1, sl marker, k2tog, * k to 2 sts before next marker, ssk, sl marker, k2, sl marker, k2tog; rep from *twice, k to 2 sts before last marker, ssk, sl marker, k1.

**Rnd 4:** K.

Cont working in rnds, dec 8 sts as set by third rnd on next and every alt rnd until 88 [96, 102, 110] sts remain.

Change to US 10 (6mm) circular needle.

**Rnd 1 (RS):** * K1, p1; rep from * to end.

**Rnd 2:** * P1, k1; rep from * to end.

Rep rnds 1–2 twice more.

BO in pattern.

Carefully graft together underarm sts.

Sew in all loose ends.

# Chapter Fourteen

♦◆♦

# Bag Ladies

### Techno Bag

Keep your laptop all cozy and warm in its custom-made carry case.

### Techno Junior

Don't let your iPod get jealous—knit it a cozy, too!

### Bandolero

Try your hand at Fair Isle, adding a chain and buckle for that finishing touch to this shoulder bag, or let your yarn speak for itself in a chunky riot of color.

# Techno Bag

Keep your laptop snug and warm in its very own stylish bag—much more fun to carry around than the stuffy old ones for the computer geeks.

**Project Rating:** Summer Fling

**Cost:** $30

**Necessary Skills:** purl (page 30); stripes (page 55); intarsia (page 56); Kitchener stitch (page 65); optional: Magic Loop method (page 33)

## Finished Size

3 x 12½ x 9½ [3 x 14 x 10½, 1½ x 17 x 10½] inches (fits 12–[14–, 17–] inch iBook)

## Materials

- Brown Sheep, Lamb's Pride Bulky (85% Wool/15% Mohair); 4 oz/113g, 125 yd/114m
- 1 skein each of colors A, B, C, and D. I used (colors are listed for gray combo, followed by green combo and orange combo in parentheses):
    A = #05 Onyx (#65 Sapphire, #04 Charcoal Heather)
    B = #04 Charcoal Heather (#120 Limeade, #57 RPM Pink)
    C = #120 Limeade (#155 Lemon Drop, #155 Lemon Drop)
    D = #170 Pine Shadows (#52 Spruce, #22 Autumn Harvest)
- 1 set of US 15 (10mm) double-pointed needles, or 1 long (over 24 in) US 15 (10mm) circular needle, if using the Magic Loop method
- Stitch marker
- Tapestry needle
- Ring binder and some magazines, or something of a similar size to your laptop computer, to place inside your bag while it is drying

## Gauge

10½ stitches and 16 rows = 4 in/10cm worked in stockinette stitch using US 15 (10mm) knitting needles, or size needed to obtain gauge

## Stitch Pattern

Corner stitch: Insert right needle knitwise into the second stitch on the left needle and knit into it without taking it off the needle, then knit the first stitch on the left needle and take both first and second stitches off the left needle at the same time.

Stripe Pattern #1 for Main Section of Bag
10 rnds color B
2 rnds color C
6 rnds color D
4 rnds color B
2 rnds color C
4 rnds color B
4 rnds color D
2 rnds color C
2 rnds color D
2 rnds color C
2 rnds color B
2 rnds color C
4 [10, 10] rnds color B

Stripe Pattern #2 for Pocket
5 rows color D
4 rows color B
2 rows color C
4 rows color B

4 rows color D
2 rows color C
2 rows color D
2 rows color C

## Instructions

### Base

Using US 15 (10mm) knitting needles and color A, CO 10 sts.

Work garter stitch (all rows k), for 60 [72, 88] rows.

Bind off.

### Main Section of Bag

Using US 15 (10mm) needle and color B, with RS facing, pick up and k 30 [36, 44] sts along first long side of base, 10 sts along first short side of base, 30 [36, 44] sts along second long side of base, and 10 sts along second short side of base — 80 [92, 108] sts.

Place marker, and begin working in rnds using stripe pattern #1. At the same time, work every rnd as follows: Work corner st, k26 [32, 40], (work corner st) twice, k6, (work corner st) twice, k26 [32, 44], (work corner st) twice, k6, work corner st.

Bind off in color B.

### Opening Section

Wind off a small apple-sized ball of color A, as you will be working with 2 ends of this color for this section.

Using the main skein of color A, pick up and k 10 sts from the row below the cast-off edge on the inside of first short side of the main part of the bag. With the RS facing you, k 1 row into back of sts.

Purl 1 row.

**Row 3 (RS):** Divide for opening: K5, then drop the yarn you were using (end #1), pick up the yarn from the small ball you wound earlier (end #2), and k rem 5 sts.

**Row 4 (WS):** Using end #2, p5; using end #1, p5.

**Row 5 (RS):** Using end #1, k5; using end #2, k5.

Rep rows 4–5 until this piece fits along the long side of the top of the bag, ending with a WS row. Cut end #2.

Cont with end #1 to close opening: K 1 row across all 10 sts.

Purl 1 row.

Bind off.

Using color A, stitch cast-off edge of opening section to inside of second short side of the main part of the bag, below the cast-off edge to match first short side. Then with wrong sides together, backstitch the long sides of the opening section to the inside of main part of the bag, just below the cast-off edge. This gives a nice, defined edge to the top of the bag.

## Handles (Worked as One Piece)

Cast on 6 sts in color sequence as folls: 1B, 1C, 2A, 2D.

Work in St st in intarsia vertical stripe as set until strip measures 104 [108, 108] in.

Bind off.

Pin strip to outside of bag, starting at join of base and bag, 3 [6, 10] sts in from corner st straight up one side of bag, leaving 22 in loose for handles, then down same side of bag 3 [6, 10] sts away from other corner st, across base. Rep on second side. Using backstitch, sew handles firmly in place.

## Pocket

Using color D, pick up and k 12 sts, between straps and 14 rows up from base on outside of bag.

Work in St st in stripe patt #2 over next 26 rows.

Bind off with color C.

Pin and stitch pocket to edges of straps.

## Finishing Instructions

### Felting

Enclose bag inside a zipped pillowcase or similar (to contain fluff), and put through a hot wash cycle of a washing machine (it helps to throw in a couple of pairs of jeans or towels for agitation).

Remove from pillowcase and check for felting/size. I usually put my felted bags through the wash cycle twice, but all machines vary.

When your bag has reached the required size (and don't worry if it looks a bit on the small side—it can be stretched, but only while it is still damp), manipulate the bag to size. I placed a ring binder and two or three glossy magazines in mine to get the size and shape I needed. It is especially important to pull the corners of the bag to form the squared shape. The pocket will probably fuse together with the bag in places, so gently pull it away from the bag.

Leave the bag to dry thoroughly. Once dry, the binders, magazines, or whatever you have used to shape your bag can be removed and a zip can be stitched into the opening if required.

# Variation

For a non-felted laptop bag, I worked a firmer fabric, made the straps double, and lined the bag for strength.

## Finished Size

2 x 14 x 10½ inches (fits 12- to 14-inch iBook)

## Materials

- Kraemer Yarns, Naturally Nazareth (85% Wool/15% Mohair); 3.5 oz/100g, 184 yd/168m: 3 skeins of color A = Winter; 1 skein of color B = Snowman; 1 skein of color C = Sleigh; 1 skein of color D = Ice Skate
- 1 set of US 8 (5mm) double-pointed needles, or 1 long (over 24 in) US 8 (5mm) circular needle, if using the Magic Loop method
- Stitch marker
- Tapestry needle

## Gauge

19½ stitches and 26 rows = 4 in/10cm worked in stockinette stitch using US 8 (5mm) knitting needles, or size needed to obtain gauge

## Stitch Pattern

Corner stitch: Insert right needle knitwise into the second stitch on the left needle and knit into it without taking it off the needle, then knit the first stitch on the left needle and take both first and second stitches off the left needle at the same time.

## Base

Using US 8 (5mm) knitting needles and color A, CO 10 sts.

Work seed stitch as folls:

**Row 1 (RS):** * K1, p1; rep from * to end.
**Row 2:** * P1, k1; rep from * to end.
Rep rows 1–2 until work meas 12½ in.
BO in patt.

## Main Section of Bag

Using US 8 (5mm) needle and color A, pick up and k 49 sts along first long side of base, 10 sts along first short side of base, 49 sts along second long side of base, and 10 sts along second short side of base–118 sts.

**Rnd 1:** Work corner st, k45, (work corner st) twice, (p1, k1) 3 times, (work corner st) twice, k45, (work corner st) twice, (p1, k1) 3 times, work corner st.

**Rnd 2:** Work corner st, k45, (work corner st) twice, (k1, p1) 3 times, (work corner st) twice, k45, (work corner st) twice, (k1, p1) 3 times, work corner st.

Rep last two rnds until work meas 12 in.

Divide for bag opening: Work corner st, (k1, p1) 23 times, (work corner st) twice, (p1, k1) 4 times, put next 49 sts on holder, turn and work on front and side panel as folls:

**Rnd 1 (RS):** (K1, p1) 4 times, p4, (p1, k1) 23 times, p4, (p1, k1) 4 times.

**Rnd 2:** (K1, p1) 4 times, (work corner st) twice, (p1, k1) 23 times, (work corner st) twice, (p1, k1) 4 times.

Rep rnds 1 and 2 once more.

**Rnd 5:** (K1, p1) 4 times, p2, then put the 10 sts just worked onto a holder, CO the next 49 sts, (k1, p1) 4 times, k1, then put the 10 sts just worked onto a holder.

*continued*

*continued*

Work the front flap from the 49 sts on a holder as folls:

**Row 1 (RS):** (K1, p1) 3 times, then knit intarsia stripe sts as folls:

Color B, 4 sts.

Color C, 2 sts.

Color D, 5 sts.

Color B, 2 sts.

Color C, 4 sts.

Color D, 2 sts.

Color B, 4 sts.

Color C, 2 sts.

Color D, 4 sts.

Color C, 6 sts.

Color B, 2 sts.

Then with color A (p1, k1) 3 times.

**Row 2:** (P1, k1) 3 times, purl intarsia stripe sts as folls:

Color B, 2 sts.

Color C, 6 sts.

Color D, 4 sts.

Color C, 2 sts.

Color B, 4 sts.

Color D, 2 sts.

Color C, 4 sts.

Color B, 2 sts.

Color D, 5 sts.

Color C, 2 sts.

Color B, 4 sts.

Then with color A (k1, p1) 3 times.

Rep rows 1–2 until flap meas 14 in, ending with a WS row. Cut colors B, C, and D and cont with color A in seed stitch only, as folls:

**Row 1 (RS):** * K1, p1; rep from * to last st, k1.

Rep row 17 more times.

BO in patt.

## Front Pocket

With RS facing, pick up and k the foll sequence of 35 sts from the tenth rnd above the base, starting from the eighth st in from the corner st:

Color C, 4 sts.

Color B, 2 sts.

Color D, 6 sts.

Color C, 2 sts.

Color B, 4 sts.

Color C, 6 sts.

Color D, 2 sts.

Color B, 4 sts.

Color C, 5 sts.

**Row 1:** P across all 35 sts in the foll sequence:

Color C, 5 sts.

Color B, 4 sts.

Color D, 2 sts.

Color C, 6 sts.

Color B, 4 sts.

Color C, 2 sts.

Color D, 6 sts.

Color B, 2 sts.

Color C, 4 sts.

**Row 2:** K across all 35 sts in the foll sequence:

Color C, 4 sts.

Color B, 2 sts.

Color D, 6 sts.

Color C, 2 sts.

Color B, 4 sts.

Color C, 6 sts.

Color D, 2 sts.

Color B, 4 sts.

Color C, 5 sts.

Rep rows 1–2 until work meas 8 in, ending with a WS row. Cut colors B, C, and D and cont with color A in seed stitch only, as folls:

**Row 1 (RS):** * K1, p1; rep from * to last st, k1.

Rep row 1 5 more times.

BO in patt.

## Strap

With RS facing and color A, work on 10 sts from a holder as folls:

*K1, p1; rep from * to end, then CO 10 sts–20 sts.

Join into the rnd, placing a marker between the first and last st and work in seed stitch as folls:

**Rnd 1 (RS):** * P1, k1; rep from * to end.

**Rnd 2:** *K1, p1; rep from * to end.

Rep rnds 1–2 until strap meas 27 in relaxed (it will stretch!).

Using Kitchener stitch, graft the first 10 sts of strap to 10 sts on holder, then sew 10 rem sts to inside base of strap.

## Finishing Instructions

Pin and slip stitch pocket sides to front of bag. Sew in all loose ends and block bag to shape.

**Lining:** Lay blocked bag on lining fabric (with bottom of bag against the fold line) to use as a template. Leaving $\frac{1}{2}$ in for seams, cut out lining pieces. With right sides together, sew lining pieces together. Then press and baste top and front flap edges $\frac{1}{2}$ in over to wrong sides. Place lining inside bag and slip stitch into place.

# Techno Junior

Keep your mobile tunes warm and snug in their own cozies. Knit one to match your Techno Bag, or go the space-dyed route and either hang your little player around your neck, or knit it a button-up cover to keep its screen clean. These babies are so quick and easy to make that you can whip up one to match every outfit, or give as gifts to all your music-lovin' friends!

**Project Rating:** Summer Fling

**Cost:** $3

**Necessary Skills:** purl (page 30); optional: I-cord (page 84); tassels (page 81); blanket stitch (page 78); crochet chain (page 86) or braided tie (page 83); Magic Loop method (page 33)

## Finished Size

Fits iPod, 4 x 2.4 x 0.4 inches

## Materials

- ◆ Knit Picks, Sock Garden (100% Merino Wool); 1.75 oz/50g, 200 yd/182m: 1 ball of #23474 Geranium (two strands of this yarn are held together throughout the knitting)
- ◆ 1 set of US 5 (3.75)mm double-pointed needles, or 1 long (over 24 in) US 5 (3.75mm) circular needle if using the Magic Loop method
- ◆ Stitch markers
- ◆ Tapestry needle
- ◆ Optional: button

## Gauge

18 stitches and 28 rows = 4 in/10cm worked in seed stitch worked in the round using US 5 (3.75mm) knitting needles, or size needed to obtain gauge

## Instructions

Using 5 US (3.75mm) needles or size needed to obtain gauge and yarn A, CO 24 sts. Make sure you're holding two strands together if using the sock yarn!

Join in a rnd and place marker between first and last st.

**Rnd 1:** *K1, p1; rep from * to end.

**Rnd 2:** *P1, k1; rep from * to end.

Rep rnds 1–2 twice more.

**Next row (RS):** Divide for circular hole: Ssk, (k1, p1) 10 times, k2tog, turn— 22 sts.

You'll be working back and forth in rows for this next bit:

**Row 1 (WS):** Ssk, (k1, p1) 9 times, k2tog, turn—20 sts.

**Row 2 (RS):** Ssk, (k1, p1) 8 times, k2tog, turn—18 sts.

**Row 3 (WS):** Ssk, (k1, p1) 7 times, k2tog, turn—16 sts.

**Row 4 (RS):** (K1, p1) 7 times, k2, turn.

**Row 5 (WS):** K1, (k1, p1) 7 times, k1, turn.

Rep rows 4–5 once more.

**Row 8 (RS):** Kfb, (p1, k1) 7 times, kfb, turn—18 sts.

**Row 9 (WS):** Kfb, (p1, k1) 8 times, kfb, turn—20 sts.

**Row 10 (RS):** Kfb, (p1, k1) 9 times, kfb, turn—22 sts.

**Row 11 (WS):** Kfb, (p1, k1) 10 times, kfb, turn—24 sts.

**Row 12 (RS):** (K1, p1) 12 times.

Rejoin rnd and place marker between first and last st.

**Rnd 1:** *P1, k1; rep from * to end.

**Rnd 2:** *K1, p1; rep from * to end.

Rep rnds 1–2 once more.

**Next row (RS):** Divide for square hole: BO 3 sts in patt, (p1, k1) 10 times, turn—21 sts.

You'll be working back and forth in rows again for this next bit:

**Row 1 (WS):** BO 3 sts, (k1, p1) 8 times, k1, turn—18 sts.

**Row 2 (RS):** (K1, p1) 8 times, k2, turn.

**Row 3 (WS):** K1, (k1, p1) 8 times, k1, turn.

Rep rows 2–3 3 more times.

**Row 10 (RS):** CO 3 sts, (p1, k1) 10 times, p1, turn, CO 3 sts—24 sts.

Join in a rnd and place marker between first and last st.

**Rnd 1:** (K1, p1) 12 times.

**Rnd 2:** (P1, k1) 12 times.

Rep rows 1–2 twice more.

Bind off in patt. **

## Optional Strap

With RS facing, pick up and k 3 sts from one side of top edge. Work an I-cord for however long you want your strap to be—noting that it will stretch with wear (mine is 34 in long).

Bind off and stitch end to other side of top edge.

## Finishing Instructions

Make two 2½-in tassels and sew securely to bottom corners. Sew cast-on edge closed, leaving a 1-in opening in the center for access to the charger slot. Sew in all loose ends.

# Variation

Don't fancy hanging your tunes around your neck? To knit a solid cozy with a front cover, you'll need 1 ball of Knit Picks Merino Style (100% Merino Wool), 1.75 oz/50g, 123 yd/112m. I used #23462 Cinnamon and a small amount of #23459 Frost, for blanket stitch trim.

Work as for space-dyed cozy to **.

## For Front Cover

Pick up and k 20 sts along side of cozy.
**Row 1:** (K1, p1) 10 times.
**Row 2:** (P1, k1) 10 times.
Rep rows 1–2 10 more times.
BO in patt.
Using contrast color yarn, blanket stitch around the top, cover, and edges of the holes. Sew on a button and make a crochet chain or braided button loop and attach it to outside edge.

# Bandolero

My inspiration for this pattern was a leather shoulder bag that my dad brought back from a business trip to Spain in the mid-1970s. I loved the way that bag smelled and its simple construction. In this design I included a Fair Isle pattern in place of the embroidery on my original and added a chain to the strap for strength, then embellished it for the 1970's hippie vibe. Adapting the pattern slightly, I created a chunky handbag with oversized button closure to stand out from the business of the space-dyed yarn.

**Project Rating:** Love o' Your Life

**Cost:** $60

**Necessary Skills:** purl (page 30); increase (page 38); decrease (page 40); Fair Isle (page 56)

## Finished Size

Width: 9 inches; height: 9½ inches

## Materials

- Kraemer Yarns, Naturally Nazareth (100% Domestic Wool); 3.5 oz/100g, 184 yd/168m:
    - 2 balls of A, Hayride
    - 1 ball of B, Moss
    - 1 ball of C, Natural
    - 1 ball of D, Twilight
    - 1 ball of E, Jack-O-Lantern
    - 1 ball of F, Beach Ball
    - 1 ball of G, Wagon Wheel
    - 1 ball of H, Ice Skate
- 1 pair of US 8 (5mm) knitting needles
- Stitch markers
- Tapestry needle
- ½ yd lining fabric
- Sewing needle and thread
- 2 D-rings, each 2-in wide
- Buckle
- 32-in chain

## Gauge

18 stitches and 20 rows = 4 in/10cm worked in Fair Isle pattern using US 8 (5mm) knitting needles, or size needed to obtain gauge

## Stitch Pattern

See figure on next page.

## Instructions

### Back

Using 8 US (5mm) needles and yarn A, CO 20 sts.

**Row 1 (RS):** *K1, p1; rep from * to last 2 sts, k2.

**Row 2:** K2, *p1, k1; rep from * to end.

**Row 3:** CO 4 sts, *k1, p1; rep from * to last 2 sts, k2—24 sts.

**Row 4:** CO 4 sts, k2, *p1, k1; rep from * to end—28 sts.

**Row 5:** CO 4 sts, (k1, p1) 3 times, k23, p1, k2—32 sts.

**Row 6:** CO 4 sts, k2, (p1, k1) twice, p25, (k1, p1) twice, k1—36 sts.

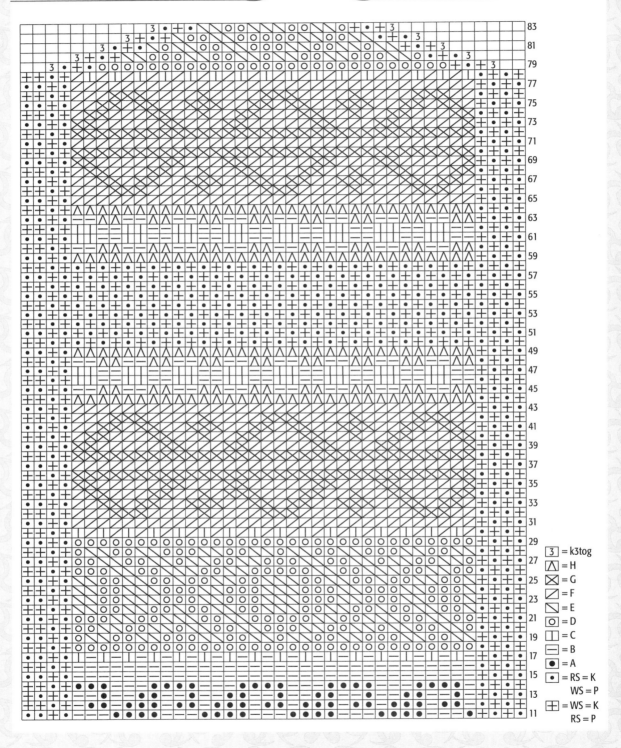

| 3 | = k3tog |
|---|---------|
| △ | = H |
| ⊠ | = G |
| ⧄ | = F |
| ⧅ | = E |
| ⊙ | = D |
| ⊞ | = C |
| ⊟ | = B |
| ● | = A |
| · | = RS = K |
|   | WS = P |
| ⊞ | = WS = K |
|   | RS = P |

**ow 7:** CO 2 sts, (k1, p1) twice, k31, p1, k2—38 sts.

**ow 8:** CO 2 sts, k2, p1, k1, p33, k1, p1, k1—40 sts.

**ow 9:** (K1, p1) twice, k33, p1, k2.

**ow 10:** K2, p1, k1, p33, k1, p1, k1.

**ows 11–83:** Follow chart for back—20 st.

**ow 84:** Using yarn A, k3tog, *p1, k1; rep from * to last 3 sts, k3tog—16 sts.

**ow 85:** K3tog, *k1, p1; rep from * to last 3 sts, k3tog—12 sts.

**ow 86:** K3tog, *p1, k1; rep from * to last 3 sts, k3tog—8 sts.

**ow 87:** K1 *k1, p1; rep from * to last st, k1.

ind off in patt.

## Front

ork as for back to end of row 43.

**ow 44:** Using yarn A, k2, *p1, k1; rep from * to end.

**ow 45:** *K1, p1; rep from * to last 2 sts, k2.

ep the last 2 rows twice more, then row 44 once more.

ind off in patt.

## Sides

sing 8 US (5mm) needles and yarn A, CO 9 sts.

**ow 1:** *K1, p1; rep from * to last st, k1.

ep this first row until work meas 3 in.

**nc row:** Kfb, *p1, k1; rep from * to last 2 sts, p1, kfb—11 sts.

**ext row:** K2, *p1, k1; rep from * to last st, k1.

ep this last row until work meas 4½ in.

**nc row:** Kfb, *k1, p1; rep from * to last 2 sts, k1, kfb—13 sts.

**ext row:** *K1, p1; rep from * to last st, k1.

ep this last row until work meas 7 in.

**nc row:** Kfb, *p1, k1; rep from * to last 2 sts, p1, kfb—15 sts.

**ext row:** K2, *p1, k1; rep from * to last st, k1.

Rep this last row until work meas 22 in.

**Dec row:** K2tog, *p1, k1; rep from * to last 3 sts, p1, k2tog—13 sts.

**Next row:** *K1, p1; rep from * to last st, k1.

Rep this last row until work meas 24½ in.

**Dec row:** K2tog, *k1, p1; rep from * to last 2 sts, k2tog—11 sts.

**Next row:** K1, *k1, p1; rep from * to last 2 sts, k2.

Rep this last row until work meas 26 in.

**Dec row:** K2tog, *p1, k1; rep from * to last 3 sts, p1, k2tog—9 sts.

**Next row:** *K1, p1; rep from * to last st, k1.

Rep this last row until work meas 29½ in.

Bind off in patt.

## Strap

Using 8 US (5mm) needles and yarn A, CO 9 sts.

**Row 1:** *K1, p1; rep from * to last st, k1.

Rep this first row until work meas 34 in.

Bind off in patt.

## Finishing Instructions

Steam block all pieces.

**Lining:** Lay blocked front, back, and side bag pieces on lining fabric to use as a template. Leaving ½ inch for seams, cut out lining pieces.

With right sides together, sew lining pieces together, then press and baste top and front flap edges ½ inch over to wrong sides.

With wrong sides together, sew bag pieces together ¼ inch in from edges using backstitch, leaving 4 inches loose at each end of sides to thread through D-rings.

Place lining inside bag and slip stitch into place. Thread a D-ring onto the top of each side piece and sew into place.

Thread ½ inch of end of the strap into each D-ring and sew into place.

Decorate and strengthen strap by sewing chain down the center of strap.

Sew buckle onto center front of bag to fasten.

Sew in all loose ends.

# Variation

If you're looking for something even easier, whip up this handbag with its oversized button closure. The finished size is 13½ inches wide by 13 inches high.

## Materials

- Lion Brand, Big Prints (80% Acylic/20% Wool); 5 oz/142g, 35 yd/32m: 3 skeins of A, #230 Spectacular Sunset
- Kraemer Yarns, Naturally Nazareth (100% Domestic Wool); 3.5 oz/100g, 184 yd/168m: 1 ball of B, Hayride
- 1 pair of US 17 (12.75mm) and US 8 (5mm) knitting needles
- Stitch markers
- Tapestry needle
- ½ yd lining fabric
- Sewing needle and thread
- Large button
- Handles (2)

## Gauge

6 stitches and 8 rows = 4 in/10cm worked in stockinette stitch using US 17 (12.75mm) knitting needles, or size needed to obtain gauge

## Back

Using 17 US (12.75mm) needles and yarn A, CO 4 sts.
**Row 1 (RS):** *K1, p1; rep from * to last 2 sts, k2.
**Row 2:** K2, *p1, k1; rep from * to end.
**Row 3 (inc):** CO 4 sts, *k1, p1; rep from * to last 2 sts, k2–8 sts.

**Row 4 (inc):** CO 4 sts, k2, *p1, k1; rep from * to end– 12 sts.
**Row 5 (inc):** CO 4 sts, (k1, p1) 3 times, k23, p1, k2–16 sts.
**Row 6 (inc):** CO 4 sts, k2, (p1, k1) twice, p25, (k1, p1) twice, k1–20 sts.
**Row 7:** (K1, p1) twice, k13, p1, k2.
**Row 8:** K2, p1, k1, p13, k1, p1, k1.
Rep the rows 7–8 9 times more.
BO tightly.
Make a second piece in the same way for front.

## Sides

Using 8 US (5mm) needles and yarn B, CO 2 sts.
**Row 1:** K.
**Row 2:** Kfb twice–4 sts.
**Row 3:** (K1, p1) twice.
**Row 4:** Kfb, k1, p1, kfb–6 sts.
**Row 5:** K1, (k1, p1), twice, k1.
**Row 6:** Kfb, (p1, k1), twice, kfb–8 sts.
**Row 7:** (K1, p1) 4 times.
**Row 8:** (P1, k1) 4 times.
Rep rows 7 and 8 until work meas 30 in from cast-on edge, ending with the second of these 2 rows.
**Row 9:** K2tog, (k1, p1), twice, k2tog–6 sts.
**Row 10:** (K1, p1) 3 times.
**Row 11:** K2tog, p1, k1, k2tog–4 sts.
**Row 12:** (P1, k1) twice.
**Row 13:** K2tog twice–2 sts.
**Row 14:** K2.
BO.

*continued*

*continued*

## Buttonhole Band

Using 17 US (12.75mm) needles and yarn A, CO 4 sts.

**Row 1 (RS):** (K1, p1) twice.

**Row 2:** (P1, k1) twice.

Rep last 2 rows 5 times.

**Row 13:** K1, p1; then using second ball of yarn, k1, p1.

**Row 14:** Using second ball of yarn, p1, k1; then using first ball of yarn, p1, k1.

**Row 15:** Using first ball of yarn, k1, p1; then using second ball of yarn, k1, p1.

Rep rows 14 and 15 for the length of your button, ending with the second of these 2 rows.

**Next row:** Using second ball of yarn only (p1, k1) twice.

**Next row:** (K1, p1) twice.

BO.

## Finishing Instructions

Steam block all pieces. With wrong sides together, backstitch sides to front and back pieces close to the edges. Sew buttonhole band onto center back top side of bag. Sew button onto center front top side of bag. Sew in all loose ends.

# Chapter Fifteen

◆◆◆

# Rug Rats

### Little Boy Blue/Alpha Female

Say goodbye to boring baby clothes. Knit these wild striped sweaters for the lil 'uns!

### Pampered Pooch Pullover

Man's best friend needs your love, too! Help Fido fight the freeze in his own styling sweater.

### Tutti-Frutti Baby Set

Work on your color changing by knitting this matching set for the baby of the bunch.

# Little Boy Blue/
# Alpha Female

This sweater was designed for my friends' daughter, Annabel. Her parents are not the type to dress their child in baby pinks and pastels, so I enjoyed playing with many different colors in this design. As small children are very clever at getting dirty, it had to be hard-wearing and easy to wash. The button-up raglan style is easy to get in and out of and you can complement the colors you choose with some interesting buttons. As an alternative to wool, I recommend knitting this sweater in cotton. Lion Brand, Lion Cotton is a good substitute.

## Project Rating: Summer Fling
## Cost: $50–$70
## Necessary Skills: purl (page 30); increase (page 38); stripes (page 55); knitting in the round (page 55); sc (page 87); optional: Magic Loop method (page 33); for Alpha Female only: intarsia (page 56)

## Finished Size
6–12 months [1–2 years, 2–3 years]
To fit chest: 22 [24, 26] inches

## Materials
♦ Cascade, 220 Superwash (100% Superwash Wool); 3.5 oz/100g, 220 yd/201m

### Little Boy Blue
A = 1 [1, 2] balls of #814 Blue
B = 1 ball of #838 Bubble Gum Pink
C = 1 ball of #824 Yellow
D = 1 ball of #849 Turquoise
E = 1 ball of #804 Purple
F = 1 ball of #850 Mint
G = 1 ball of #809 Red

### Alpha Female
A = 1 [1, 2] balls of #804 Purple
B = 1 ball of #836 Lt. Pink
C = 1 ball of #849 Turquoise
D = 1 ball of #824 Yellow
E = 1 ball of #848 Teal
F = 1 ball of #838 Bubble Gum Pink
G = 1 ball of #814 Mid Blue
H = 1 ball of #809 Red
I = 1 ball of #850 Mint

♦ 1 long (over 24 in) US 5 (3.75mm) circular needle for Magic Loop method, or 1 set of US 5 (3.75mm) double-pointed needles
♦ 1 long (over 24 in) US 6 (4mm) circular needle for Magic Loop method, or 1 set of US 6 (4mm) double-pointed needles
♦ Buttons (4)
♦ Stitch markers
♦ Stitch holders
♦ Tapestry needle

## Gauge

21 stitches and 27 rows = 4 in/ 10 cm worked in stockinette stitch using US 6 (4mm) knitting needles, or size needed to obtain gauge

**Note:** This pattern is worked from the top down, knitted straight to the armholes then in the round to the bottom. The sleeve stitches will be kept on stitch holders while the main part of the body is knitted.

## Stitch Pattern

### Stripe Pattern #1 (Little Boy Blue Only)

2 rows yarn B
2 rows yarn C
2 rows yarn D
2 rows yarn E
2 rows yarn F
2 rows yarn G

### Stripe Pattern #2 (Alpha Female Only)

2 rows yarn B
2 rows yarn C
2 rows yarn D
2 rows yarn E
2 rows yarn F
2 rows yarn G
2 rows yarn H
2 rows yarn I
2 rows yarn A

## Chart for Alpha Female Only

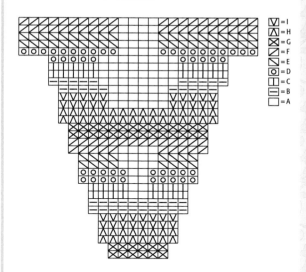

V = I
⊠ = H
⊠ = G
⊠ = F
☒ = E
⊘ = D
□ = C
— = B
□ = A

## Instructions

### Neck

Using size 5 US (3.75mm) needles and yarn A, CO 70 [86, 102] sts.

**Row 1 (RS):** *K1, p1; rep from * to end.

Rep row 1 another 5 times for rib.

Change to size 6 US (4mm) needles.

**Note:** On the next 26 [28, 30] rows, the first 2 sts on RS rows and the last 2 sts on WS rows will be worked in yarn A in garter stitch (every row knit), which will be the placket. The rest of the sts will be worked in

St st (RS rows knit, WS rows purl) and in stripe patt, as above, for either style. Be sure to twist the yarns around one another when changing colors to prevent holes from appearing.

## Little Boy Blue Only

**Row 7 (RS):** K2 A, pm, start first color in stripe patt, kfb, k19 [23, 27], kfb, pm, k2, pm, kfb, k7 [11, 15], kfb, pm, k2, pm, kfb, k20 [24, 28], kfb, pm, k2, pm, kfb, k7 [11, 15], kfb, pm, k1 — 78 [94, 110] sts.

**Row 8:** K1, p to last 2 sts, k2 A.

## Alpha Female Only

**Row 7 (RS):** K2 A, pm, kfb, k19 [23, 27], kfb, pm, k1, change to first color in stripe patt, k1, pm, kfb, k7 [11, 15], kfb, pm, k1, change to color A, k1, pm, kfb, k20 [24, 28], kfb, pm, k1, change to first color in stripe patt, k1, pm, kfb, k7 [11, 15], kfb, pm, k1 — 78 [94, 110] sts.

**Row 8:** K1, p to last 2 sts in colors as set, k2 A.

## Both Styles

**Row 9 (RS):** Following stripe patt, and maintaining garter st in A over first 2 sts, k to end, inc into st after first, third, fifth, and seventh markers and into st before second, forth, sixth, and eighth markers — 86 [102, 118] sts.

**Row 10:** K1, p to last 2 sts in colors as set, k2 A.

## Alpha Female Only

**Rep** rows 9–10 10 [11, 12] times — 166 [190, 214] sts.

**Next row (RS):** K2 A, kfb, k21 [24, 27], using color G k6 — starting the first row of the chart, then change to color A and continue the row as set including the inc — 174 [198, 222] sts.

**Next row:** K1, p to last 2 sts in colors as set, k2 A.

**Next row (RS):** CO 2 sts, k21 [24, 27], then using color H, k8 from third row of chart, then continue in color A, k21 [24, 27], turn, CO 4 sts, turn, put next 37 [43, 49] sts for first sleeve onto a holder, k across next 50 [56, 62] sts for back, turn, CO 2 sts, turn, put last 37 [43, 49] sts for second sleeve onto a holder — 108 [120, 132 sts].

**Join** into a rnd, placing marker between first and last st.

**Next 29 rnds:** Cont to k every st, following chart, maintaining intarsia stripe patt, starting with second row.

**When** intarsia patt is completed, k all rnds in color A only until body meas 10½ [12, 13] in from cast-on edge.

**Change** to size 5 US (3.75mm) needles.

**Next rnd:** *K1, p1; rep from * to end.

**Rep** last rnd another 4 times.

Bind off in rib.

## Sleeves

Using next color in stripe sequence, where you left off for the sleeve, CO 2 sts, then k across 37 [43, 49] sts from holder, turn, CO 2 sts—41 [47, 53] sts.

Knit 8 rnds, maintaining stripe patt.

Next rnd (dec): K1, k2tog, k to last 3 sts, ssk, k1—39 [45, 51] sts.

Knit 7 rnds.

Rep last 8 rnds 2 [3, 3] times, then rep dec rnd once more—33 [37, 43] sts.

## Second and Third Sizes Only

Work a further [2, 6] rnds without shaping.

## All Sizes

Change to size 5 US (3.75mm) needles and color A.

Next rnd: K2tog, p1,* k1, p1; rep from * to end.

Next rnd: * K1, p1; rep from * to end.

Rep last rnd another 3 times.

Bind off in rib.

Rep for second sleeve.

## Little Boy Blue Only

Rep last 2 rows 11 [12, 13] times—174 [198, 222] sts.

Next row (RS): Using color A only, CO 2 sts, k50 [55, 60], turn, CO 4 sts, turn, put next 37 [43, 49] sts for first sleeve onto a holder, k across next 50 [55, 60] sts for back, turn, CO 2 sts, turn, put last 37 [43, 49] sts for second sleeve onto a holder—108 [118, 128] sts.

Join into a rnd, placing marker between first and last st.

Working in color A only, k every rnd until body measures 10½ [12, 13] in from cast-on edge.

Change to size 5 US (3.75mm) needles.

Next rnd: *K1, p1; rep from * to end.

Rep last rnd another 4 times.

Bind off in rib.

## Sleeves

Using color A, CO 2 sts, then k across 37 [43, 49] sts from holder, turn, CO 2 sts—41 [47, 53] sts.

Join into a rnd, placing marker between first and last st.

Working in color A only, k 8 rnds.

Next rnd (dec): K1, k2tog, k to last 3 sts, ssk, k1—39 [45, 51] sts.

Next rnd: K 7 rnds.

Rep last 8 rnds 2 [3, 3] times, then rep dec rnd once more—33 [37, 43] sts.

### Second and Third Sizes Only

Work a further [2, 6] rnds without shaping.

### All Sizes

Change to size 5 US (3.75mm) needles.

Next rnd: K2tog, p1,* k1, p1; rep from * to end.

Next rnd: * K1, p1; rep from * to end.

Rep last rnd another 3 times.

Bind off in rib.

Rep for second sleeve.

## Finishing Instructions

Sew up underarm seams.

Buttonholes: With RS facing, start at the top of the front raglan placket and single crochet a row of 24 [27, 30] sts to bottom of opening, turn, then chain 2, skip the first loop, then single crochet 1 st (chain 3, skip 2 loops and single crochet 4 [5, 6] sts) rep twice, chain 3, skip 2 loops and single crochet 1 st. Cut yarn and draw through loop.

Sew 4 buttons onto other side of raglan opening to match placement of button-holes. Sew in all loose ends.

### Variation

This pattern can be the base for many types of baby sweaters. To make a comfy and cozy roll-neck sweater, start the neck with two to three rows of stockinette stitch. Finish the cuffs and the bottom sweater edging the same way. Rather than work the intarsia alpha symbol, work the child's initial in intarsia or work in your own motif.

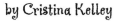

# Pampered Pooch Pullover

### by Cristina Kelley

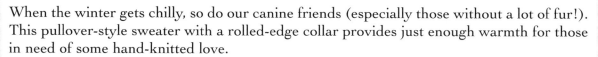

When the winter gets chilly, so do our canine friends (especially those without a lot of fur!). This pullover-style sweater with a rolled-edge collar provides just enough warmth for those in need of some hand-knitted love.

**Project Rating:** Summer Fling

**Cost:** $12–$24

**Necessary Skills:** purl (page 30); pick up stitches (page 67); increase (page 38), optional: Magic Loop method (page 33)

## Finished Size

Fits chest: 14 [18, 22, 26, 30] inches

## Materials

- Harrisville Designs, New England Highland (100% Pure Wool); 3.5 oz/100g, 200 yd/182.88m:
    - MC: 1 [1, 2, 2, 3] skeins #07 Tundra
    - CC: 1 [1, 1, 1, 1] skein #41 Sandalwood
- 1 pair of US 6 (4.25mm) needles
- 1 pair of US 7 (4.5mm) needles and 1 set of US 6 (4.25mm) double-pointed needles, or 1 long US 6 (4.25mm) circular needle if using the Magic Loop method
- Stitch holders

## Gauge

14 stitches and 24 rows = 4 in/10cm worked in stockinette stitch using US 7 (4.5mm) needles, or size needed to obtain gauge

## Instructions

### Collar

The sweater is worked in one piece, from the collar down.

Using smaller needles and CC, CO 35 [47, 55, 63, 73] sts. Work in St st for 2½ [3, 3½, 4, 4] in, ending with a purl row.

### Body

Change to MC and larger needles.

Starting with a knit row, work 2 rows in St st.

**Next row (inc):** K1fb, k to last 2 sts, k1fb, k1.

**Next row:** P.

Rep these 2 rows 6 [7, 10, 13, 15] more times—49 [63, 77, 91, 105] sts.

Work even until piece measures 3½ [4, 4½, 5½, 6] in from color change.

## Foreleg Holes

The sweater will be seamed down the front and belly; one foreleg hole is made on each side. Sleeves will be picked up and knit later.

On next WS row: P5 [7, 9, 11, 13] sts, BO next 5 [7, 9, 11, 13] sts, p29 [35, 41, 47, 53] sts, BO 5 [7, 9, 11,13] sts, p rem 5 [7, 9, 11, 13] sts.

Starting with a k row, work 8 [10, 16, 18, 22] rows in St st on the first 5 [7, 9, 11, 13] sts. Break yarn and move sts to holder.

Starting with a k row, work 8 [10, 16, 18, 22] rows in St st on center 29 [35, 41, 47, 53] sts. Break yarn and move sts to holder.

Starting with a k row, work 8 [10, 16, 18, 22] rows in St st on the last 5 [7, 9, 11, 13] sts. Do not break yarn.

On next row (RS): K5 [7, 9, 11, 13] sts, CO 5 [7, 9, 11, 13] sts, k to end of back section, CO 5 [7, 9, 11, 13] sts, k5 [7, 9, 11, 13] sts.

Work these three sections for the leg openings at the same time for 8 [10, 16, 18, 22] rows, ending on a purl row.

Work without shaping until piece measures 7 [10½, 13, 17, 21] in from color change.

Change to smaller needles and CC and work in k1, p1 ribbing for 1 [1, 1½, 1½, 2] in.

Bind off all sts.

## Sleeves

With RS of work facing you, using size 6 dpns, pick up 24 [30, 42, 48, 60] sts evenly spaced around the four sides of the armhole.

Place marker, join rnd, and work in k1, p1 ribbing for 1 [1, 1½, 1½, 2] in.

Bind off loosely in ribbing.

Work second sleeve same as first.

## Finishing Instructions

Sew center front seam, from top of collar to bottom of sweater (including hem). Sew in all loose ends.

---

## Variation

Instead of k1, p1 ribbing for sweater hem, try garter, seed, or moss stitch. Add in stripes for the body and/or different colors for the sleeves. You could finish the body 2–3 inches shorter (your dog can try it on before you bind off if he's patient) for a more cropped look if your boy tends to wet his sweater.

With contrasting yarn, embroider your pet's initial on the back of the sweater!

# Tutti-Frutti Baby Set

### by Alison Stewart-Guinee

Worked in mosaic knitting, this pattern offers an opportunity to achieve the look of complex color work without having to carry or strand your yarn. Designed to be fun and whimsical, the set is sure to send those winter blues packing and transition easily to a summer beach set for your favorite little bathing beauty.

**Project Rating:** Summer Fling

**Cost:** Blanket, $50; hat and bag, $15 to $25 each

**Necessary Skills:** purl (page 30); three-needle bind-off (page 69)

## Finished Size

Blanket: 32 inches square

Hat: fits 6 to 12 months

Bag: 13½ inches wide by 13 inches high (to bag top)

## Materials

- Tahki Cotton Classic (100% Mercerized Cotton); 1.75 oz/50g, 108 yd/100m:

    MC1: 5 skeins #3401 Tangerine (blanket, 3; hat and bag, 1 each)

    MC2: 5 skeins #3456 Berry pink (blanket, 3; hat and bag, 1 each)

    CC1: 4 skeins #3947 Red purple (blanket, 2½; hat, 1; bag, ½)

    CC2: 4 skeins #3723 Chartreuse (blanket, 2; bag, 2; hat, partial skein)

- For blanket: 1 set of US 4 (3.5mm) double-pointed needles; 1 US 5 (3.75mm) 24-in and 1 40-in circular needle

- For hat: 1 set of US 4 (3.5mm) and 1 set of US 5 (3.75mm) double-pointed needles; 1 US 5 (3.75mm) 16-in circular needle

- For bag: 1 set of US 4 (3.5mm) double-pointed needles; 1 US 4 (3.5mm) 16-in needle; 1 US 5 (3.75mm) 24-in circular needle

## Gauge

22 stitches and 28 rows = 4 in/10cm worked in stockinette stitch using US 5 (3.75mm) circular needle, or size needed to obtain gauge

## Stitch Pattern

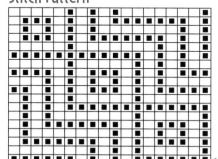

← Begin row 1 here

Mosaic knitting is a method of two-color slip stitch knitting. Each row is comprised of knitted and slipped stitches. One strand of yarn is used alone across a row and back. Colors are alternated every two rows and the color not in use is left untouched at the beginning of the row. Slipped stitches are always slipped as if to purl with the yarn at the wrong side of the work. Work even-numbered rows exactly like the preceding row, slipping the slipped stitches and working the knitted stitches.

To maintain garter stitch when knitting in the round, as for the hat and bag, stitches are knit and slipped on odd rounds and are purled and slipped on even rounds. When knitting flat, as for the blanket, stitches are slipped and knit on both right- and wrong-side rows.

The mosaic chart is 18 sts by 36 rows. Each of the 18 rows in the chart represents two rows or rounds of work. Begin by reading the chart from bottom to top. When knitting the blanket, the mosaic section is knitted flat and thus the chart is read from right to left on right-side rows and from left to right on wrong-side rows. When knitting in the round, as for the hat and bag, the chart is worked from right to left on both even and odd rounds. White squares represent MC1; black squares represent MC2.

Each triangle is worked separately and then knitted on to the piece. On smaller double-point needles, CO 2, turn, K2, turn, *yo once, k to end, turn, rep from * until you have the desired number of sts (14 for the blanket and 9 for the bag and hat). The last row of each triangle will be worked plain (purled on the blanket and hat triangles and knit on the bag triangles). Do not bind off; cut yarn, leaving triangles on needle. Repeat for desired number of triangles. Knit triangles to piece by placing the needle with the triangles in front of your work (the tail of the triangle should be coming from the right side of triangle).

If you're knitting the triangles on double-pointed needles and leaving them on needles, you need to slip all of the triangles (with same side facing) onto a spare (smaller diameter) circular needle, since you can't fit 18 triangles onto a few dpns.

## Instructions

Knit the first triangle st together with the first st of the piece. Continue across triangle sts.

### Garter Ridge

Rnd 1: K.

Rnd 2: P.

On the blanket only, 2 inc are worked at each corner of the purl rows.

Inc rnd for garter and stockinette rows: Inc will be worked every other rnd as you k out to the edge of the blanket. One inc will be made before and after each corner st (8 inc per inc rnd). In garter stitch sections, the inc will always occur on a p rnd. *K corner st, k, and then p into the next st, p to 1 st before the marker, p and k into the st before the marker, pass marker, rep from * to end of rnd. On the stockinette sections, inc will be worked the same way except that the sts between inc will all be knitted.

## Beaded Ridge

**Rnd 1:** *Sl 1, k1; rep from * around.

**Rnd 2:** Sl the slipped sts and p the knit sts.

Inc will continue on beaded rnds as before, however, it requires a little adjustment. Inc on the beaded ridge will always be worked on rnd 2. Knit corner st at the beginning of the rnd. Use the point of the right needle to pick up the bar from the previous rnd on the left side of the corner st. The bar will be the same color as the slipped sts. Keep the bar on the right needle to be worked on the next rnd. P1, sl 1 across to next marker, pick up the bar to the right of corner st, pass marker, k corner st, and pick up the bar to the left of the corner st. Cont in this manner, working 2 inc at each corner and ending by picking up the second inc for the initial corner st of the rnd.

## Blanket

**With** the 24-in US 5 (3.75mm) circular needle and MC1, CO 56 sts. This includes 2 selvedge sts with 3 patt repeats in between.

**Row 1 (RS):** Join MC2 and k1, place marker, *work first row of chart, knitting sts to be worked with MC2 (black squares) and slipping sts to be worked with MC1 (white squares), place marker, rep from * twice more, end with k1 in MC2.

**Note:** Selvedge sts will always be knitted with the working yarn for each row. This forms the first RS row.

**Row 2 (WS):** Cont with MC2, work back across row 1, knitting and slipping the same sts that you did on the first pass of this row. Yarn is always on the WS of the work when slipping sts. Remember to maintain garter stitch when knitting flat; the sts to be worked will be knitted on both RS and WS rows.

**Row 3:** With MC1, k1, pass marker, work second line of chart (working up from the bottom), this time knitting the MC1 sts and slipping the MC2 sts, pass marker, end k1 MC1.

**Row 4:** Cont with MC1, work another pass of line 2 of chart.

**Cont** in this manner for the remainder of the chart. Rep the 36 rows of the mosaic twice more. End by rep line 1 of the chart once more, keeping in mind that one line of the chart produces 2 rows of knitting (110 rows total).

**With** RS facing, knit across with MC1. This is the last row that will be knit flat. From here sts will be picked up on the remaining three sides and the work will be knit in the round.

**Change** to the 40-in US 5 (3.75mm) circular needle. Cont with MC1, *place a marker, rotate the piece to the right, and pick up 56 sts along this edge. Rep from * twice more. Once 56 sts on the third side have been picked up, place a marker of a different color from the other three. This will mark the beg of the rnd. Pass this marker, pick up 1 st by knitting into the bar between the first two sts of the previous rnd, p across the 56 live sts on the needle (these sts made up the final row of the mosaic), *pass marker, pick up 1 corner st kwise as before, p the 56 sts picked up on the previous rnd, rep from * twice more. You will have 57 sts between markers, 228 sts in all.

Garter stitch and stockinette bands comprise the remainder of the piece. The garter stitch band sections are made up of garter ridges and beaded ridges. The stockinette bands form the background for the triangle sections. On the blanket, all sections include inc worked every other rnd. Inc are made as described in the previous "Stitch Pattern" section, before and after the corner sts on every other rnd, creating 8 new sts every 2 rnds. Inc are always worked on the even rnds. These will be the purled rnds of the garter and beaded ridge sections. Move to longer circular needles as needed.

**Garter section 1:** 1 garter ridge CC1 (236 sts), 1 of MC2 (244 sts), 2 of CC1 (260 sts), 1 beaded ridge MC1 (268 sts), 2 garter ridge CC1 (284 sts), 1 of MC2 (292 sts), 1 of CC1 (300 sts), 1 of MC1 (308 sts), and 1 of MC2 (316 sts).

**Triangle section 1:** With US 4 (3.5mm) dpns and CC1, make 20 triangles as described above (14 sts each). With MC2, k first 2 blanket sts, *join triangle by knitting it and the corresponding blanket sts tog, k1 blanket st, rep from * across (there will be 1 st in between each triangle). At each corner

you will k the corner st and 1 st on either side of it plain. After joining all 20 triangles, k 12 rows MC2, working inc every other rnd as for garter ridge (364 sts).

**Garter section 2:** 1 garter ridge MC1 (372 sts), 1 of CC2 (380 sts), 1 of CC1 (388 sts), 2 of CC2 (404 sts), 1 beaded ridge MC2 (412 sts), 2 garter ridge CC2 (428 sts), 1 of CC1 (436 sts), 1 of CC2 (444 sts), 1 of MC1 (452 sts), 1 of CC1 (460 sts).

**Triangle section 2:** With MC2, make 32 triangles. Using CC1, attach triangles, omitting the st between triangles and maintaining the 3 single knit sts at the corners. K 12 rows CC1 continuing in established pattern (508 sts).

**Garter section 3:** 1 garter ridge CC2 (516 sts), 1 of MC1 (524 sts), 1 of MC2 (532 sts), 2 of MC1 (548 sts), 1 beaded ridge CC2 (556 sts), 2 garter ridge MC1 (572 sts), 1 of MC2 (580 sts), 1 of MC1 (588 sts), and 1 of CC2 (596 sts).

**Triangle edging:** With CC1, k 40 triangles. Beg at the marker and using CC1, k the triangles to the blanket, knitting 1 blanket st between each triangle except for at each of the four corners. Cont with CC1, BO blanket edge.

## Hat
The hat is worked in the round throughout.

**Rnd 1:** With CC1 and US 4 (3.5mm) 16-in circular needle, CO 90 sts, place marker, join rnd, taking care not to twist sts.

**Rnds 2–7:** P.

**Rnd 8:** K1 CC2, Sl 1 around.

**Rnd 9:** P1 CC2, Sl 1 around.

**Rnds 10–12:** With CC1, p.

## Closing the Hatband

With the RS facing, reach behind the work with the point of the left needle. Pick up the first st of the cast-on row. Using CC1, k this st together with the first live st on the left needle. Cont around, picking up sts from the cast-on row one at a time, and knitting them tog with the corresponding live sts on the needle, forming a tube for the hatband.

## Mosaic Band

With larger 16-in circular needle and MC1, k 1 rnd.

**Next rnd:** Cont with MC1, *P4, inc 1 (k and p into the same st), rep from * six times to end of rnd (108 sts).

Join MC2 and work through chart (36 rnds). The mosaic band will measure approx 3 in from the hatband.

Work 1 garter ridge CC1.

With CC2, k 12 triangles of 9 sts each as described previously. P last row. Attach to hat by knitting each triangle st tog with a corresponding hat st. Each triangle is attached one right next to another with no spare sts placed between, knitting with CC1 for the rest of the project.

Knit 1 rnd, placing a marker after every twelfth st.

**Next rnd:** *K10, k2tog, pass marker, rep from * to end of rnd—99 sts.

**Next rnd:** K.

**Next rnd:** *K9, k2tog; rep from * to end of rnd—90 sts.

**Next rnd:** K.

Working in St st, decrease 9 sts every other rnd as established (and moving to dpns when circular becomes too long), until 9 sts rem. K in rnds on these 9 sts for a further 3 in. BO and knot the top.

## Bag

With CC2 and smaller dpns, CO 6 sts. Divide evenly onto 3 needles. Join, placing a marker after each st. P 1 rnd.

**Rnd 1:** K1, make 1, pass marker—12 sts.

**Rnd 2:** P.

Cont alternating these 2 rnds until you have 27 sts per section (162 sts total), moving to 16-in and 24-in circular needles as needles become crowded.

With smaller dpns and MC2, make 18 triangles of 9 sts each. K the last row of each triangle.

With larger 24-in needle and CC1, k triangles to bag by knitting triangle sts tog with the corresponding sts on the bag.

Cont with larger circular needle and CC1, p 1 rnd.

Garter ridge CC1 once, MC1 once, MC2 once, CC1 once.

Beaded ridge CC2 once.

Garter ridge CC1 once, MC2 once, MC1 once, CC1 twice, end MC1 once.

Work mosaic chart all the way through, from bottom to top twice as follows. After knitting through all of the lines of the chart once (36 rnds), begin again at the first line of the chart and work through it a second time from bottom to top (another 36 rnds, for 72 rnds total). This section is worked over 162 sts, making 9 repeats of the mosaic around the bag. End by repeating the first line of the chart (74 rows and approx 6 in).

With smaller 24-in circular needle, work garter ridge MC2 once, CC1 twice, MC1 once, and CC2 twice. The length from the triangle edging to the top edge of the bag is approx 9 in.

## Bag Top and Handles

Bind off 10 sts, k 61 sts and put on holder for later, BO 20 sts, k 61 sts, BO remaining 10 sts. Cut yarn, leaving a long tail for weaving in later.

Handles are worked back and forth in rows. With WS facing, join CC2 to the 61 sts rem on needle and work first handle as follows:

Row 1: K.

Row 2: Sl 1, ssk, k to the last 3 sts, k2tog, k1—59 sts.

Row 3: Sl 1, k to end.

Rep these last two rows until 15 sts remain (approx 4 in).

Knit back and forth on these 15 sts, always slipping the first st, for a further 6 in. End with a WS row, leaving sts on needle. Handle length will be approx 10 in.

Rep for second handle.

Connect handles by working a three-needle bind-off with the right sides of the work together.

## Finishing Instructions

Weave in all ends, lightly block blanket, line blanket and/or bag if desired.

## Variation

Knitted mosaics not your thing? Omit the mosaic panel and knit it solid, striped, or in a textural stitch pattern. Or let the yarn do the work for you by knitting these patterns with a combination of novelty yarns such as eyelash and ribbon yarns, along with basic dk weight yarns, to produce a project that is both fun and texturally interesting.

# Chapter Sixteen

◆◆

# Home Buddies

### Hearts & Stars

Large intarsia motif cushions are knitted in one piece and buttoned up at the back.

### Loopy Landing

By wrapping yarn around your thumb, do your feet a favor and knit up the softest-ever bath or shower mat.

### Indulge

Keep your hands warm and your pleasure cold with these ice cream and beer cozies.

# Hearts & Stars

Dress up your sofa with some bright and cheerful cushions. Choose colors that either match or complement your décor. These covers are knitted in one long piece, then folded, seamed, and buttoned up on their stripy backs.

**Project Rating:** Summer Fling

**Cost:** $30 for each cover

**Necessary Skills:** purl (page 30); intarsia (page 56); stripes (page 55); buttonholes (page 70)

## Finished Size
Fits 15¾-inch-square cushion pad

## Materials
- Brown Sheep, Lamb's Pride Bulky (85% Wool/15% Mohair); 4 oz/113g, 125 yd/114m:
  - 2 skeins of color A (I used M81 Red Barron for Heart and #120 Limeade for Star)
  - 2 skeins of color B (I used #150 RPM Pink for Heart and #155 Lemon Drop for Star)
- 1 pair of US 10½ (6.5mm) knitting needles
- Tapestry needle
- Buttons (4)
- Cushion pad (15¾ x 15¾-in)

## Gauge
13½ stitches and 18 rows = 4 in/10cm worked in stockinette stitch using US 10½ (6.5mm) knitting needles, or size needed to obtain gauge

## Stitch Pattern
See figures on pages 219–220.

## Instructions

Using US 10½ (6.5mm) knitting needles or size needed to obtain gauge and color A, CO 50 sts.

Work in seed stitch as folls:

**Row 1 (RS):** K1, * p1, k1; rep from * to last st, k1.

**Row 2:** K2, * p1, k1; rep from * to end. (I like to knit the first and last st in every row to give a firm and even edge.)

Rep rows 1–2 once.

**Row 5:** Using color A (k1, p1) twice, using color B k42, using color A k1, p1, k2.

**Row 6:** Using color A k2, p1, k1, using color B p42, using color A (p1, k1) twice.

**Row 7:.** Using color A (k1, p1) twice, k43, p1, k2.

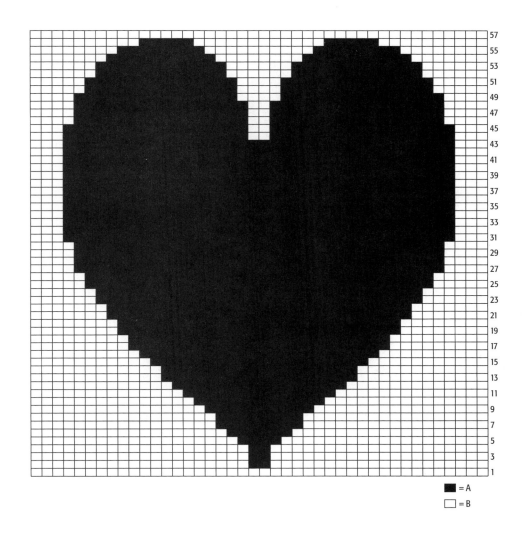

57
55
53
51
49
47
45
43
41
39
37
35
33
31
29
27
25
23
21
19
17
15
13
11
9
7
5
3
1

■ = A
□ = B

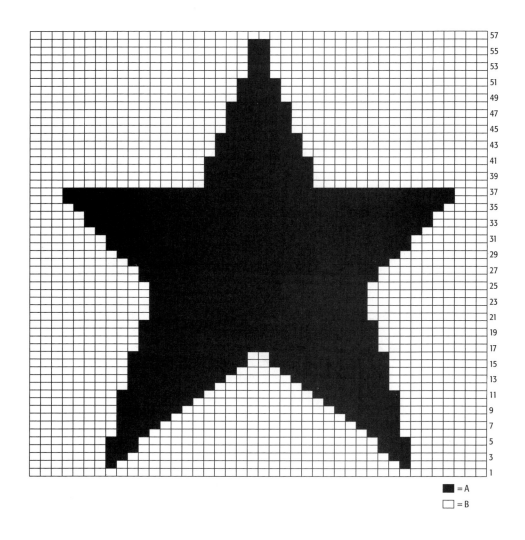

57
55
53
51
49
47
45
43
41
39
37
35
33
31
29
27
25
23
21
19
17
15
13
11
9
7
5
3
1

■ = A
□ = B

**Row 8:** Using color A k2, p1, k1, p43, k1, p1, k1.

Rep rows 5–8 10 times.

Rep rows 5–6 once.

Using color A, rep rows 1–2 3 times.

Purl 1 row.

**Next row (WS):** Work as for row 2.

**Next row (RS):** Work as for row 1.

Rep last 2 rows twice.

**Next row (WS):** Work as for row 6.

**Next row (RS):** Work as for row 5.

**Next row (WS):** Work as for row 6.

Keeping the 4 sts at both sides of work as set in patt and color A, follow the graph for intarsia design (57 rows).

**Next row (WS):** Work as for row 6.

**Next row (RS):** Work as for row 5.

**Next row (WS):** Work as for row 6.

**Next row (RS):** Work as for row 1.

**Next row (WS):** Work as for row 2.

Rep last 2 rows twice.

Purl 1 row.

**Next row (WS):** Work as for row 2.

**Next row (RS):** Work as for row 1.

**Next row (WS):** Work as for row 2.

Rep last 2 rows.

Rep rows 5–8 4 times.

**Next row (RS):** Work as for row 5.

**Next row (WS):** Work as for row 6.

**Next row (RS):** Work as for row 1.

**Next row (WS):** Work as for row 2.

**Buttonhole row:** (K1, p1) 3 times, yon, k2tog, (k1, p1) 5 times, yon, k2tog, (k1, p1) 5 times, yon, k2tog, (k1, p1) 5 times, yon, k2tog, (k1, p1) twice, k2.

**Next row (WS):** Work as for row 2.

**B**ind off in patt.

## Finishing Instructions

**U**sing P rows as fold lines, fold work so that buttonhole band overlaps button band at start of work. With wrong sides together, and matching k st bumps at edges of work, pin then backstitch cushion cover sides together, sewing though all 3 thicknesses at button and buttonhole bands.

**S**ew in all loose ends neatly.

**B**lock, then sew buttons opposite buttonholes.

# Variation

Using this pattern as a base, design your own fun and funky cushion covers with wild and wonderful colors and textures. Make up your own intarsia charts by drawing your design directly onto graph paper–visit these sites for printing your own graph paper to suit your gauge:

- ◆ www.tata-tatao.to/knit/matrix/e-index.html
- ◆ www.thedietdiary.com/knittingfiend/KnittersGraph.html

Or check out www.microrevolt.org/knitpro.htm to upload your design and see your image magically morphed into a chart ready for you to knit!

Cover your cushions in stripes, cables, or bobbles. Use the stitch from Loopy Landing (see next pattern) to make a plush cover in snuggly-soft yarn.

# Loopy Landing

Step out of the shower onto this gorgeously soft, plush mat. I made mine in organic cotton in a natural ecru shade that will fit into any color scheme; you could go for a bolder look with a solid color or stripes. Your feet will thank you for it! The absorbent quality of cotton makes this yarn ideal for the bathroom. One of my students wants to make a matching toilet seat cover!

**Project Rating:** Flirtation

**Cost:** $37–$74

**Necessary Skills:** slip stitch (page 67)

## Finished Size

Shower mat: 24 x 16 inches; bathmat: 24 x 32 inches

## Materials

- Blue Sky Organic Cotton (100% Organic Cotton), 3.5 oz/100g, 150 yd/137m; color #80 Bone:
    - 4 balls (for shower mat)
    - 8 balls (for bathmat)
- 1 pair of US 7 (4.5mm) knitting needles

## Gauge

14 stitches and 22 rows = 4 in/10cm measured over loopy stitch using US 7 (4.5mm) knitting needles, or size needle to obtain gauge

## Loopy Stitch Pattern

**Row 1 (RS):** K1 without slipping st from left needle. Bring yarn from back to front between the needles. Wrap yarn counterclockwise around tip of left thumb to create a loop, then bring yarn to the back between the needles. K into the same st once more, bringing it up and off the left needle. (You now have 2 sts on the right needle.) Insert the point of the left needle into the first st on the right needle, then pass first st over second and off the needle.

**Row 2:** K.

Rep these 2 rows until you reach length required.

## Instructions

Using US 7 (4.5mm) knitting needles, CO 84 sts.

**Foundation row (WS):** K into the back of every st.

Work in loopy stitch pattern until mat measures 16 in for shower mat or 32 in for bathmat, or longer if you want a bigger mat.

Bind off.

### Finishing Instructions

Fold bound-off edge to back of mat just after last row of loops, then, using a tapestry needle threaded with a long length of yarn, slip stitch into place. This leaves a nice loopy finished edge to match the loops at the cast-on edge.

## Variation

- Go for that kitchy look in your bedroom by knitting up the bathmat-sized rug in some bright-colored Lion Brand Fun Fur.

- Knit up a hearth rug in a color to match your living room décor for a more sophisticated vibe with a warm and cozy yarn like Brown Sheep, Lamb's Pride, which comes in a huge selection of colors.

- Use the loopy stitch for cushion covers by working up a 12 x 24-inch rectangle, then fold, seam, and stuff with a 12-inch cushion pad to liven up the couch.

- Pick up stitches around the edge of a hat or mittens and knit 4 to 6 rows of loopy stitch for a shaggy trim.

# Indulge

### by Claudine Monique

We've all done it: taken the pint of ice cream out of the freezer, pulled a spoon out of the drawer, and sat down in front of the TV. Before you know it your hand is really cold. Haven't you ever wondered what you could do to prevent the hand freeze? Wonder no more. Go ahead, indulge in the pint. This is a quick project and a great way to use up some yarn from your stash! It only takes a few hours to make and would be a fabulous last-minute present.

**Project Rating:** Flirtation

**Cost:** About $15 (or you can make a few cozies out of a skein using yarn from your stash)

**Necessary Skills:** duplicate stitch (page 74); decrease (page 40); optional: Magic Loop method (page 33)

## Finished Size

Cuff: about 9 inches, length: 4½ inches

## Materials

### For Version 1
- MC: Patons Classic Merino Wool (100% Wool); 3.5 oz/100g, 223 yd/205m, 1 skein of #00222 Sage
- CC: Cascade 220 (100% Wool), 3.5 oz/100g, 220 yd/201m, 1 skein of #8010 Cream

### For Version 2
- MC: Patons Classic Merino Wool (100% Wool); 3.5 oz/100g, 223 yd/205m, 1 skein of #00226 Black
- CC: Kraemer Yarns, Naturally Nazareth (100% Wool); 3.5 oz/100g, 184 yd/168m, 1 skein of Bloom

- 1 set of US 5 (75mm) double-pointed needles, or 1 long (over 24 in) US 5 (3.75mm) circular needle if using Magic Loop method
- Stitch marker

## Gauge

20 stitches and 32 rows = 4 in worked in stockinette stitch using US 5 (3.75mm) needles, or size needed to obtain correct gauge. This gauge is intentionally tight to soak up any condensation and keep your hand really warm.

## Stitch Pattern

See figure on pages 226–227.

## Instructions

Using MC, CO 48 sts with smaller needles. Being careful not to twist sts, join for working in the rnd, placing marker between first and last st. Beg by working 4 rows in a k2, p2 rib. Switch to St st (k every rnd) and work even until piece measures 4½ in from cast-on row. You are now finished with the body of the cozy. P1 rnd; this forms the ridge at the base of the pint. K3 rnds even. Begin dec for base of pint.

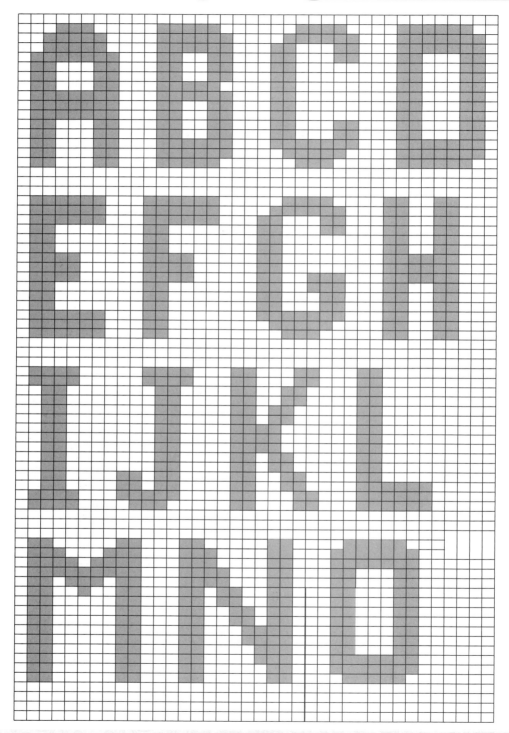

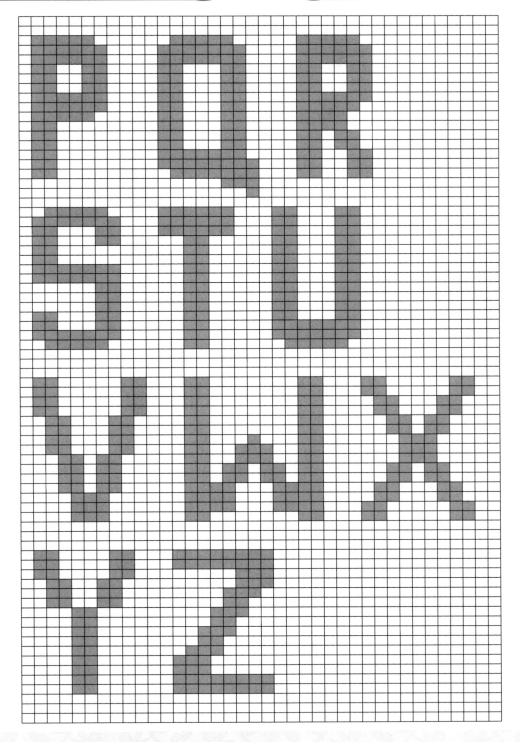

**Rnd 1:** *K6, k2tog* rep from * to end—42 sts.

**Rnd 2:** *K5, k2tog* rep from * to end—36 sts.

**Rnd 3:** *K4, k2tog* rep from * to end—30 sts.

**Rnd 4:** *K3, k2tog* rep from * to end—24 sts.

**Rnd 5:** *K2, k2tog* rep from * to end—18 sts.

**Rnd 6:** *K1, k2tog* rep from * to end—12 sts.

**Rnd 7:** *K2tog* rep from * to end—6 sts.

## Finishing Instructions

Break yarn, leaving about 6 in, and thread through remaining 6 sts. Pull through to WS. Weave in all ends.

Using the chart provided and CC yarn, begin duplicate stitch with the initial of your choice about 8 rnds from the bottom ridge.

Weave in all ends, and enjoy!

## Variation

Have you ever put your beer down at a party for only a few minutes, only to return to find four beers where you put yours down? A good way to help prevent beer bottle identity theft is to make a beer cozy using the initial chart. CO 36 sts in the same gauge as for Indulge and work for 4½ inches, then beg the dec starting with rnd 3 as stated previously.

Some other good ideas to use up your stash would be to do a stripe pattern, or chose yarns in the same color family with different textures.

# · Part Three ·

## Junk in the Trunk

# Chapter Seventeen

◆◆◆

# Make the Buy

When you are as passionate about knitting as I am and some of my creative friends are, you find yourself wanting to read everything you can on the subject. Luckily for us there are growing numbers of publications filling the shelves of bookshops, trying to entice you into being the one you take home. But how do you choose from such an array?

You already have this book in your hands, so hopefully that means that you own it. If not, what are you waiting for? Run to the checkout and buy it, for heaven's sake! Good.

Now, you want another book to keep this one company at home, right? Then I'll give you my choices.

## Book Reviews

As a sweater designer, I often use stitch pattern books when searching for different textures I can play with. The whole look of a piece can be dramatically altered by simply changing the stitch. Try knitting small swatches of one yarn in many stitches and you see for yourself how different one yarn can look knitted up.

The first knitting book I ever bought was *The Harmony Guide to Knitting Stitches, Volume One* (Lyric Books Ltd., 1988). This was quickly followed by *Volume Two*. I used them constantly during my four years of studying knitwear design, and I still use them today. They are well written, easy to understand, and have good, clear photographs of hundreds of different stitches ranging from simple knits and purls through color work and more intricate lace and cable stitches. My designs would not have been so successful if I had not used these valuable additions to my library.

I was recently given the first two books in the series of four by Barbara G. Walker: *A Treasury of Knitting Patterns* (Schoolhouse Press, 1998). Thanks to the amazing work of the very talented Ms. Walker, these books contain a wealth of stitches, many a lot more complicated than the *Harmony Guides*. Don't be afraid to try out new stitches. By knitting only a small swatch, you can quickly see how much fun it is to watch the texture pattern appear before choosing your favorite and trying it out on a full-sized piece.

If you are only going to buy one stitch book, I would recommend *The Ultimate Sourcebook of Knitting and Crochet Stitches* from *Reader's Digest* (2003). It includes a lot of the same stitches from the *Harmony Guides,* but they are all in one book and categorized by weight. Having crochet as well as knitting stitches all together helps a designer find what she needs without having to pull several books from the shelf.

For any beginner, I would recommend Maggie Righetti's *Knitting in Plain English* (St. Martin's Press, 1986). Not only does she let you in on many tricks of the trade in a down-to-earth, conversational tone, but this woman is funny—we all need to laugh more—why not have a good old chuckle while you're learning a new craft? This book opens with the chapter "You can always tell what's wrong with the garment by the way the model is posed." Too true!

What can I write about Debbie Stoller that hasn't already been said? I love this woman—she's just fabulous! Her *Stitch 'n Bitch—The Knitter's Handbook* (Workman Publishing, 2003) has turned many a young thing onto the knitting buzz. Her unique writing style has you hanging on every word. The directions are easy to understand, and this book contains just about everything a beginner could need. The good variation of patterns contributed from designers around the globe are cute and imaginative. This book was a definite breath of fresh air for all knitters.

Ms. Stoller's second knitting book, *Stitch 'n Bitch Nation* (Workman Publishing, 2004), takes you on to the next step by introducing the reader to the basics of sweater design. The even "hipper" patterns are a little more complicated, to keep up with the knitter's growing skill level. Check out a couple of the patterns by a certain blonde English designer—she's *hot* (hehehee)!

I rarely buy a book for the patterns alone, but when the very innovative and lovely Teva Durham wrote *Loop-d-Loop* (Stewart, Tabori & Chang, 2005), I just had to have my very own copy. Her designs are fresh and imaginative—no boring sweaters here. She offers interesting techniques mixed with flattering silhouettes—many wearable sweaters without row upon row of boring stockinette stitch!

When you are ready to design your own patterns, I would heartily recommend you read *Knitting from the Top* by Barbara G. Walker (Schoolhouse Press reprint, 1996). Although lacking in pretty pictures, this book teaches you how to knit sweaters, skirts, and trousers in all their variations and with the minimal amount of seaming—all, believe it or not, from the top down. The reason I love this method is that you can try on the garment every now and then as you are knitting it to make sure you achieve the correct fit—brilliant!

# Magazines

I love knitting magazines. I can lose myself in them, especially in the multitude of ads! I spend hours leaning against the racks in bookshops trying to decide which ones to buy. These are my favorites:

- ♦ **Rowan.** This is the only magazine I subscribe to (which is not entirely true, as my Mum has the subscription—she has a good look through it then sends it over the Atlantic to me with notes on which patterns she'd like me to knit for her—clever, 'ey?). This is my little piece of England. I love the photography, the images of the rolling green countryside, the dry stone walls, and the ancient farmhouses. The styling is often better than the designs, but they are a good mix of basic sweaters and crazy pieces all using the delicious yarns that Rowan is famous for (see "Suppliers of Featured Yarns" later in this chapter).

- ♦ **Rebecca.** Fresh-faced, happy, and healthy-looking young models are seen running and jumping around in colorful hand-knits. Beautifully photographed, this magazine is translated from its native German, making the patterns a little tricky to understand, which can be a turnoff for beginners, but persevere and your hard work will reap rewards. Using many different yarn weights and textures, the designs are hip and fresh, although, if you are a devout follower, you may notice that they sometimes come close to repeating themselves.

- ♦ **Vogue Knitting.** Want to knit the latest trend? Then take a look at this magazine. It is still one of the best sources for fashionable patterns. It's interesting to see what the "big names" design for hand-knitters. Choose wisely, as by the time you have finished your project, the trend may have passed and you will be out of style.

- ♦ **Interweave Knits.** The patterns in *Interweave* tend to be more classic and reusable. I do like the way the patterns are placed right next to the photographs instead of all being stuffed in the back pages, as seems to be the norm with other magazines. This magazine also includes many well-written, interesting articles and useful "how-tos" on all aspects of knitting.

The French yarn company Phildar publishes several magazines each year with wonderful designs using their yarns. They have fabulous patterns, but you need to be able to translate them into English. I get my Canadian boyfriend to buy them for me when he visits his hometown of Montreal. They are also available over the Internet and, I believe, there are plans to release English versions soon.

I also love Japanese designers, and there are a number of very cute magazines on the market that we need to have translated into English, although it can be fun to try one out yourself with the help of a phrase book or the Internet!

## Enter the Internet

Everyone knows about eBay, right? For those of you who have been too busy knitting to keep up with what's happening in the world, www.ebay.com is a mammoth online auction. People from all over the world sell their unwanted items to the highest bidder over the Internet.

There's no shortage of knitting yarn and supplies, and you can nab yourself some incredible bargains if you know what you're looking for.

It's not just people like you and me who are de-stashing in this manner. There are also online shops with cheap lots of really good yarn for hugely discounted prices. But buyer beware— only bid on yarn if it's a type you have previously used, seen in a yarn shop, or have been given the all-clear by a friend who has bought a similar yarn, as you can't see the color properly or give it a good fondle while it's in cyberspace!

## Free Is for Me

You can spend huge amounts of cash on your crafting, so it's nice to get something for free once in a while—and once again, there's no place better for that than our good friend, the Internet.

As I mention in Chapter 18, "Knitters of the World Unite," the Knitter's Review (www. knittersreview.com) is an online world of reviews, chat, and information for every kind of knitter. You could spend days on this site, so before you visit you'd better clear your schedule!

Then there's Knitty (www.knitty.com). Oh, how I love Knitty! It's a fabulous online magazine with articles, tips, and a huge archive of wonderful patterns designed by its readers. Log onto their "coffeeshop" and join in on all kinds of knitting-related conversations. They have a special section for KAL (knit-a-longs), where any number of people can share their experiences while all knitting the same pattern.

For more specialized online groups, check out www.theanticraft.com, www.menknit.net, www.socknitters.com, groups.yahoo.com/group/laceknitters, or do a search for something more to your taste.

Another fantastic bonus the Internet has to offer is a never-ending supply of *free* knitting patterns. You can find patterns for just about anything you could be looking for, plus thousands of other patterns to download that you know you will never ever knit! Use your favorite search engine to find the pattern you are looking for or try any of these: www.woolworks.org, www.knittingpatterncentral.com, or check out yarn manufacturers' Web sites for free patterns using their yarns.

Other fabulous places to visit include:

♦ **www.knittinghelp.com.** This Web site is full to bursting with free videos to teach you all types of knitting techniques, from the basics to the more advanced, including how to knit in the round using the Magic Loop method (a particular favorite technique of mine, which I use whenever possible).

- **www.knitting.about.com.** Without all the fancy bells and whistles of some of the trendier Web sites, this one is incredible—you could spend days and days jumping from link to link lapping up all the information offered. If you can't find what you're looking for here, then it probably doesn't exist!

## Suppliers of Featured Yarns

**Berroco Inc.**
14 Elmdale Rd.
P.O. Box 367
Uxbridge, MA 01569
508-278-2527
www.berroco.com

**Blue Sky Alpacas**
P.O. Box 387
St. Francis, MN 55070
888-460-8862; 763-753-5815
www.blueskyalpacas.com

**Brown Sheep Company, Inc.**
100662 County Rd. 16
Mitchell, NE 69357
800-826-9136
www.brownsheep.com

**Cascade Yarns**
1224 Andover Park East
Tukwila, WA 98188
206-574-0440
www.cascadeyarns.com

**Coats and Clark**
P.O. Box 12229
Greenville, SC 29612
800-648-1479
www.coatsandclark.com

**Debbie Bliss**
Designer Yarns Ltd.
Unit 8-10 Newbridge Industrial Estate
Pitt Street, Keighley
West Yorkshire BD21 4PQ England
Tel: +44 01535 664222
www.debbieblissonline.com
(In U.S.: See Knitting Fever Inc.)

**Fiesta Yarns**
5401 San Diego NE
Albuquerque, NM 87113
505-892-5008
www.fiestayarns.com

**Harrisville Designs**
Center Village
P.O. Box 806
Harrisville, NH 03450
800-338-9415
www.harrisville.com

**Jo Sharp**
P.O. Box 1018
Fremantle 6959
Western Australia
Tel: +61 8 9430 9699
www.josharp.com.au

**Karabella**
1201 Broadway
New York, NY 10001
800-550-0898
www.karabellayarns.com

**Knitting Fever Inc.**
315 Bayview Ave.
Amityville, NY 11701
516-546-3600
www.knittingfever.com

**Knit One, Crochet Too, Inc.**
91 Tandberg Trail
Unit 6
Windham, ME 04062
207-892-9625
www.knitonecrochettoo.com

**Knit Picks**
13118 N.E. 4th St.
Vancouver, WA 98684
800-574-1323
www.knitpicks.com

**Kraemer Yarns**
P.O. Box 72
Nazareth, PA 18064
800-759-5601
www.kraemeryarnshop.com

**Lion Brand Yarn**
135 Kero Rd.
Carlstadt, NJ 07072
800-258-9276
www.lionbrand.com

**Patons**
320 Livingstone Ave.
South Listowel, ON
Canada N4W 3H3
Tel: 888-368-8401
www.patonsyarns.com

**Plymouth Yarn Company**
P.O. Box 28
Bristol, PA 19007
215-788-0459
www.plymouthyarn.com

**Rowan**
Green Lane Mill
Holmfirth
HD9 2DX England
Tel: + 44 (0) 1484 681881
www.knitrowan.com
In U.S.: See Westminster Fibers:
4 Townsend West
Unit 8
Nashua, NH 03063
603-886-5041

**Sheep's Clothing (for Morehouse Merino)**
2 Rock City Rd.
Milan, NY 12571
866-470-4852
www.morehousefarm.com

**Tahki Stacy Charles, Inc.**
70-30 80th St.
Building 36
Ridgewood, NY 11385
800-338-9276
www.tahkistacycharles.com

**Trendsetter**
16745 Saticoy St.
Suite #101
Van Nuys, CA 91406
800-446-2425; 818-780-5497
www.trendsetteryarns.com

# Chapter Eighteen

◆◆◆

# Knitters of the World Unite

**W**hat kind of image does the word "knitter" conjure up in most people's minds? I think it's a fairly safe bet to say that a shawl-wearing granny rocking to and fro in a chair by the fire would be the most popular image, and sure as cashmere is soft, in many cases they'd be right on target! No offense to dear old granny, but times, they are a changin'.

In my circle of more than 30 knitters, there are no Dickensian caricatures; some are partial to a bit of shawl wearing, but that's their business! The crafters I meet with regularly are a youthful mix of interesting, intelligent, independent, generous, caring, creative, and fun people from all walks of life. The females outnumber the males by quite a high ratio, but men are catching on that there's more to this pastime than continually looping yarn with the aid of a pair of sticks.

## All the Fun, with Added Group Benefits

Knitting is no longer a private activity to be done solely fireside. Groups of like-minded crafters are meeting up in public to share their passion, knowledge, and spirit of all things wooly.

I *love* my knitting group and look forward to attending meetings every week. We gather to show off our latest projects, yarn, gadgets, and patterns. The knitting is a constant while the topics of conversation vary widely from the sublime to the ridiculous, and we always find plenty of things to laugh about. The group's skills vary from total beginners to life-long knitters, but we are continually learning from one another. It's a wonderful feeling to pass on to others the knowledge and techniques that we pick up along the way. Since joining the group a couple of years ago, I have acquired more than a bit of knitting company on Tuesday evenings; we have developed some strong friendships. Wherever my life takes me, I feel confident that the love of knitting that brought us together will be the cement that keeps the foundation of our relationships together for life.

Join an established group or start your own. If you're not ready to knit in public, you could meet in a group member's home, but for maximum exposure and group-expanding opportunities, it's favorable to meet in a comfortable, friendly, public space. My group has moved its location several times while I have been a member. We currently meet in a small knitting shop that has its own onsite café. The staff are friendly, helpful, and very accommodating—our group can easily take over the whole space on a busy night! We have also met in coffee shops; the best ones are roomy with good lighting and comfy seating. Don't be afraid to ask café owners if you can hold meetings in their establishments; they are usually happy to accept the business. Just don't forget to repay the favor in buying drinks or snacks—no one likes a freeloader!

Some groups also meet in bars, but unless you can knit without looking, the lack of good lighting can make progress tricky—and after a few dirty martinis, who knows how your knitting will turn out?

Advertise your meetings on the Internet—set up a group on the Stitch 'n Bitch Web site (www.stitchnbitch.org/snb_groups.htm). Post eye-catching fliers at your nearest yarn shops, library, café, gym, yoga studio, and anywhere you feel may attract attention. Spread the word at work, and be willing to grab any knitters you see on the bus, train, or at the doctor's office to tell them about your fabulous new group.

## Swap Shop

Aside from the camaraderie, exchange of knowledge, and taking your craft out of the home, there are other things your group can do together. Our group has held two very successful yarn swaps. This is where you gather together all of your unwanted yarn that's taking up valuable space in your home (or in my case, my apartment, my friends' attics, my parents' house, and my office!). Take it to a meeting place (this time it's best to get together at one person's home), and exchange your yarn within the group.

We set out our yarn offerings on a table, then after everyone had arrived and taken a few minutes to glance over the evening's offerings, one member of the group acts as auctioneer (in our case, the lovely Claudine!). As each yarn is held up and described, interested bidders raise their hands if it absolutely needs to go home with them. If more than one person has their hand in the air, the dueling bidders have to stake their claim by describing the project they have in mind for the yarn; the rest of the group then decides to whom the yarn should go. This continues until all the yarn has found a new owner.

## Daytrippers

When planning a trip, who among us looks for places to buy yarn as a high point of the visit? You are far from alone my fiendish fiber friend! My group also gets together for outings, mostly in the pursuit of more yarn, needles, patterns, and books, but sometimes just for a change of scenery and a new space in which to sit, knit, and chat.

The most popular place to visit among us is the New York Sheep and Wool Festival, held one weekend each October during peek leaf-peeping season in Rhinebeck, a picturesque rural town that is invaded for that weekend by crazed yarn fanatics. We cram ourselves into a minivan and set off upstate for a day of unadulterated fiber fun.

It's not just sheep and wool, either; there are alpacas, goats, and Angora rabbits showing off their fabulously soft coats, and for the non-yarn freaks there are sheep-dog trails, demonstrations, and all the deliciously naughty fairground food you can eat!

Barnfulls of vendors offer their multicolored wares to the hungry masses. There is stall after stall of soft and fluffy bundles of yarn and roving, as well as patterns, books, and tools for all types of fiber crafters. What makes it all the more special is that you can chat with the people who raise the animals, or those who spin and dye the yarn, and find out about all the processes involved—something to think about as you knit the yarn and then use the finished item. You can't get that at your local yarn shop!

The festival also offers various workshops, including knitting, crocheting, spinning, and felting, for those who seek further enlightenment. When you're as obsessed with knitting and all things fiber-related as we are, this is the type of outing you look forward to all year!

There are all sorts of shows and festivals around the country to tempt a hungry knitter out of her (or his) armchair. To find one near you, check online at the Knitter's Review (www. knittersreview.com) or in the classifieds section at the back of knitting magazines.

# A Knitted Gift Exchange

We spend hours, days, months, and sometimes years to lovingly create one-of-a-kind knitted masterpieces. Only another knitter knows the time and mental energy it takes to finish our works of art.

If you plan on knitting a gift for a non-knitter, don't be surprised if your recipient's excitement upon receiving your offering isn't as enthusiastic as you feel it deserves. Moments like this can often lead to heartbreak as people who do not knit, or don't live with a knitter, really have no clue how much we really put into our craft. This is why the knitted gift exchange, invented by my lovely knitting pal, Kara, is such a fabulous idea!

Gather your knitting friends together and ask everyone to knit a gift to be exchanged within the group. If someone doesn't have time to complete a project, they can wrap up some yarn, needles, or other knit-related gift to exchange.

# Cyber-Knitting

If knitting in public is not an option, there are plenty of people willing to be your knitting friends over the Internet. Hours and hours of my precious time (time that could be spent knitting!), are spent surfin' the 'Net. It's a goldmine of information and silliness all within easy reach. I write this from under a blanket, prostrate on the settee in my tiny Manhattan apartment with my 12-inch laptop perched atop a cushion, and from here I can reach Web sites from all over the world. However did we manage without it?

There are thousands of online knitting groups, a great number of which can be found via your favorite search engine. Find one (or more), that takes your fancy and you'll have valuable information, chat, pattern swapping, help, and advice from thousands upon thousands of like-minded souls from all over the world, directly at your fingertips. My favorites are Stitch 'n Bitch (worldwide groups; www.stitchnbitch.org/snb_groups.htm), The Knitlist (www.knitlist.com), Knitty (www.knitty.com), UK Handknitters (groups.yahoo.com/group/UKHandKnitters), and the Knitter's Review (www.knittersreview.com). Everything you ever wanted to know—and a whole lot you didn't—can be found there.

Need help with a particular pattern? Advice on what to knit with yarn you purchased on a whim? Or just want to show off your newly finished project? Then these types of sites are for you.

## Blogging

Immerse yourself deeper into the lives of your virtual friends by reading about their knitting exploits on their weblogs—or blogs for short. By adding photographs and links to patterns or other Web sites, bloggers document their lives and their projects, journal style, for all to read.

When I have the time, I like to catch up with some of my group members by reading their blogs. A few that volunteered to be mentioned here are www.avocadofever.blogspot.com, www.passionknitly.blogspot.com, and www.yarnmonster.blogspot.com. Bloggers of note that have reached "celebrity" status for their entertainment value are www.masondixonknitting.com and www.yarnharlot.ca/blog.

Purely for research purposes, I started my own blog. I wanted to see how easy it really was (for a non-techie like me) to launch one before I could write about it. I went to www.blogger.com and followed the clear instructions, and in no time at all my blog was there in cyberspace for all to see! As all my free time is currently being spent on writing this book, I'm not revealing my blog's title, but it really was easy to get the basic layout and start posting. In order that your blog be visually pleasing, you really can't do without a digital camera—but almost everyone's got one of those these days.

# Appendix

◆◆◆

# Reference Tools

## Abbreviations

To keep patterns short and sweet, designers use common abbreviations for writing their directions. Here is a list in alphabetical order of the main ones you will need to know. Any special abbreviations for cabling or lacework will be included in the patterns.

| | | | | |
|---|---|---|---|---|
| alt | alternate | dpn | double-pointed needle |
| approx | approximately | dtr | double treble crochet |
| beg | begin(ning)(s) | e | every |
| bet | between | eon | end of needle |
| BO | bind off | eor | every other row (round) |
| but | buttonhole | fin | finish(ed) |
| cab | cable | foll(s) | follow(ing)(s) |
| CC | contrast color | g | gram |
| ch | chain | g st | garter stitch |
| cm | centimeter(s) | grp(s) | group(s) |
| cn | cable needle | hdc | half double crochet |
| CO | cast on | hk | hook |
| col | color | htr | half treble |
| cont | continue(s); continuing | in(s) | inch(es) |
| dbl | double | inc | increase(s); increasing |
| dc | double crochet | incl | include |
| dec(s) | decrease(s); decreasing | inst | instruction(s) |
| diag | diagonal | k | knit |
| diam | diameter | k-b | knit stitch in row below |
| DK | double knitting | kbl (k tbl) | knit through back of loop |

*continued*

241

| | | | |
|---|---|---|---|
| kfb | knit into front and back of stitch | rib | ribbing |
| k2tog | knit two stitches together | rn | right needle |
| kwise | knitwise | rnd(s) | round(s) |
| l | left | RS | right side |
| lg | large | RT | right twist |
| LH | left hand | sc | single crochet |
| ln | left needle | sel(v) | selvage |
| lp(s) | loop(s) | sk | skip |
| LT | left twist | skn | skein |
| m | meter(s) | skp | slip one, knit one, pass slip stitch over |
| MB | make bobble | sl | slip |
| MC | main color | sl st | slip stitch |
| med | medium | sm | small |
| mm | millimeter(s) | sp | space |
| m1 | make one | ssk | slip, slip, knit |
| mult | multiple | st(s) | stitch(es) |
| no | number | St st | stockinette stitch |
| opp | opposite | tbl | through back of loop |
| oz | ounce | tch | turning chain |
| p | purl | tog | together |
| patt(s) | pattern(s) | tr | treble |
| p-b | purl into the stitch below | WS | wrong side |
| pfb | purl into the front and the back of stitch | wyib | with yarn in back |
| pm | place marker | wyif | with yarn in front |
| pnso | pass next stitch over | yb | yarn back |
| psso | pass slip stitch over | yd | yard(s) |
| p tbl | purl though back of loop | yf | yarn forward |
| p2tog | purl two stitches together | yfon | yarn forward over needle |
| p2tog-b | purl two stitches together through back of loop | yfrn | yarn forward round needle |
| | | yo | yarn over |
| pwise | purlwise | yon | yarn over needle |
| r | right | yo2 | yarn over twice |
| rem | remain(ing) | yrn | yarn round needle |
| rep | repeat | ytb | yarn to back |
| rev St st | reverse stockinette stitch | ytf | yarn to front |
| RH | right hand | | |

# Knitting Needles Inventory and Conversion Table

Use this table to keep track of all of your knitting needles. Write the length of your needles in the columns against the needle size. You can also use the table to convert the sizes of your needles from mm to UK or US sizes.

| MM | UK* | US | Single Point Needles | Double-Pointed Needles | Circular Needles |
|----|-----|----|----|----|----|
| 2 | 14 | 0 | | | |
| 2.25 | 13 | 1 | | | |
| 2.75 | 12 | 2 | | | |
| 3.25 | 10 | 3 | | | |
| 3.5 | - | 4 | | | |
| 3.75 | 9 | 5 | | | |
| 4 | 8 | 6 | | | |
| 4.5 | 7 | 7 | | | |
| 5 | 6 | 8 | | | |
| 5.5 | 5 | 9 | | | |
| 6 | 4 | 10 | | | |
| 6.5 | 3 | 10½ | | | |
| 7 | 2 | - | | | |
| 7.5 | 1 | - | | | |
| 8 | 0 | 11 | | | |
| 9 | 00 | 13 | | | |
| 10 | 000 | 15 | | | |
| 12 | - | 17 | | | |
| 15 | - | 19 | | | |
| 19 | - | 35 | | | |
| 25 | - | 50 | | | |

* UK sizes are not being made anymore, but a lot of the old UK needles are still in use.

# Designer Bios

**Lynn Burdick** Lynn taught herself to knit when she was 11 years old. Knitting comes naturally to her, although some of her techniques aren't "by the book." She considers herself "your average obsessed knitter" who owns way too much yarn. Her current project is a line of patterns for adventurous knitters and a workbook for creative design. To find out more, contact Lynn at knit1gal@yahoo.com.

**Cristina Kelley** Cristina grew up listening to the sound of her mother's sewing machine. She taught herself how to knit, quilt, sew, and crochet, and is a veteran "eyeballer." Cristina is a true dilettante, having been an actor, writer, musician, superhero, animator, p.a., pet sitter, and dog wrangler extraordinaire. A California native, she is currently doing time in Brooklyn, New York, with one dog, three cats (two domestic, one semi-feral) and one boyfriend (also semi-feral). Check out www.bigbgoodies.com.

**Jessamyn Lee** As a little girl, yarn and needles were Jessamyn's crayons and paper. Now, as a busy teacher in New York City, knitting relieves the stress of her day and provides stimulation. Her non-knitting husband, Ben, has become a willing accomplice, pointing out inspiration in handmade garments in fancy boutique windows and on hip New Yorkers. Jessamyn considers knitting her gateway to a wonderful, diverse community of people from different industries, cultures, and countries. Check out Jessamyn's blog, www.sweetgirlknits.blogspot.com/.

 **Claudine Monique** Although she made potholders as a child, Claudine became hooked on knitting about six years ago, when she bought a sweater from a chain store and wore it to work the next day, only to discover that three coworkers were wearing the same sweater. That Christmas Claudine asked her mother to re-teach her how to knit, thinking that she would make a scarf and maybe a hat and that would be it. She hasn't put her needles down since.

 **Katy Moore** Katy learned how to knit when she was about 6, but soon forgot everything. After college, her godmother bought her a "Teach Yourself to Knit" book, size-8 metal needles, and some gray acrylic yarn, and asked Katy to knit her a pair of house slippers. Katy made the slippers, and she's been knitting ever since. She knits mostly on the subways in NYC and while waiting for her computer to think. Visit Katy's blog at katyknitsnyc.blogspot.com.

 **Ruthie Nussbaum** Ruthie's grandmother taught her how to knit when Ruthie was 15. Through high school and college she knit and read everything about knitting she could find in secret for fear of being labeled a dork by her friends. Today Ruthie lives in New York City, where she's a reading teacher and medical editor, as well as a knitting instructor and burgeoning knitwear designer. See Ruthie's latest work at www.ruthieknits.com.

 **Jeanette Sherritze** Jeanette brings passion into her textile, canvas, and jewelry designs. She began painting as a young child and designed her own clothes as a teenager. Now, even as a professional artist, she continues her quest for beauty through her knit designs. Choosing mostly a palette of natural fibers such as wool, cashmere, and llama, Jeanette knits constantly. Her fun blog, "Knit Styles of the Mentally Insane," can be found at http://knittinginsteadofhousework. blogspot.com/.

 **Anna Sorrentino** A graphic and Web designer by day and a self-taught fiber artist by night, Anna spends every second of her spare time manically knitting, spinning, creating beaded stitch markers, and futilely attempting to complete her ridiculously large number of WIPs. She lives in London with her boyfriend, no cats, and more yarn than she'll ever know what to do with. Her creations can be viewed and bought at www.annerella.co.uk.

**Alison Stewart-Guinee** Alison first learned to knit from her mother, but a move to Michigan in her early 20s and some talented knitting friends took her dalliance to the next level. Alison teaches knitting at Yarns Unlimited in Bloomington, Indiana, and is currently working on a collection of children's patterns. When she's not knitting, she weaves a line of art-to-wear wraps sold through galleries, tries to keep up with three busy kids, and travels as much as possible.

**Jane Thornley** Jane is a Nova Scotian knitwear and jewelry designer whose Web site celebrates texture, design, and color in wearable art. Her exuberant knitwear designs spring from a passion for mixing yarns in interesting ways and combining fiber with beads. Jane is currently working on a book called *Adventure Knitting*. Her patterns, available on her Web site (www.janethornley.com), feature watercolor "stitch & color maps" mixed with narrative as well as traditional instructions. She aims to encourage the "pattern-challenged" knitter. Jane's Night Falls Scarf design is featured online at www.wiley.com/go/NYMknitting.

**Jennifer Thurston** Jennifer's knitting hobby began about seven years ago with the experimental creation of a stripy scarf. In 2003 she founded her own Web page, www.xtreme-knitting.com, which has helped turn a hobby into an obsession! She has since had patterns published in online knitting magazines *Knitty* and *Magknits*, and offers many designs on her Web page. When she's not knitting, she enjoys sewing, cooking, and thinking about knitting!

**Melissa Webster** Melissa moved to New York City in the early 1990s, where she became roommates with Heather, the author of this book. Patient and talented Heather took the task of teaching her the sticks. With a baby on the way, Melissa plans to get into more complicated items like booties and sweaters. She wishes to thank her grandmother for being a knitting and personal inspiration, and her husband-to-be, Robb, who's still waiting for his knit nude-colored bodysuit!

**Jennifer Wendell** Jenn started knitting in fall 2004 after wondering how her grandmother had made a poncho. She taught herself with books and the Internet. Knitting not only gave her something to do in her post-college daze, but it gave her a way to be productive while undertaking the quixotic task of finding employment in New York City. She regularly attends the lower Manhattan SNB, where she commiserates with like-minded yarn addicts. Her blog can be found at http://passionknitly.blogspot.com.

# Index

tog (together), 242
together (tog), 242
tr (treble), 242
*A Treasury of Knitting Patterns*
    (Walker), 232
treble (tr), 242
Trendsetter, yarn supplier, 236
tube method, 33
Tulip Lace, stitch pattern, 43
turning chain (tch), 242
Tutti-Frutti Baby Set
        pattern, 211–216
        variation, 216
twisted
        stitches, 90
        tie, 83
two-row buttonhole, 70

## U

*The Ultimate Sourcebook of Knitting
    and Crochet Stitches*, 232
unfinished stitches, 90
unknitting, 89

## V

vegetable yarn, 15
vertical double decrease, 41
vertically picking up stitches, 68
*Vogue Knitting* magazine, 233

## W

Wave Stitch, stitch pattern, 44
weaving, loose ends, 71–72
whipstitch, 79
Wildflowers
        sweater pattern, 175–181
        variation, 181

with yarn in back (wyib), 242
with yarn in front (wyif), 242
wood needles, 11
wool yarn, 14
wrong side (WS), 41, 242
WS (wrong side), 41, 242
wyib (with yarn in back), 242
wyif (with yarn in front), 242

## Y

yard(s) (yd), 242
yarn, 94
        acrylic, 15
        alpaca, 14
        angora, 14
        animal, 14–15
        back (yb), 242
        to back (ytb), 242
        boucle, 16
        buying, 234
        cashmere, 14
        categories of, 17
        chenille, 16
        cotton, 15
        eyelash, 16
        forward (yf), 242
        forward (yf or yfwd), 39
        forward over needle (yfon),
            242
        forward round needle
            (yfrn), 242
        to front (ytf), 242
        hemp, 15
        holding the, 25–26
        joining, 53–55
        label, 18–19
        linen, 15
        measuring length of, 54
        metallic, 16
        mohair, 14

novelty, 16
nylon, 16
over (yo), 39, 242
over buttonhole, 71
over needle (yon), 242
over twice (yo2), 242
polyester, 16
price of, 13
qivuit, 15
rayon, 16
round needle (yrn), 39, 242
selecting, 13–14
silk, 14–15
soy, 15
subbing, 20
suppliers, 235–236
synthetic, 15–16
tangle management, 57
tension, 26
thickness, 16–17
types, 14–16
vegetable, 15
weight system, 17
yb (yarn back), 242
yd (yard(s)), 242
yf (yarn forward), 39, 242
yfon (yarn forward over needle),
    242
yfrn (yarn forward round
    needle), 242
yfwd (yarn forward), 39
yo (yarn over), 39, 242
yo2 (yarn over twice), 242
yon (yarn over needle), 242
yrn (yarn round needle), 39, 242
ytb (yarn to back), 242
ytf (yarn to front), 242

## Z

Zimmerman, Elizabeth, 84

# There's lots more in store with *Not Your Mama's*™ Craft Books!

Hip and savvy *Not Your Mama's* books are designed for confident crafters like you who don't need to start at the beginning and don't want to go back to basics and slave over every pattern and page. These books get right to the point so you can jump right into real projects. With easy-to-follow instructions plus hints, tips, and steps for customizing projects, you'll quickly have something to show for your efforts—fun, trendy items to add sass and class to your wardrobe or home.

0-471-97382-3

0-471-97381-5

0-471-97380-7

It's knitting with a trés chic attitude. Projects include Pirate Socks, Boot-i-licious (boot jewelry), Girly (a sexy cardigan), Macho Picchu (a man's sweater), Techno Bag (a laptop case), Pampered Pooch Pullover, Hearts & Stars (cushions), and more.

Creative crochet is in today! Patterns include an Uber-Femme Capelet, Pseudo Kimono, Daisy Chain Neck Warmer, When the Jeans Don't Fit (recycled denim rug), Straight-Laced Tank and Shrug, Wowie Zowie Eco-Tote, Crocheted Bling, two super-cute plush toys, and more.

Do the bling thing. Projects include Financial Freedom (recycled credit card necklace), Tough Cuff, Catch Your Own Bouquet ring, Tipple Rings (wine stem markers), Girls Gone Bridaled (a tiara), Security Anklet, push pins with pizzazz, and more.

**All *Not Your Mama's*™ Craft Books**
$14.99 US/$17.99 CAN/£9.99 UK • Paper • 240-264 pp.
7 3/8 x 9 1/4 • Lots of illustrations and color photos

Available wherever books are sold.

**WILEY**
Now you know.
wiley.com

Wiley, the Wiley logo, and Not Your Mama's are trademarks or registered trademarks of John Wiley & Sons, Inc. and/or its affiliates in the United States and other countries.